WHAT ABC

Most young people considering studying law, or pursuing a legal career, have very little idea of what learning law involves and how universities teach law to their students. This new book provides a 'taster' for the study of law; a short, accessible presentation of law as an academic subject, designed to help 17- and 18-year old students and others decide whether law is the right choice for them as a university subject, or, if they have already made the choice, what to expect when they start their law degree. It helps answer the question 'what should I study at university?' and counters the perception that law is a dry, dull subject.

What About Law? shows how the study of law can be fun, intellectually stimulating, challenging and of direct relevance to students. Using a case study approach, the book introduces prospective law students to the legal system, as well as to legal reasoning, critical thinking and argument.

This is a book that should be in the library of every school with a sixth form, every college and every university, and it is one that any student about to embark on the study of law should read before they commence their legal studies.

All of the authors have long experience in teaching law at Cambridge and elsewhere and all have also been involved, at various times, in advising prospective law students at open days and admissions conferences.

What About Law?

Studying Law at University

Catherine Barnard, Janet O'Sullivan
and Graham Virgo (editors)

Authors:

Catherine Barnard
David Feldman
Kevin Gray
Janet O'Sullivan
Graham Virgo
Tony Weir

·HART·
PUBLISHING

OXFORD AND PORTLAND, OREGON
2007

Published in North America (US and Canada) by
Hart Publishing
c/o International Specialized Book Services
920 NE 58th Avenue, Suite 300
Portland, OR 97213-3786
USA
Tel: +1 503 287 3093 or toll-free: (1) 800 944 6190
Fax: +1 503 280 8832
E-mail: orders@isbs.com
Website: www.isbs.com

Edited by Catherine Barnard, Janet O'Sullivan and Graham Virgo
© The various authors 2007.

Hart Publishing, 16C Worcester Place, OX1 2JW
Telephone: +44 (0)1865 517530 Fax: +44 (0)1865 510710
E-mail: mail@hartpub.co.uk
Website: http://www.hartpub.co.uk

British Library Cataloguing in Publication Data
Data Available

ISBN-13: 978-1-84113-632-5 (paperback)

Typeset by Compuscript Ltd, Shannon
Printed and bound in Great Britain by
TJ International Ltd, Padstow, Cornwall

Foreword

The two questions most often asked of a barrister about his or her profession are, 'How can you defend someone if you know they are guilty?' and 'What should I (or my son/daughter) read in order to decide whether to study law?'. This book now provides the answer to the second enquiry, leaving more time for discussing the first.

You can learn something about legal studies by reading the law reports in *The Times* or attending a trial at your local Crown Court or watching classic films such as *Twelve Angry Men*. But like a tourist in a foreign country where you do not speak the language, it can help to have a professional guide. The authors of this volume expertly identify and communicate the essence of the subject: its broad scope, covering a wide range of social, political and moral problems; its intellectually satisfying methods of analysis, based on logic, precedent and judgment; and, above all, its entertainment value.

The law addresses everyday concerns and its reasoning is often no more than applied common sense. But we lawyers do not make it easy for others to understand what we are talking about. Lawyers still have, as Jonathan Swift observed nearly 300 years ago, 'a peculiar cant and jargon of their own, that no other mortal can understand'. This can be confusing, even intimidating, to others. One of the great merits of this volume is that the authors demystify the process. They strip away the obscurities and explain what the study of law is really all about.

I very much hope and expect that the information, and enthusiasm, contained in these pages will encourage potential law students. Our society may not need more lawyers. But we certainly need more lawyers who think clearly about the meaning and the content of the laws that govern all our lives.

David Pannick QC
Blackstone Chambers
Temple, London
EC4Y 9BW
18 June 2007

Preface

What about Law? is primarily intended to be a 'taster' for the study of law as an academic subject, with a view to helping prospective students decide whether reading Law at university is for them. It also aims to provide an introduction to the main subjects students will study for a Law degree. We hope that many other sorts of reader will find something in it to interest them too, perhaps school careers' advisers or parents wishing to understand what their children are studying, or planning to study, at university. Indeed, we hope that any intelligent non-lawyer who has ever wanted to know a bit more about English law will find this book a valuable tool.

However, this book comes with a health warning: it does not provide a comprehensive review of the nuts and bolts of the legal system. There are plenty of such books on the market. Nor is it packed full of useful tips as to how to be a good student of law (how to write good essays, how to prepare for exams, etc). Rather, it explores what the law is, how it has developed, how the judges interpret it and *why* it is that way. It does so by examining seven cases, each one taken from the subjects forming the 'core' of any law syllabus (criminal, contract, tort, land, equity, constitutional and EU law). These seven core subjects are the minimum which students must study, and pass, in order to be able to undertake their professional training to become practising solicitors or barristers. Sometimes students consider these subjects dry and technical. The aim of these chapters is to show that they are anything but.

In analysing the seven cases, the various authors examine the legal issues raised, the legal reasoning employed by the judges in the different courts, and the relationship between the particular area of law and some of the broader social, political, philosophical, ethical and economic debates at stake. But, of course, each chapter inevitably moves beyond the one chosen case, exploring other aspects of the relevant legal landscape, such as related decisions of other courts and legislative developments.

Putting it another way, the aim of this book is to use the cases in the same way as newspapers write features on the 'life in the day' of a particular celebrity: each case is used to illustrate issues which have ramifications beyond the immediate subject in hand. The subjects of many of these cases are not celebrities, certainly not in the tabloid sense of the word, but ordinary people suffering the vicissitudes of life. And because each case is known by the name of the parties (and not by a sterile reference number or date as often happens on the Continent) these individuals acquire a certain celebrity status among law students. If you are interested in what you are told about these celebrities, you can read the actual cases themselves on the companion website (www.whataboutlaw.com/www.whataboutlaw.co.uk).

As you will discover, the cases studied in the core subjects are the foundations to understanding any branch of law and for learning that elusive skill—how to 'think like a lawyer' (and this certainly does not mean how to charge clients a lot of money). Of course the study of law is academically demanding (this should never be forgotten), but it is also intellectually stimulating, controversial, of daily relevance and very often highly entertaining.

Each of the authors of the chapters in this book is a leading academic with, cumulatively, over a century of university teaching and research experience. We hope that we have managed to convey some small part of our own boundless enthusiasm for our subjects—if so, we will have achieved our objective.

Catherine Barnard, Janet O'Sullivan and Graham Virgo
Cambridge, July 2007

Acknowledgements

This project has had a long gestation period. The editors are extremely grateful to Richard Hart and his team for their enthusiasm for our book and for their support for this rather unusual venture. While many of our friends, colleagues and students have given us help, advice and inspiration, we should like to express particular thanks to Albertina Albors-Llorens, Tony Arnull, Caroline Blyth, John Cary, Charles Cook, Phil Fellows, Daniel Francis, Amy Goymour, Jonathan Hilliard, Dominic Hockley, Emily Haystead, Angus Johnston, Magnus Jones, James Lawson, Jake Rowbottom, Jens Scherpe and Rob Veale.

The editors would also like to express sincere thanks to their colleagues and friends, David Feldman, Kevin Gray and Tony Weir, for writing the constitutional, land law and tort chapters respectively, and for their constant encouragement and support for this project.

Contents

Authors

Catherine Barnard—Reader in European Union Law, Jean Monnet Chair in European Union Law and Fellow of Trinity College, Cambridge. Author of *EC Employment Law* (3rd edn, Oxford University Press, Oxford 2006) and *The Substantive Law of the EU: The Four Freedoms* (2nd edn, OUP 2007).

David Feldman—Rouse Ball Professor of English Law, FBA, Fellow of Downing College, Cambridge, Chairman of the Faculty of Law; Judge of the Constitutional Court of Bosnia and Herzegovina since 2002 and a Vice-President since 2006. Formerly Legal Adviser to Parliamentary Joint Select Committee on Human Rights, Houses of Parliament. Author of *Civil Liberties and Human Rights in England and Wales* (2nd edn, OUP 2002) and editor of *English Public Law* (OUP 2004).

Kevin Gray—Professor of Law, FBA, Fellow of Trinity College, Cambridge. Co-author of Gray and Gray, *Elements of Land Law* (4th edn, OUP 2005) and *Land Law* (5th edn, OUP 2007).

Janet O'Sullivan—Senior Lecturer in Law, Fellow of Selwyn College, Cambridge, winner of Cambridge University Pilkington Teaching prize for excellence in university teaching; associate editor, Tottel's *Journal of Professional Negligence*; previously solicitor, Slaughter and May. Author of O'Sullivan and Hilliard, *The Law of Contract* (2nd edn, OUP 2006).

Graham Virgo—Professor of English Private Law, Fellow of Downing College, Cambridge, winner of Cambridge University Pilkington teaching prize, Law Faculty Access Officer; barrister. Author of *Principles of the Law of Restitution* (2nd edn, OUP 2006).

Tony Weir—Emeritus Reader in Law, Fellow of Trinity College, Cambridge. Author of *A Casebook on Tort* (10th edn, Sweet & Maxwell, London 2004), *An Introduction to Tort Law* (2nd edn, OUP 2006) and *Economic Torts* (OUP, 1997).

1

Introduction to Law

Catherine Barnard, Graham Virgo
and Janet O'Sullivan

STARTING TO THINK ABOUT LAW

Picture this. Laura, who is 17, organises a party at the family home while
her parents are away for the weekend. It gets out of hand. For Laura and
her parents, it is a nightmare. But for a lawyer, there are as many questions as there are empty bottles strewn the next morning across the prized
living room carpet.

What if the party was very noisy? It might have caused a nuisance
to neighbours living nearby and those neighbours might have con-
tacted the local authority, whose noise-prevention officers have powers to close the party down or reduce the noise in some other way.
If the party was large enough—and loud enough—to cause a serious
nuisance across a wide area, Laura and her guests might even be prosecuted for the crime of public nuisance and eventually punished.

What if the partygoers damaged the house or stole some of the family's possessions? These are obviously criminal offences, but what happens if the perpetrators can't be identified? Can guests be forced to give
evidence of what happened? Can they get into trouble if they don't name
names? If the perpetrators are easily identified and have lots of money,
Laura's parents might even consider suing them for compensation to
cover the cost of all the damage. If the parents choose not to bother,
but claim instead on their household insurance policy, can the insurance

2 Introduction to Law

company recoup some of the money it pays out from those responsible for the damage?

What if one of the invited guests, Mark, was seriously injured when he tripped over a loose paving stone on the patio, that Laura's parents knew was dangerous and had been meaning to get fixed? He might want to sue the parents for compensation, but would it make any difference to his chances of success if the parents had expressly banned their daughter from inviting anyone to their home while they were away? And what if Mark was drunk or messing about when he tripped, but the paving stone was sufficiently dangerous that he would, more likely than not, have tripped and suffered the same injury even if he had been perfectly sober? Do people nowadays resort too readily to litigation when injured, unwilling to accept that they have no-one to blame but themselves for what happened?

How would the arrival of gate-crashers affect the position? What was their legal status while in the house—were they trespassers? If so, what does that mean? They might be guilty of a crime, such as burglary, if they intended to steal property. Could they be forcibly ejected by the hostess's friends, even if this requires physical violence? What if the hostess turned a blind eye to their arrival or appeared to welcome them, but later wanted to throw them out? And what if a gatecrasher is injured tripping on that same dodgy paving stone?

The internet adds a new dimension to the problem. Perhaps Laura publicised the party on an internet chatroom, or maybe some of her so-called friends hacked into her account and publicised the party without her permission. Would this generate any legal liability in itself? What about any responsibility of the company supposed to monitor the chatroom? Is it asking too much to expect a traditional, national legal system to cope with the challenges of an online world?

Did Laura buy alcohol for the party, even though there are supposed to be laws preventing that happening? Or did she raid the parental drinks cabinet? Are there any laws that penalise *serving* drinks to under-age people at private parties, or any licensing requirements that apply to such private gatherings? We all know about the problem of binge drinking, but some countries have laws imposing 'social host liability'—this means that if a host has served alcohol and then allows an obviously drunk guest to drive home, the host might be liable to pay compensation if the drunk driver later injures or kills someone on the road. Should the same laws be introduced in the UK and, if so, should they apply just to commercial premises, like pubs, or should they apply to private parties too? And should they apply if the person killed or injured is not an innocent third party but the drunk driver himself?

Meanwhile, back at the party, what if some guests did things they deeply regretted next morning? If a woman consented to sex when drunk, but the man knew that she wouldn't have consented if she had been sober, is he guilty of rape? And can a drunken consent to sex really be considered consent? What if a man believes a woman is consenting, but only because he is too drunk to realise that she isn't? The legal age of consent to sex is 16, so what are the criminal law consequences of a 19-year-old man having sex with a 15-year-old girl who said she was 17, or of a 15-year-old boy having consensual sex with a girl his own age? Is it right for the law to attach such overwhelming significance to the age '16' in this context? Is it practicable to have laws that are so difficult to enforce?

As the party descended into chaos, there was a fight and a man was hurt. Can he sue for damages, even though he was a willing participant in the fight? If the fighting spilled out onto the street, can the police arrest the perpetrators for causing a breach of the peace or for drunk and disorderly conduct? Are there any additional protections for under-age suspects?

Finally, the police raided the party and found that illegal drugs were being taken. Is it illegal to take drugs, to share them, or just to supply them? Is it economically and politically sensible to tackle drug-taking using the criminal law?

Laura is clearly going to be in trouble with her parents, but can she be held legally responsible for any of these disastrous events, even if she spent all night cowering in her bedroom, terrified and unable to do anything to bring the party to an end? And should her parents be regarded as legally responsible, even though they were not there and were horrified to discover the chaos when they got home?

***

One party, but so many diverse and fascinating legal issues. Some are about what the law *is*, others about *why* it is that way and whether it should be that way. Lawyers have to think in those terms all the time. For many of the questions, there is no obvious 'right' answer, because the law is surprisingly open to more than one interpretation and because considerations of policy and fairness do not always point in the same direction. Lawyers and law students need to think about all these issues, and this book will give you a taste of the opinions and arguments that result.

We have taken seven cases—one from each of the core subjects that you must study if you wish to start out on the career path of becoming a lawyer. These subjects are essential building blocks for a proper understanding of law, regardless of whether you go on to pursue a legal career. First, however, we need to provide you with some of the basic tools of the trade to help make sense of the cases that follow. Why not start with a fundamental (and very difficult) question—what is law?

THE TOOLS

What is Law?

The *Oxford English Dictionary* describes law as:

> The body of rules, whether formally enacted or customary, which a particular State or community recognises as governing the action of its subjects or its members and which it may enforce by imposing penalties.

This definition is perfectly satisfactory as far as it goes, but it doesn't tell us much about what law really is, either as an academic subject or in the way it works for lawyers and members of the public. So let's think in detail about where law comes from and the role it plays in different sorts of disputes. We will return to the essential question of what we really mean by 'law' in the final chapter, once you have read the rest of the book. It seems simple, but it is actually one of the most difficult and controversial questions raised by the philosophy of law (known as *jurisprudence*).

The Sources of Law

English law comes from a number of *sources*. First, because we do not have a written constitution in the United Kingdom, the laws with the highest authority in this country are *statutes,* passed by

Parliament and given 'royal assent' by the Queen. Statutes, also known as Acts of Parliament, are referred to as *primary* sources of law. There is more detail on this in chapter 7. These primary laws may be supplemented by *secondary* sources, known as secondary or delegated legislation, usually in the form of Statutory Instruments (SIs). These are the nitty-gritty, detailed, technical rules fleshing out in more detail a provision laid down in a particular Act of Parliament. SIs are subject to less detailed parliamentary scrutiny. To give you an example, the right for parents with young children and those with caring responsibilities to request flexible working hours is laid down in general terms in the Employment Rights Act 1996. But you will find all the details in various SIs such as the Flexible Working (Eligibility, Complaints and Remedies) Regulations 2002. However, when adopting Acts of Parliament and SIs, Parliament no longer enjoys the total freedom it once had: it must ensure that the rules do not contravene either European Community law (considered further in chapter 8) or the European Convention on Human Rights.

The statutory rules may also be accompanied by other documents which are not always legally binding but offer guidance to judges and other officials striving to apply these rules. These include planning guidance and codes of practice such as the Advisory and Conciliation Service's (ACAS) Code of Practice on Disciplinary and Grievance Procedures at Work.

The second source of law is the *common law*, much of it made a long time ago by judges. It continues to develop as judges have to decide new and different cases. It is all rather mysterious, because in strict theory judges don't make new law, they merely declare and apply the existing law when deciding a case (although this is a bit of a chicken and egg puzzle because every common law rule must at some point in ancient legal history have been invented for the first time). This *declaratory* theory is certainly accurate insofar as it relates to judges in the ordinary or *lower* courts (we will return to the structure of the courts later). These are judges who preside over criminal trials and who decide initially which party wins a civil dispute. However, when the losing side is unhappy with the result and takes the case further, to the higher or appellate courts, the senior judges who decide the appeal often do things that look very much like making new law, such as deciding to expand a rule to cover a new area or reverse an earlier rule because it is now out-of-date or didn't work very well. The appellate judges are adept at being creative with the existing law, managing to respect the declaratory theory while, in reality, changing the law slightly.

The basics of many important areas of law, like contract, tort and equity (which are considered later in this book), are governed by judge-made law, although even these traditionally common law areas are increasingly being altered by statutory developments. Sometimes this happens when Parliament thinks that the common law is going in the wrong direction. At other times, politicians want to introduce a wholly new law in a particular area. Judges (however creative they are) cannot make major reversals or big changes to the common law—this requires legislation. A good example of statutory intervention is the Unfair Contract Terms Act, passed by Parliament in 1977, which provided that certain very unreasonable contract terms and notices were no longer to be legally effective. Included among these were those which say that one person is exempt from any liability for negligently causing death or personal injury to another person. The courts had struggled for years to find common law solutions to protect people from onerous exclusion clauses and notices of this kind, but parliamentary intervention was able to do the trick in an instant. From the moment this statute was passed, it replaced all the old common law on the question of the validity of such notices and clauses. When passing the Unfair Contract Terms Act, Parliament had the benefit of guidance from the *Law Commission*. This body, consisting of judges, barristers, solicitors and academic lawyers, considers whether particular areas of law need reform, puts proposals for change out to consultation with lawyers and other interested parties, and produces reports detailing its final conclusions. Parliament is not obliged to implement the Law Commission's recommendations, but frequently does so.

Today, many statutes are also passed to give effect to the UK's commitments to the European Union. So, for example, in July 1985 the European Community adopted a Directive on Product Liability requiring Member States to implement domestic legislation providing that manufacturers would be liable, even if not at fault in the traditional sense, for any personal injury or damage to property caused by their defective products. This Directive means the 27 Member States of the European Union all have compatible, harmonised product liability regimes. The

UK government implemented the Directive by passing the Consumer Protection Act 1987.

Most statutes, even those introducing completely new rules, assume and build on the existing common law in some way—they rarely arrive out of a clear blue sky. For example, statutory provisions protect *employees* from being unfairly dismissed, but the question 'who is an employee' is answered by reference to the common law's understanding of a *contract* of employment. In addition, the common law still has a role to play when a statute is enacted in a particular area. Judges may need to interpret what a particular statutory provision means and, having decided what it means, this interpretation will then become law in its own right and be applied in future cases.

By now, you will have worked out that existing common law cases, and the rules set down in them, are important in deciding new cases. They not only influence the result in the new case, but also dictate what that result will be, because the fundamental basis of the common law system is the doctrine of *precedent*. To grasp fully the importance of this doctrine, we must first understand the structure of the courts in England.

At its simplest, the structure of the courts (see Fig. 1.1 on page 10, below) consists of trial judges at the lowest level, then the Court of Appeal and finally the House of Lords. The doctrine of precedent requires the lower level courts to be *bound* by the decisions of superior courts on matters of *law*—they have no choice but to follow the rule set down in those superior decisions. Don't ignore the words 'of law' in the previous sentence—trial judges often have to decide between conflicting pieces of evidence and work out the *facts* of the case, and in this aspect of their decision-making the doctrine of precedent has no role to play. But where issues of law are concerned, a trial judge is bound by decisions of the Court of Appeal and the House of Lords, and the Court of Appeal is bound by the decisions of the House of Lords. Also, courts of a particular level are generally bound by decisions of other courts at the same level. So, for example, the Court of Appeal is bound by other, earlier, decisions of the Court of Appeal, although on very rare occasions it is possible for the Court of Appeal to overrule one of its own earlier decisions. Likewise, the House of Lords can in theory overrule its own, earlier, decisions, but like the Court of Appeal, it does so only on very rare occasions and for exceptional reasons. On the other hand, higher courts are *not* bound by decisions of lower courts. So, for example, the House of Lords can, and frequently does, overrule decisions of the Court of Appeal in earlier cases, just as it can reverse the result in the particular case being appealed to it and allow the appeal.

This book focuses on the law of England, which includes the law of Wales. This system is primarily common law based. Scottish law is different. It is derived from Roman law, which is the tradition which also applies in continental Europe. The Scottish system, also sometimes called the *civilian* system (not to be confused with the more common meaning of the phrase 'civil' law as the opposite of criminal law, which is discussed below), is based on formal written Codes prescribing the detail of the law. In contrast to the common law, civilian judges have no law-making function at all, other than in interpreting and applying the Code. However, the law of England and Wales, on the one hand, and Scotland, on the other hand, is not as different as would first appear. In areas which have not been devolved to the Scottish Parliament or the Welsh Assembly, statutes passed by the Westminster Parliament in London apply to all three jurisdictions and the interpretation of those statutes by the Scottish courts has persuasive effect on the English courts. Further, and somewhat surprisingly, decisions of the House of Lords bind the courts throughout the United Kingdom, including Scotland, and (as we shall see in chapter 4) the House of Lords is the highest appeal court for Scottish cases as well as those from England and Wales.

At present, Northern Ireland's legal system is very similar to that of England and Wales, applying the common law in an identical judicial structure (with final appeals to the House of Lords), though with some differences in dealing with criminal offences involving terrorism. The Northern Ireland Assembly, which was reactivated in May 2007, has legislative power and so in future there may well be significant changes in the legal system and procedure operating in Northern Ireland.

All this discussion of domestic law should not blind you to the variety of other sources of law which have a significant impact on domestic law. We have already mentioned the important influence of European Community law on the United Kingdom (this is considered further in chapter 8). In addition, the European Convention on Human Rights, incorporated into domestic law by the Human Rights Act 1998, provides litigants with an important way of challenging the validity of acts and decisions taken by the government. Other *international law* rules are also important. International law concerns treaties binding on states, such as the Law of the Sea Convention and the UN Convention on the Rights of the Child. Occasionally, English courts refer to international law to assist in the interpretation of ambiguous provisions of national law.

Classification

We have already seen some of the classifications lawyers use, such as statute/common law and national/EC law. Another important distinction is between the civil and criminal systems, which is reflected in the structure of the court system itself. *Criminal law* is the power of the state to punish people for causing harm or for being involved in other forms of unacceptable conduct. Most minor crimes are dealt with in Magistrates' Courts; more serious cases are heard in the Crown Court by a judge and jury (see figure 1.1 below). Appeals in Crown Court cases can go to the Court of Appeal (Criminal Division) and then to the House of Lords. In criminal cases the accused, referred to as the defendant, is *prosecuted* by the state in the name of the Queen (*Regina*). In practice, the prosecution is dealt with by the Crown Prosecution Service, a body of professional prosecutors acting in the name of the Queen. The cases are therefore referred to as *Regina* (abbreviated as R) *versus* (abbreviated as *v*) [the name of the defendant]. So, if John Smith is being prosecuted his case would be called *R v Smith*. It would be written this way too, but when talking about a case lawyers generally say 'and' instead of '*v*', so the case would be called 'R *and* Smith' but, more usually, simply by the name of the defendant ('*Smith*'). If the prosecutor is successful the defendant is found *guilty*.

Civil cases are all those cases which are not criminal, such as cases involving contract, tort, employment, commercial, trusts or property law. Civil cases start in either the County Court, for cases involving smaller sums of money, or the High Court, for cases involving larger sums. The vast majority of civil cases are heard by a judge without a jury (defamation cases being a notable exception). Appeals on the law go to the Court of Appeal (Civil Division) and then, with permission, to the House of Lords. In civil cases the *claimant* (who used to be known as the plaintiff)

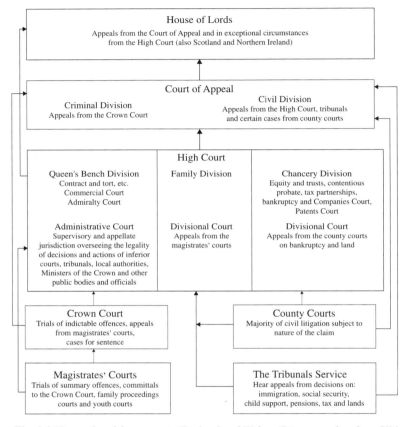

Fig. 1.1 *Hierarchy of the courts in England and Wales. (Diagram taken from HM Courts Service's website and reproduced with kind permission of HM Courts Service.)*

sues the *defendant*. If the claimant is successful then the defendant is held *liable*. For this reason, lawyers often talk about *liability*, saying things like 'these facts give rise to negligence liability' or 'if contractual liability is established, the defendant must pay damages'—remember that this simply relates back to the notion of the defendant being legally responsible.

Civil cases are usually referred to by the names of the parties (eg, *Smith v Jones*). On appeal, parties are called the *appellant* and the *respondent.* When writing the name of a case it is usual to underline or italicise the names. As we saw above, when speaking about a case or reading out the case name *Smith v Jones* will be referred to as 'Smith and Jones'.

Apart from the different courts which hear the cases and the different terminology used, another major distinction between civil and criminal cases is the burden of proof. In criminal cases, the prosecutor must prove that the defendant is guilty beyond all reasonable doubt: if there is any remaining flicker of reasonable doubt about the defendant's guilt then the magistrate or jury must not convict. In civil cases, the claimant has to prove a case only to the lower standard of 'balance of probabilities', meaning that the defendant's liability is more probable than not. The higher standard in criminal cases reflects the fact that, if convicted, defendants can lose their liberty and be sent to prison.

The other distinction which is commonly drawn by commentators who write about law is between public and private law. Public law deals with the powers of the state and, in particular the relationships between the different arms of the state, namely the legislature (law-makers), the executive (government, and the arms of the executive such as the police) and the judiciary. In some countries, such as the USA and Germany, these relationships are laid down in a written constitution. In the UK we do not (yet) have such a document but the equivalent principles and conventions have developed over the years and form our unwritten constitution, which is considered in chapter 7. Public law includes administrative law, which regulates the relationship between the individual citizen and the state. In this context, the 'state' can take a number of forms (central government, local authorities and agencies).

Private law deals with the rights and duties of individuals towards one another, such as the duty to carry out a contract or to avoid injuring another person by negligent acts or omissions, as well as the remedies which the courts can order when rights are infringed or duties breached, such as ordering the defendant to pay money to the claimant to compensate for loss suffered (damages) or, much less commonly, ordering the defendant to stop committing some ongoing harm (an injunction).

Case Law

Citing a Case

When you are studying law, you need to be able to find cases easily. Not all cases are reported in law reports, but those which are have a *citation*. The first case which forms the subject matter of a chapter in this book is the criminal case of *R v Brown and others*. This is a decision of the House of Lords and is reported at [1994] 1 AC 212. [1994] refers to the year of publication of the report (the case was actually decided in 1993). AC is an abbreviation of one set of law reports called 'Appeal Cases' and the numbers mean that *Brown* is reported in the first volume from 1994 on page 212. There are many series of law reports but the Appeal Cases form part of the official law reports, the most prestigious series.

Since 2001 a new, official mode of citation has been developed, called the system of *neutral citation*. This is a universal system: it does not refer to a particular set of published law reports, but rather is a citation which tells you the year in which judgment was given and also which court gave the judgment. This is then followed by a number which is unique to that case. So, for example, a case may have a reference [2007] UKHL 54, meaning that the judgment was given in 2007, in the United Kingdom House of Lords and was the 54th judgment of that court in that year. The neutral citation is an especially useful way of finding cases online.

The internet has revolutionised the way that the common law system works. For students, life is now much easier, because they can search for a case and find the text of it online, even if they can remember the name of only one of the parties, without having to venture into a law library. There are also online journals and sets of specialist law reports that are never published in paper form. The internet has been helpful in a substantive sense too. The doctrine of precedent means that a new case becomes part of the common law as soon as the court gives its judgment. However, before the internet the *text* of a new case was hard to find at first and often wasn't published in a law report for several months, even years, after being decided. Now, the texts of new cases are available on the internet within hours of being decided. It is also much easier for practising lawyers to find every precedent that might have some relevance to their client's case. However, this aspect of the internet is not viewed by everyone as an advantage. For example, judges were not happy when barristers in court began to cite hundreds of cases of very minor relevance to the issue they were dealing with, simply because the barristers had found them online. Eventually a new rule of civil procedure was introduced to limit the number of precedents that either side in a dispute is allowed to cite in court.

Reading a Case

When you have found a case, you need to be able to read it carefully. That means not simply getting from beginning to end but understanding the different elements included.

Most law reports start with a head-note, a summary of the facts and the decision, prepared by a law reporter. It does not constitute any part of the judgment and is not a source of law in its own right. However, the head-note has a use in enabling you to work out what the case is actually about and whether it is going to be relevant to your inquiry. You must never fall into the trap of believing that reading the head-note means that you do not need to read the whole case, although its summary of the *facts* may be beneficial, helping you to focus your energy on reading, thinking about and maybe even criticising the legal reasoning in the judgments that follow.

Studying law in a system based on precedent involves being able to work out precisely what a case decided. This is known as the *ratio decidendi*, or sometimes simply the *ratio*—the 'nugget of law' that the court used to reach its decision on the particular result. Discovering the *ratio* of a case requires you to work out what the key facts were and what rules were applied to those facts. It may surprise you but this can be a difficult and controversial task, one that lawyers may struggle with long after a case is reported, sometimes for decades. Indeed, the skill of discerning what exactly a difficult case decided and stands for is one which lawyers can spend entire careers perfecting.

Where more than one judge delivers an opinion it is particularly hard to work out the actual legal ruling. These areas of disagreement give lawyers room for manoeuvre later when arguing a subsequent case for their client. They might seek to persuade the judge that the ratio of a case was X and not Y. Alternatively, they might argue that the facts of the present case are so different from the earlier case that the earlier case should be *distinguished.* In other words, the ruling in the earlier case should not be applied to the present dispute.

If you are dealing with a decision of the House of Lords you may have to read as many as five speeches, and occasionally more (the Law Lords give speeches, not judgments, reflecting the fact that currently they sit in the judicial Chamber of the House of Lords: soon they will be moving to a separate Supreme Court). Even a decision of the Court of Appeal may contain up to three judgments. So, although it is common for one or more of the appellate judges simply to agree with the detailed reasoning of one of the others and add nothing more of detail, sometimes all the judges want to give us the benefit of their detailed views.

It gets particularly interesting where there is disagreement among the panel of judges, so that for example three or four Law Lords want to allow the defendant's appeal but one or two would prefer to refuse it. That leaves you trying to work out which judges form the majority and which are in the minority. It is only the judgments of the majority which constitute the law that derives from the case, but a speech given by a judge in the minority (usually known as a dissenting speech or a *dissent*) can nonetheless be well worth reading in detail. Not only does it help you to understand the controversies behind the majority decision and decide whether you agree with it, but it may also turn out to be more important in the future. For example, the Court of Appeal had to decide in the 1950s whether a negligent accountant could ever be liable to a claimant who suffered financial loss because the claimant relied on incorrect statements made by the accountant, where that claimant was not the accountant's own client (so that there was no contract between them). The majority said that no claim was possible, but Lord Denning dissented and explained in his speech why he thought there *should* be liability in this case and in others like it. More than 10 years later, the House of Lords overruled the 1950s' decision and said in strident terms that Lord Denning had been right all along.

You may also read part of a judgment which is not strictly relevant to the decision on the facts, but involves the judge expressing his or her opinion on a related legal issue. This is known as an *obiter dictum* (or *obiter dicta* if there is more than one such expression of opinion). An *obiter dictum* does not form part of the *ratio* of the case and does not bind other judges, but it might persuade other judges to adopt that approach in a future case where the particular issue arises.

Courts and Other Means of Resolving Disputes

It is important to be aware that the different levels of courts have different types of judge. The lower courts typically have just one judge presiding (referred to as 'judge' and whose name would be written: Bloggs J). The Court of Appeal sits in chambers of three and the judges are referred to as Lord Justices (so: Bloggs LJ). The two most senior of the Lords Justice are the Master of the Rolls for civil cases and the Lord Chief Justice for criminal cases. The House of Lords is the superior court in the United Kingdom. In this context, the 'House of Lords' does not mean all the hereditary and life peers, but only very senior judges appointed to be 'Lords of Appeal in Ordinary', commonly known as Law Lords. This court hears appeals only on questions of law. Typically, appeals in the House of Lords are heard by five judges. However, there are well-developed plans to create a new Supreme Court to replace the House of Lords as a judicial court. We are still waiting for details about how this new Supreme Court will work.

While we have concentrated so far on the main courts, it is important to be aware that there are other methods of resolving legal disputes. There are other courts throughout the system, like the Small Claims Court which provides a quicker and more informal method of dispute resolution for relatively minor civil disputes. There are also other state tribunals which deal with specialised disputes, such as tax appeals and employment disputes; cases decided in these tribunals can be appealed to the High Court or equivalent if the losing party wishes to challenge the decision. Another important option in practice, particularly for commercial disputes, is for the dispute to be decided by *arbitration* rather than in the courts. Arbitration will take place where the parties have agreed in their contract that, if there is a dispute between them, then an independent, qualified and often highly specialist arbitrator will be appointed who will decide the dispute and that the arbitrator's decision will bind the parties. This is particularly useful in resolving complex commercial disputes and it is cheaper and quicker than having a protracted trial in the High Court.

Some organisations also have their own tribunals to consider disciplinary matters, such as sports tribunals, which deal, for example, with doping allegations involving competitors, and professional bodies, such as the Solicitors' Disciplinary Tribunal which deals with complaints about solicitors. Certain industries and public bodies (such as local government, insurance and pensions) have what is called an ombudsman: an independent and qualified official whose job it is to resolve, if possible, complaints from members of the public without the need for litigation.

At the other end of the spectrum, there are also two key courts in Europe, namely the European Court of Justice (ECJ) based in Luxembourg and the European Court of Human Rights (ECtHR) based in Strasbourg. They are often confused with each other but it is vitally important to remember that these are two completely different bodies with entirely different functions. The ECtHR gives authoritative interpretations of the European Convention on Human Rights, to which the United Kingdom is a party. The ECJ, on the other hand, has much less to do with human rights; rather (as we shall see in chapter 8) it hears *references* from the national courts, which are questions as to the meaning and validity of European Community law on, for example, free trade issues, as well as deciding other sorts of issue concerning Community law.

LEGAL METHOD

The discussion so far might make you think that studying law as an academic subject will involve simply looking up rules and regulations in dusty old books, but there is an awful lot more to it than that. This perception of law as an academic subject is based on the popular misconception that there must be a 'right' answer to any legal question if only you look hard enough and read enough books. As you will soon discover, while some aspects of the law are clear, others are far from certain, particularly when dealing with questions of precedent. Lawyers and law students frequently need to tackle some very complex and subtle questions when working out what the law is, or should be, in a given situation. In this section we consider various skills you will need to do this.

Description

The most straightforward aspect of studying law is when you are simply asked to describe the law in one particular area. If you need to consider what the law says on a particular point you will have to look at various books, law reports and statutes to find the current state of the law. So, for example, you may need to describe the law on what is the crime of murder, what counts as a valid contract, or when squatters acquire rights over the land they are occupying. It goes without saying that any description you produce needs to be expressed in elegant, often simple, but grammatically correct English.

Sometimes the description of a particular area of the law is straight-forward, because it has been accepted and settled for many years. Here it might be sufficient to rely on a reputable textbook for a concise statement of the law. However, the law is never entirely static: legislation is repealed and replaced; old cases are overruled or applied to surprising new areas; new cases are decided in unexpected ways. This is one of the fascinating things about the law—you will be studying a dynamic, developing organism not a fossilised and unchanging text—and means that what once might have been accepted as straightforward law may now be much more controversial. It also means that you can never entirely rely on a textbook, even one that was published relatively recently, for the correct state of the law. Moreover, sometimes there simply is no consensus about what the state of the law is on a particular point, so even the usually straightforward task of describing the law may in fact prove very complicated.

Applying the Law

Identifying the Nature of the Problem

Although it is of some interest to be able to describe the state of the law, law is never studied in a vacuum. Law is meant to be applied, so when you study law you spend a lot of time applying the law to real or hypothetical problems. This requires, first of all, careful identification of the nature of the problem with which you are dealing. You then need to work out what law applies to the problem and then apply that law to determine the result. This is how lawyers in practice have to approach problems, since they need to advise clients who want their disputes resolved by the law or who want to be able to structure their business or personal affairs to avoid legal difficulties in the future.

The process of applying the law varies, depending on the field of law. For example, a number of the private law core subjects, such as contract, tort and equity, involve, as central issues, the commission of some form of wrongdoing by the defendant, for which the claimant seeks a legal remedy. In such circumstances it is vital to know what the nature of the wrong is, to determine what area of the law you are concerned with. This will require you to identify what is called the *cause of action*. This is the basic set of elements which need to be in place before the claimant can establish that the defendant is liable. For example, let's go back to where we began—to Laura's party and the guest tripping on an uneven patio slab. He suffered a serious injury and now wishes to sue the owner/ occupier of the house for damages. He may be able to bring a claim under the Occupiers' Liability Act 1957, but only if he can establish all the elements required by the statute for that cause of action. In this example, the injured claimant would have to show that (1) he was a lawful visitor on the premises (a more recent, stricter statutory regime applies to claims by trespassers); (2) the occupier failed to take reasonable care to ensure that visitors would be reasonably safe on the premises; and (3) the claimant suffered personal injury as a result of that failure by the occupier. If the claimant can establish all these things, he will have a cause of action for damages in tort.

However, establishing the cause of action is not necessarily the end of the story, because the defendant might be able to respond by establishing a *defence* to the claim, meaning an excuse recognised by law which would enable the defendant to escape liability. You are probably familiar with some of the defences in criminal law, such as provocation and self-defence, but there are equivalents in civil cases. For example, the defendant may try to prove that the party guest expressly consented to run the risk of tripping on the patio stone, though that is not very likely to succeed. Much more plausible is the defence of contributory negligence, in which the defendant argues that his liability should be reduced in some way to reflect the fact that the claimant was partly to blame for his injuries. Finally, you will need to consider what type of *remedy* will be available to the claimant if he or she can prove all the elements of the cause of action and fend off the defendant's defences. The most common remedy is financial, awarding damages to compensate the claimant for the loss suffered by the wrong. But for other causes of action different remedies may be available, such as a court order to make the defendant do (or not do) something. This is called an injunction. There are also remedies which enable the claimant to recover money or property from the defendant.

This analysis of the law as involving causes of action, defences and remedies only works for private law subjects involving obligations and property. In this book, these are the foundation subjects of contract, tort, land law and equity. For the other foundation subjects different approaches may need to be adopted, but it is still necessary to identify the nature of the problem carefully and break the law down into its key elements to be able to apply the relevant legal rules to resolve the problem.

Drawing Distinctions

A system based on precedent is not always wholly straightforward, despite the simplicity of its basic premise that like cases must be treated alike. In practice, cases often arise that are very *similar* to an existing case but not absolutely identical. A lawyer then has to decide whether and to what extent the (sometimes subtle) differences matter: is this case none-theless sufficiently similar to the existing precedent that we should *apply* the same rule, or are the differences significant enough that we should *distinguish* the existing rule and not apply it, maybe recognising a new exception to the existing rule at the same time? This process of drawing distinctions is one of the most important skills for a lawyer, one sufficiently fundamental that we will return to it in more detail in chapter 9. For now, one simple example will give the flavour. If you promise in a contract not to do something but then do that very thing, the court will normally order you to stop doing what you promised not to do by grant-ing an injunction. However, if the agreement is a contract of work and you promised not to work for anybody other than the employer, then the court will be reluctant to grant an injunction to make you work for the employer, because this would have the effect of making you work for somebody when you do not want to do so; this would be tantamount to slavery. Consequently, in *Warren v Mendy*, the court distinguished the general rule and refused to grant an injunction to make the defendant work for the employer. Instead, the employer was granted a monetary remedy for the breach of contract in the form of damages to compensate him for the loss he had suffered.

Making Predictions

As the previous paragraph showed, there are times when you might be faced with a particular problem and find that there appears to be no statute or case which covers that particular area or, if there is some law in the area, that it is contradictory or confused. Now you need to work out what judges would say if they were faced with the problem. This requires you to put yourself in the position of the judge and survey the existing law to try to find clues as to how the problem would be resolved. Finding the solution requires looking at any rules that do exist, working out the purpose and policy behind those rules and then, if necessary, drawing analogies from other areas of law to see if they support a plausible conclusion.

The following example will give a taste of this process. It has long been an established part of the law that it is straightforward to sue for damages if the defendant's negligence caused the claimant to suffer personal injury. So if a doctor negligently failed to diagnose the claimant's medical condition correctly, with the result that the claimant is left with a permanent injury instead of being totally cured, the doctor is liable. It was, in contrast, traditionally very difficult, if not impossible, for a claimant to sue a public authority for damages if he or she 'lost out' because that authority negligently failed to perform one of its public responsibilities properly (like running hospitals, highways, social services, etc). Then in the 1990s the courts were faced with two wholly new sorts of negligence case, dealing with issues that simply did not exist when the precedents were decided. These were claims for damages brought by children in two situations. The first concerned children who had been taken into care because the council's social workers negligently thought the children were the victims of child abuse by their parents at home when, in fact, the parents were not abusing their children. The second situation concerned children who were dyslexic but whose dyslexia was not diagnosed during their school days as a result of the negligence of the council's educational psychologists. There were no English precedents covering either of these areas, or even analogous areas, so the lawyers advising the parties had to engage in a lot of (educated) prediction about what the courts would decide.

Interestingly, very few lawyers successfully predicted the eventual House of Lords' decisions on either issue. Even specialist negligence practitioners and academics found the decisions startling and surprising.

In 1995, their Lordships decided that children whose future prospects were adversely affected because educational psychologists negligently failed to diagnose their dyslexia were owed a duty of care in negligence and were thus entitled to damages. However, in contrast, the House of Lords decided at the same time that no duty of care was owed to children who suffered ongoing child-abuse when social workers negligently failed to spot what was happening and take them into care. This was mainly because the Law Lords thought that if social workers were to have potential negligence liability hanging over them, this would unduly hamper their independence and decisiveness when dealing with child-protection cases although, as many commentators pointed out, their Lordships had not actually had the benefit of any concrete evidence to back up this view.

Many lawyers believed these results were the wrong way round, and that the law of negligence had got into a position of having, or appearing to have, its values and priorities muddled up. Happily, the European Court of Human Rights has since decided that the abused children did not obtain an adequate remedy from the UK courts when the House of Lords rejected their negligence claims, so the law is now that both sorts of claimant can in theory claim damages (although, of course, to get such damages they must also be able to prove that the defendants were actually negligent—no easy task and one that the tabloid newspapers virtually always overlook when complaining about the 'compensation culture').

Interpretation

Sometimes the meaning of the rules in an area of the law is not clear. As a lawyer, you need to be able to interpret the law before you can describe it and then apply it. Different approaches apply when you are interpreting the meaning of cases and the meaning of statutes.

As we have already seen, when you read a case there may be a variety of questions which arise involving interpretation. It may not be obvious what a case decides because, perhaps, a variety of issues were considered in the case or there was disagreement among the judges and it is necessary to determine which judges were in the majority. The judges' words may also be ambiguous or be context-specific, and so you are required to interpret them very carefully.

Reading a statute may also bring problems of interpretation. The wording of the statute may not be clear, leaving you to work out what the words mean. One of the big questions of statutory interpretation concerns whether the words should be interpreted *literally* or whether the ambiguity can be resolved by considering the *purpose* of the provision. A similar dilemma applies when interpreting the meaning of complex written contracts.

A good example is the case of *J Pereira Fernandes SA v Mehta*, which involved the interpretation of a very old statute called the Statute of Frauds 1677. Fraud was fairly widespread in the seventeenth century, and the purpose of the statute was to reduce the problem by requiring certain sorts of contract, such as transactions involving the sale of land and the sale of goods, to be made in writing and signed by the parties. If a transaction did not comply with the statutory requirements, it was unenforceable. In fact, the Statute of Frauds is still in force, although over the years the list of transactions to which it applies has been whittled away, but crucially it still applies to '*agreements of guarantee*'.

In *J Pereira Fernandes SA v Mehta* the defendant promised to guarantee payment of a company's debts to the claimant (in other words, he promised that if the company did not pay its debts, the defendant would pay them instead). Section 4 of the Statute of Frauds requires the guarantee to be in writing and with the guarantor's signature. The problem was that the defendant made the offer of the guarantee to the claimant by email, which the claimant then accepted orally. The defendant's name did not appear in the email, but his email address was automatically inserted by an internet service provider. Obviously, when the Statute of Frauds was enacted electronic communication was not contemplated, so could the statutory requirement of writing be interpreted to include the sending of an email? The trial judge concluded that it could, but he went on to explore the additional requirement from the Statute of Frauds that the document had to be signed. In his view, a signature required an intention to authenticate the document (ie, to establish the document as genuine) and so he did not regard the inclusion of an email address by the internet provider as sufficient. Consequently, the requirement of the Statute of Frauds was not met and so the guarantee was not enforceable: in other words, the claimant could not sue the defendant to pay up. This case illustrates elegantly what is called 'purposive interpretation' of a statute. The court had to look at the purpose behind the requirement of writing and a signature and work out whether the inclusion of an email address met that purpose.

Another example of statutory interpretation is found in *Serco v Redfearn* concerning the interpretation of the Race Relations Act (RRA) 1976 in the workplace context. This Act prohibits discrimination on 'racial grounds', a phrase which the courts have previously interpreted broadly to cover not just obvious cases in which employees from ethnic minorities are given less favourable treatment, but also to protect white employees who are *instructed* by their employers to discriminate against fellow employees from ethnic minorities. Redfearn was dismissed from his job as a bus driver when it was discovered that he was a local councillor for the British National Party (BNP). The BNP's constitution states that it is wholly opposed to any form of integration between British and non-European peoples. The bus company justified dismissing Redfearn on health and safety grounds (a lawful reason for dismissal), arguing that its staff and passengers, many of whom were Asian, would be anxious in Redfearn's presence and also that he might be attacked at work. Redfearn argued that his dismissal was really on racial grounds, and therefore in breach of the RRA 1976, but the Employment Tribunal disagreed and found that the 'health and safety' grounds were genuine. However, on appeal, the Employment Appeal Tribunal (EAT) overturned this decision because the Employment Tribunal had not explored whether those health and safety grounds were themselves influenced by racial considerations.

The EAT's reasoning raised the spectre of a provision, which had been interpreted to protect white employees from having to do racist things, being invoked by a racist to protect himself. The Court of Appeal was horrified by this possible outcome. Looking at the objectives of the Race Relations Act 1976, Mummery LJ said that Redfearn's 'sweeping proposition is wrong in principle, is inconsistent with the purposes of the legislation and is unsupported by authority'. He said that it produced the absurd consequence that an employer who, in trying to improve race relations, dismissed an employee whom he discovered had been guilty of racist abuse, would be liable for race discrimination. Redfearn therefore lost his case.

Serco v Redfearn shows how different judges at different levels in the judicial hierarchy can reach very different conclusions on the same set of facts and applying the same legal provisions. It also demonstrates how a simple examination of the dictionary meaning of words may not be sufficient to decide the outcome of a particular case. Mummery LJ recognised this and, when interpreting the statute, called upon the values behind the legislation as well as considering the absurd consequences of ruling in favour of Redfearn. This purposive approach to interpretation is also characteristic of European Community law. As both the *J Pereira Fernandes SA* and *Serco* cases demonstrate, it is increasingly being used by English judges too. Whether the flexibility this brings is invariably an entirely good thing, or whether it sometimes comes at the expense of clarity and certainty in working out the legal rules, is an open question.

Imagination

When asked to list the skills needed to make a good lawyer, few people would think of putting 'imagination' on their list—the law seems far too technical to need such a creative skill. But in fact lawyers need to use their imagination all the time. For example, when a claimant sues a defendant for damages for negligence, one of the relevant issues for the court to decide is whether the defendant breached the *standard of care* expected when doing whatever the defendant was doing when the claimant was harmed. This is an objective test—the question is not whether the defendant was careless by his or her own standards, but rather whether he or she came up to the standard of a *reasonable person* engaged in that particular activity. Traditionally this hypothetical, reasonable person was labelled 'the man on the Clapham omnibus', but today this phrase is considered outdated, so tends to be avoided.

In any event, the lawyer acting for the claimant has a lot more work to do than simply reminding the court of the law and convincing the court that the claimant's version of the facts is the correct one. As well as proving what the defendant actually did, the claimant's lawyer must also show what the hypothetical reasonable person *would have done* in the same situation, which in turn means (because of the objective standard of care) that this is what the defendant *should have* done. The claimant must also prove that if the defendant had followed this hypothetical path instead, the claimant would not have been harmed. This hypothetical version of events is sometimes called the *counterfactual*. Very often this counterfactual enquiry about the standard of care is too obvious even to be noticed: if the defendant failed to stop at a red light and smashed into the claimant on a pedestrian crossing as a result, it is obvious that the hypothetical reasonable driver would have stopped and the accident would have been avoided. But sometimes it is not so obvious. This is where imagination comes in, on the defendant's side as well as the claimant's. After all, this sort of argument is not about the facts (what actually happened), but nor is it really a legal argument either— precedents can only help us so far in working out what the reasonable person would have done in a given situation.

For example, in *Surtees v Kingston Upon Thames Borough Council and another* a foster mother was caring for a two-year old child; at bath time she left the child sitting on the laundry basket in the bathroom for a moment while going to fetch a towel from just outside. The child managed to knock the hot tap on the basin and badly scalded her foot, so sued her foster mother (and the local authority) for damages in negligence (this may sound bizarre, but if successful the child's damages would come from an insurance policy, not the foster mother's own pocket). The court had to decide whether the foster mother had come up to the standard of the reasonable foster mother in that situation, or whether she had taken an unreasonable risk. The claimant's lawyer had a relatively easy task, detailing why it was dangerous to leave a two-year-old child in the vicinity of the hot tap. But the defendant's lawyer retorted with lots of very imaginative arguments as to why the foster mother had *not* acted *un*reasonably. These included the fact that she was looking after lots of other children, so if she carried the claimant around everywhere she would have neglected the others; that it is not necessarily a good idea to cushion children from *all* risks, because that way they grow up with no idea of how to assess risks and therefore might end up more seriously injured in the future; that carrying the child out of the bathroom might itself have been more dangerous; and that demanding too high a standard from foster parents might put people off volunteering for the role, which would be detrimental to more children in the long term. These imaginative factual and policy arguments convinced both the trial judge and the Court of Appeal, so the child's claim failed.

Generalisation

If your study of the law was confined simply to describing, applying and interpreting the law, with a bit of imagination thrown in, you would soon be faced by a very confusing mass of seemingly unconnected legal rules derived from a lot of legal sources. So there is a further dimension to the study of law, which is usefully called *generalisation* or, sometimes, the search for principle. Lawyers spend a lot of time examining a mass of rules and then try to identify a principle which explains those rules and which links similar cases at a higher level of generalisation. The identification of these principles makes the law much more manageable, but also gives a much better idea of the real point of the particular area of law, allowing both patterns and inconsistencies to appear.

This process of generalisation is a bit like looking at a television screen or an impressionist painting. If you get very close to the screen you can see lots of individual pixels or dots, but you cannot make out a picture. For that, you need to step back to put the pixels or dots together to see the big picture. In the same way, the process of generalisation of the law requires you to step back to see the bigger picture. Once you have identified some principles, you can then step back even further to link the different pictures together to produce an even bigger picture. This is a bit like looking at an aerial photograph on a website. You could focus on your house in your road, but that will not enable you to see how that road fits in with the neighbourhood. So you can draw back to see the whole town and then back further to see the county, and further to see the country, and further to see the continent and further to see the world.

This sort of generalisation process goes on throughout the law, at all sorts of different level. For example, parliamentary draftsmen, when preparing the wording of new statutes, invariably have to think in general terms, so as to draft statutory wording that deals with problems at a high level of generality: far better than having to include exhaustive lists of every possible example that will be covered by the legislation. Likewise appellate judges, especially in the House of Lords, often have to generalise in the sense of examining lots of earlier, seemingly disparate, cases and pointing out that they are in fact linked by a principle that had not been recognised before, so as to assist in deciding the particular case that has been appealed to them at the time and to make the law clearer in future cases.

One of the best examples, as we will see in more detail in chapter 4, is the development of the modern law of negligence. In the nineteenth century there were a number of unrelated situations (for example, those involving 'occupiers and their guests' and 'horse-drawn carriages and pedestrians') in which the defendant was liable to compensate the claimant for harm suffered as a result of his negligence, but nobody had yet spotted that these different cases might be better regarded as examples of one more general principle. It wasn't until 1932, in perhaps the most famous case in the English law reports, *Donoghue v Stevenson* (about a snail in a bottle of ginger beer), that the House of Lords examined all of these different cases and synthesised the law, recognising for the first time the general principles that underpin the law of negligence today.

Academic lawyers and law students are frequently better placed to recognise general principles than judges and lawyers who concentrate on dealing with the specifics of the case in front of them. Indeed, judges come in for criticism if they focus too much on the implications of their decisions for other areas of the law. Academic lawyers and students, however, have the freedom to compare one area of the law with another, which often enables them to spot patterns and inconsistencies, connections and general principles that have gone unrecognised by practitioners and judges. A good example is the area of law now known as *restitution for unjust enrichment* (not a core subject in undergraduate law courses, but very important nonetheless). For over two centuries the law recognised a lot of different situations where the defendant was liable to pay something back or return something to the claimant, including where money had been paid to the defendant by mistake. Each case shared the common feature that the defendant's obligation to repay was not contractual (after all, he never promised to make the payment), but beyond this no obvious common thread linking the various examples had been spotted. It was not until the publication of a seminal book in the 1960s, *The Law of Restitution*, and later academic writing, that these cases were linked at the level of general principle, creating what was, in effect, a new legal subject (a bit like the introduction of new scientific disciplines like psychotherapy in the nineteenth century and just as hotly disputed). Finally, in 1991 English law officially caught up with this academic progress, when the House of Lords acknowledged in *Lipkin Gorman v Karpnale* that all these different situations could be explained by a principle to prevent the defendant from being unjustly enriched. Most lawyers think the development of the general principle of unjust enrichment has allowed a better understanding of how the law operates and what it achieves in individual cases.

Policy Underpinning the Rule

It is all very well to be able to state what the law is and to be able to apply it to particular problems, but the study of law as an academic subject involves another dimension, namely having regard to the *policy* which underpins the law. This method of legal study is often more theoretical and may also involve engaging with other academic disciplines. For example, we may be concerned with issues of social policy, such as whether a woman, who has cohabited with a man, should have any rights to the house in which they both lived but which was registered only in his name. This is considered further in chapter 5. Elsewhere, lawyers may be concerned with economic issues, in that we are seeking to ensure that the law promotes results which are economically efficient. For example, if you have sold part of your land to a purchaser who made an enforceable contractual promise not to build houses on the land, but who later breaches this promise and builds houses, should you be entitled to enforce that promise and obtain a court order for the destruction of those houses, even at a time of housing shortage?

At other times, lawyers may be concerned with political issues, such as the right balance between freedom of expression and national security, or with ethical issues, such as whether it is appropriate to take body parts from somebody who has just died if it will save somebody else's life, even though the deceased had not given prior consent. Sometimes we may be concerned with philosophical issues, such as whether the law properly respects basic principles of individual autonomy, or with sociological issues, such as whether applying a rule equally to everyone may in fact disadvantage certain groups such as women or ethnic minorities whose social or educational background means that they cannot take advantage of that rule.

These illustrations show that choosing to study law certainly does not close off other avenues of interest in academic terms; far from it, since to master law you really need to understand many other policy issues in society. Much of the real interest in studying and applying law lies in its impact on society. And what is interesting is the extent to which law is, or can be, a vehicle for social change. Take the example of the Sex Discrimination Act 1975 and the Race Relations Act 1976. These statutes were adopted at a time when it was commonplace for sexually and racially discriminatory policies to be applied, especially at work. The Acts were significant catalysts of social change because they contained the important statement that the state disapproves of discrimination on the grounds of sex and race. It is hard to prove cause and effect but attitudes to women and ethnic minorities have certainly changed significantly in the last thirty years.

ONE FINAL EXAMPLE

The application of all the different approaches to the study of law outlined above can be illustrated by the following problem which, as hypothetical legal problems often do, might stretch your sense of credulity. David has just been dumped by his girlfriend. He decides to kill her. He goes to a local craft shop to buy some modelling clay and some pins. He moulds the clay into the shape of his girlfriend and then sticks 10 pins into it. Why? Because he believes in voodoo and thinks that this will kill her. In fact, it has no effect on her at all. Is David guilty of a criminal offence?

First, we need to describe the law in this area. There is a crime of murder which is committed whenever the defendant kills the victim, intending either to kill or to cause serious injury. Clearly, David is not guilty of this offence because his girlfriend is not dead. But there is another crime of *attempted* murder. This is governed by the Criminal Attempts Act 1981, which creates an offence where the defendant does a more than merely preparatory act with the intention to commit a crime. The Act specifically states that it is irrelevant that it is impossible to commit the offence in the circumstances. Reviewing all the cases which have been decided under this statute, it is clear that none of them relate to trying to kill somebody by voodoo. So the simple description of the law does not reveal whether David is guilty of an offence.

We therefore need to move on to the application of the law to the facts. Analysis of the statute reveals that there are three elements to the offence. First, the defendant must have intended to kill his girlfriend. Although intention can be difficult to define, it is clear on our facts that the defendant wanted to kill his girlfriend and so intention can be identified. But the application of the other two elements is less straightforward. What is meant by 'a more than merely preparatory act' and how should the notion of 'impossibility' be defined? Answering these questions requires the statute to be interpreted. Reviewing the cases which have interpreted the statute merely reveals that 'a more than merely preparatory act' means an act which has gone further than merely preparing for the crime. As David has done all that he believes he needs to do to kill his girlfriend, since he stuck all the pins into the model of his girlfriend, it is certainly arguable that he has done a more than merely preparatory act. In reaching this conclusion, we might perhaps distinguish *Campbell*, where the defendant, who had an imitation firearm with him, was arrested by the police just before he entered a post office. He was charged with attempting to rob the post office, but was acquitted because he had not gone beyond preparing for the commission of the crime of robbery. The result would have been different had he gone into the post office before he was arrested. In David's case, he appears to have got beyond preparing for the commission of the crime. But we would also need to consider any possible defences that David might wish to rely on. For example, if his mental state was wholly unhinged at the time (and a belief in voodoo might suggest it was), then perhaps this would excuse David from criminal culpability?

But the central question remains: if it is impossible to kill by voodoo, can the crime of attempted murder really have been committed? To answer this question we need to predict how the courts would decide a case involving voodoo, an issue which has never come before the courts directly. Since the statute is clear that impossibility to commit a crime is no defence, perhaps the judges would feel they had no choice but to conclude that the offence has been committed. But others might argue that there is a meaningful distinction between the sort of impossibility involved in an attempt to kill using a replica gun (which the defendant believed to be loaded) and the sort of impossibility we are dealing with in the voodoo example.

We would also need to consider whether a conviction would be appropriate, just as the courts would do when deciding the case. In considering this it is useful to identify any rules or principles which can be generalised from the cases on criminal attempts. The general principle appears to be that attempting to commit a crime exists as a separate crime in itself in order to punish defendants who want to cause harm to somebody else and who have done some acts towards the commission of this goal, even if the goal can never actually be achieved. It is the *desire* to reach the goal which is most significant and makes the conduct culpable even though no harm has actually been caused to the intended victim. This would justify conviction in David's case.

We might then to go on to consider whether there is any policy which underpins the offence. One policy might be that it is better to arrest and convict a defendant before any harm is committed, so we need a crime of attempt to do this. But this policy would suggest that David should not be convicted because he would never succeed in killing his girlfriend using voodoo. In the light of this clash between policy and principle, we would then need to consider whether the application and interpretation of the law in this case really is defensible. This would turn on whether we consider that it is fair and just to convict a defendant of a crime when he or she has not caused any harm and will not do so using that method. Other issues might arise, such as whether it is a good use of scarce public resources to prosecute someone who has no prospect of causing harm by his chosen method, or whether the mental health system might be more appropriate than a criminal prosecution for dealing with David's situation. So many different questions, suggesting so many conflicting answers: that's what makes law exciting and challenging.

CONCLUSIONS

Learning law is about lots of reading: cases, statutes, textbooks, academic articles, but it is also about thinking: what is the relevant legal rule here? Does it apply to this case or can it be distinguished? Should it apply? If not, why not, and what rule should apply instead? All lawyers need to think—logically, clearly and critically. This is what judges have to do, what practising lawyers have to do when giving legal advice to their clients, and what all law students must do too. The aim of this book is to give you a flavour of this process in action.

Cases

Donoghue v Stevenson [1932] AC 562

J Pereira Fernandes SA v Mehta [2006] 1 WLR 1543; [2006] EWHC 813 (Ch)

Lipkin Gorman v Karpnale [1991] 2 AC 548

R v Campbell [1991] Crim LR 268

Serco v Redfearn [2005] IRLR 744 (EAT); [2006] EWCA Civ 269; [2006] IRLR 623 (Court of Appeal)

Surtees v Kingston Upon Thames Borough Council and another [1991] 2 FLR 559

Warren v Mendy [1989] 3 All ER 103

Websites

For many important cases which are freely available: <http://www.bailii.org>.

For the English and Welsh Law Commission: <http://www.lawcom.gov.uk>, and for the Scottish: <http://www.scotlawcom.gov.uk>.

For links to the many legal resources available on the web: <http://www.law.cam.ac.uk/resources.php>.

Further Reading

On Law

Honoré, *About Law: An Introduction* (Oxford University Press, Oxford 1995)

On Legal Study Skills

Askey and McLeod, *Studying Law* (Palgrave Macmillan, Basingstoke 2006)

Bradney, Cownie, Masson, Neal and Newell, *How to Study Law* (5th edn, Sweet & Maxwell, London 2005)

Holland and Webb, *Learning Legal Rules: A Students' Guide to Legal Method and Legal Reasoning* (6th edn, Oxford University Press, Oxford 2006)

McBride, *Letters to a Law Student* (Pearson, Harlow 2007)

McLeod, *Legal Method* (5th edn, Palgrave Macmillan, Basingstoke 2005)

Smith, *Glanville Williams' Learning the Law* (13th edn, Sweet & Maxwell, London 2006)

2

Criminal Law

Graham Virgo

We hear about crimes all the time and many of us probably feel that we have a pretty good idea of what conduct is criminal, whether it is murder or rape or theft. It may also be pretty obvious why we want to punish people for committing such crimes. But when you study criminal law you cannot rely on gut reaction: you need to think carefully about how crimes are defined, how they should be defined and why it is appropriate for the state to punish somebody. For example, should people who smoke cigarettes in pubs be punished for doing so? Should we punish people who sell drugs? But why don't we punish people who break a contract, or prostitutes for selling sexual services?

THE ELEMENTS OF A CRIME

When lawyers consider whether a crime has been committed they usually break a criminal offence down into three separate elements. First, they consider whether the prohibited conduct and result have occurred. This is known as the external elements of the crime and they are often described by using the Latin term *actus reus*. So, for the crime of murder, the *actus reus* is that the victim is dead and that his or her death was caused by the defendant. Secondly, most crimes also involve a fault element, which is often known as the *mens rea*. Not every crime needs a *mens rea*, but many do, especially serious crimes, because it is the fact that the defendant was at fault which makes him or her blameworthy and justifies the state in punishing the defendant. Relevant fault elements include intention, recklessness and negligence. For the crime of murder the relevant fault element is that the defendant intended either to kill or to cause serious injury. If this cannot be established, the defendant cannot be convicted of murder, although he or she might still be guilty of a less serious offence, such as manslaughter. Once the external and fault elements have been established, the third and final element is whether the defendant has any defences to the crime. For the crime of murder there are a number of full or partial defences which might be available. For example, if the defendant was attacked by the victim, the defendant could plead self-defence. If this defence is successful the defendant would be acquitted of the crime completely, so this is a full defence. Alternatively, the defendant might plead defences such as provocation or diminished responsibility. If one of these partial defences is successful the defendant would be convicted of the less serious offence of manslaughter rather than murder.

THE REASONS FOR PUNISHMENT

Assuming that the defendant has been convicted of a crime, he or she can expect to be punished. The criminal law recognises a variety of forms of punishment including imprisonment, fines and community sentences. Different reasons for punishment can be identified depending on the nature of the punishment, but there are four main reasons why the state wishes to punish a defendant who has been convicted of an offence. First, there is the need to protect the public from dangerous criminals, which can be satisfied by locking the defendant up for a substantial period of time. Secondly, there is the need to deter the defendant and other potential defendants from committing crimes. Thirdly, there is the need to rehabilitate defendants to seek to ensure that they do not commit crimes in future. Finally, there is the need for retribution: society wishes to mark certain types of conduct as wrongful and reassert the accepted social order by punishing the wrongdoer.

REASONS FOR CHARACTERISING CONDUCT AS CRIMINAL

In addition to considering the definition of offences and the reasons for punishment, criminal lawyers also consider another crucial question, namely why certain conduct is criminal and other conduct, which we might dislike, is not treated as criminal. In considering this question there are two separate principles which are involved and which contradict each other. The first is the principle of autonomy. According to this principle, individuals should be free to do whatever they like. But if we allowed this principle to operate without any check we would end up with a society which is lawless and where anarchy prevails. Society needs rules to operate by and so the autonomy of individuals needs to be restrained in some way. We can do this by means of a second principle, which is called the welfare principle. According to this principle, the needs of society must prevail over the interests of individuals. Of course, if we allowed this principle to operate without check we would end up with a totalitarian state where the interests and rights of individuals would always be subordinated to the interests of the state. Whenever we consider whether or not certain conduct should be criminalised we are really considering to what extent, if at all, the autonomy of individuals should be restricted for the benefit of the state and the protection of other individuals. We sometimes describe this restriction on autonomy in other ways. One way is by reference to the doctrine of utilitarianism, where the interests of the majority are more important than the interests of the individual. Also, there is the doctrine of paternalism, where the state intervenes to restrict the autonomy of the individual because the state is acting in the best interests of the individual.

This tension between autonomy and welfare is illustrated by a number of long-running debates in the criminal law. One of the best examples concerns the use of certain types of drug. If we wished to adopt an approach which is simply based on the autonomy of the individual, we would allow all drug-taking to be legal since it would be up to the individual to decide if they wanted to take drugs. However, the state has determined that there are certain types of drug the possession of which should be criminalised because of the dangers posed by drug addicts to other people (the utilitarian argument) and to themselves (the paternalism argument).

The implications of these three distinct issues of the definitions of offences, the reasons for punishment and the reasons for criminalising certain conduct were raised by the very important decision of the House of Lords in a case called *Regina v Brown*.

FACTS OF *BROWN*

Brown concerned a group of more than 40 sado-masochistic homosexuals. Some of these men were sadists who obtained sexual satisfaction from causing pain. Others were masochists who enjoyed having pain inflicted on them. The activities were wide-ranging, but essentially involved branding, piercing and beating sensitive parts of the body. Certain features of the men's activities need to be emphasised. They occurred in private; injuries were inflicted but they did not result in any permanent disability; no infection was caused; the participants had safety words to use to ensure that the activities did not get out of hand; no medical attention was required; and no complaint was made to the police. Crucially, all of the participants consented to the activities.

The police discovered the activities of this group in the course of a separate investigation, called Operation Spanner, into the sale of obscene videos. In the course of this investigation the police discovered private videos of the sado-masochistic activities carried out by Brown and his friends and consequently the participants were charged with various criminal offences.

THE KEY OFFENCES

The defendants were charged with two specific offences contrary to sections 47 and 20 of the Offences Against the Person Act 1861. To be convicted of the section 47 offence it must be shown that the defendant has assaulted the victim so as to cause him or her actual bodily harm. This offence can be broken up into four distinct elements, all of which need to be satisfied to convict the defendant of the offence:

1. Assault: this means either causing the victim to apprehend immediate and unlawful harm to the person (known as common assault) or unlawfully touching the victim (known as battery).
2. Actual bodily harm (otherwise known as ABH): this means that the victim suffered an injury which interfered with the health or comfort of the victim but was more than transient or trifling. So, for example, this would include a broken finger and bruising which was painful to the touch.
3. Causation: that the actual bodily harm was caused by the defendant's conduct.
4. The fault element: the defendant must have intended to assault or batter the victim or foresaw that this might happen as a possibility.

If the defendant is convicted of this offence he or she can be sentenced to imprisonment for a period up to five years. The other relevant offence in *Brown* was maliciously wounding or inflicting grievous bodily harm contrary to section 20. This offence can also be broken up into a number of distinct elements:

1. Either wounding, which means doing something which penetrates all the layers of the victim's skin, so a pin-prick could count as a wound; or
2. Inflicting grievous bodily harm, known as GBH. This injury is defined simply as serious injury. It is clearly worse than ABH and includes broken limbs as well as serious internal injuries. This harm needs to be inflicted. The meaning of this word 'inflicts' has proved to be controversial but it seems that it simply means that the defendant caused the victim GBH.
3. The fault element for this offence is malice, regardless of whether the defendant has wounded or inflicted GBH. Malice here means that the defendant foresaw the possibility of some harm occurring, but that harm need not be as serious as the harm which did actually occur. So, for example, if the defendant punched the victim in the face thinking that the victim would only suffer bruising, but her nose was badly broken, the defendant could be guilty of the section

20 offence because he has inflicted GBH and foresaw the possibility of some harm being caused.

The maximum sentence for this offence is five years' imprisonment, just as for the section 47 offence, even though that offence involves less serious harm. However, in practice, if the defendant is convicted of a section 20 offence then he or she is likely to get a longer sentence than if he or she was convicted of the less serious section 47 offence.

THE ISSUE IN *BROWN*

The key issue for the courts in *Brown* was whether it was appropriate to convict the defendant sadists of harming the masochist victims where the victims wanted to be harmed. In other words, should the consent of the victim operate as a defence? English law accepts that, as a general rule, where the victim consents to harm then that is a valid defence. So, for example, if the defendant tattoos the victim at her own request, the victim's consent means that no crime has been committed. This defence of consent even extends to cases where the victim cannot be shown to have specifically consented to the harm but that harm occurs in circumstances where the victim can be deemed to have consented to it. So, for example, if the defendant slaps the victim on the back as a greeting at a party, that is the type of touching to which everybody can be assumed to have consented. Similarly, if the defendant is playing football with the victim and trips the victim up in order to get the ball, that would usually be the sort of touching to which all football players consent, at least if the defendant has not gone beyond what a player could reasonably have regarded as having been consented to by taking part in the sport. But should any limit be imposed upon the type and circumstances of harm to which the victim can consent? That is the key issue with which the judges in *Brown* had to grapple.

THE TRIAL

The defendants were tried in a Crown Court before a judge and jury. In such a trial the judge has to decide questions of law, such as the proper interpretation of elements of the crime, but the jury has to decide questions of fact in the light of the judge's directions and rulings about legal questions. In *Brown* the jury was asked to consider whether the elements of both the sections 47 and 20 offences had been satisfied to secure a conviction. For the most part this was simply a question of fact. But there was a key question of law, namely that if, as the Defence argued, the victims had consented to the harm, then, because of the extreme circumstances in which that harm was caused, was this consent a valid defence? The judge ruled that it was not and so, even if all the victims did consent, it followed that the defendants were guilty. Following this ruling the defendants pleaded guilty and various sentences of imprisonment were imposed on them, ranging from one to three years.

The Court of Appeal

Following the defendants' conviction they wanted to appeal against the judge's ruling that the defence of consent was not available. This involved appealing to the Court of Appeal (Criminal Division). The argument before the Court of Appeal focused simply on a question of law rather than fact, namely whether the actual consent of the victims meant that the defendants could not be found guilty of the crimes. The judges reviewed earlier cases and concluded that they were bound by these authorities to rule that the victims' consent was not a valid defence. Consequently, the defendants' appeal was rejected. However, their sentences were reduced to between three and six months because they did not know that their conduct was criminal.

The House of Lords

The defendants then appealed to the House of Lords. Three of the five judges decided that the appeal should be rejected and the other two dissented, concluding that the appeal should be allowed. The decision of the majority prevails and so the appeal was rejected, which meant that the defendants' convictions were affirmed.

Since, however, there were three speeches given by the majority, it is not immediately obvious what counts as the 'official' reason for rejecting the appeal. It is, therefore, necessary to analyse these speeches very carefully, and by doing so it is possible to identify a central principle which justifies the decision of the majority. As we saw in chapter 1, this is called identifying the *ratio decidendi*, otherwise known as the *ratio*. The *ratio* of *Brown* is as follows:

- Where the victim has suffered harm which is actual bodily harm or worse, then the victim's consent to that harm is no defence.
- But this principle is subject to an exception, namely that the consent can operate as a defence if the circumstances of the harm can be justified by a good reason.

Since, on the facts of *Brown*, the harm was at least actual bodily harm and because satisfaction of the sado-masochistic libido was not considered by the majority to be a good reason for causing such harm, it followed that the victims' consent was not relevant and the defendants were properly convicted.

The majority identified four key reasons in support of this decision.

Earlier Authorities

Although this was a decision of the House of Lords, which is not bound by earlier decisions of lower courts such as the Court of Appeal, the majority judges in the House of Lords considered it important that their decision was consistent with such earlier authorities. These earlier cases were interpreted as recognising that the consent of the victim to actual bodily harm or worse could be justified only if the conduct was consistent with public policy. So, an earlier decision of the Court of Appeal had held that causing harm in the course of a fight in public was not an acceptable reason even if the victims had consented. This case had recognised that acceptable reasons for consenting to harm would include medical interventions and properly conducted sports. However, the judges in the House of Lords could have decided to overrule these earlier cases if they thought that the principles involved were not acceptable. Indeed, it is even possible for the House of Lords to overrule its own earlier decisions if it is felt that those decisions were incorrect or no longer appropriate.

Technical Reasons

The majority accepted that it was easier to differentiate between no injury and some injury than it was to distinguish between degrees of injury.

Consequently, it was accepted that the appropriate line to be drawn between when the victim's consent should always be a defence and when it should only be a defence if the conduct was consistent with public policy is the line between battery and actual bodily harm, rather than between actual bodily harm and grievous bodily harm. This is, however, highly dubious reasoning, because the criminal law distinguishes between injuries constituting actual bodily harm and grievous bodily harm all the time, since it is the difference between these degrees of injury which underlies the separate offences of section 47 and section 20.

Policy Reasons

A number of policy reasons were identified by the majority for their decision. These included:

- the dangers of more serious injury being caused if the defendant's activities became too exuberant;
- the dangers of infection being transmitted, particularly of the HIV virus; and
- the danger that young men would be corrupted by involvement in sado-masochistic activities.

But all of these factors involve potential harm, none of which was found to have occurred on the facts. It is difficult to justify the decision in *Brown* on the basis of what might have happened, rather than what did actually happen, particularly because the defendants had introduced various safeguards to ensure that very serious injuries were not caused and that any diseases were not transmitted. Further, if there had been any evidence that young men had been corrupted into performing sado-masochistic activities, this would suggest that they were not consenting, which would unquestionably constitute an offence against the person, and may also involve a sex offence in its own right.

Morality

None of these reasons is therefore altogether convincing. However, careful reading of the majority speeches reveals a fourth reason for the decision, namely that the majority perceived the case as involving conduct which was so immoral that it could not be tolerated by society and had to be punished. For example, Lord Templeman said that '[p]leasure derived from the infliction of pain is an evil thing' and Lord Lowry spoke in emotive terms of activities resulting from 'perverted and depraved sexual desires'. Whether reliance on gut reactions to perceived immorality is a sufficient reason to criminalise conduct is a difficult question. The danger of such an argument is that the notion of what is immoral is virtually impossible to define and depends very much on personal perceptions and beliefs rather than legal principle. It is difficult to see, therefore, that this is a sufficient reason in its own right to justify conviction.

APPLICATION OF THE DECISION

Despite concerns about the reasons behind the decision of the majority, we are left with *Brown* representing the law in England as to when the victim's consent can operate as a defence. When you are considering whether an important decision is correct, it is always useful to test the implications of that decision by applying it to hypothetical situations in an attempt to determine whether the results are acceptable or absurd. In considering the application of *Brown* it is important to consider those circumstances where harm might be considered to be justified by public policy and those where it might not.

Good Reasons for Consenting to Harm

In a case decided before *Brown*, the Court of Appeal recognised that a victim could validly consent to harm involving actual bodily harm or worse where the harm occurred in the course of properly conducted games and sports, lawful chastisement and correction, reasonable surgical interference, and dangerous exhibitions, which would presumably cover the case of an incompetent knife-thrower at a circus who misjudges the throw and wounds his assistant.

The test of properly conducted sports encompasses boxing, because such a sport must be conducted within the Queensbury Rules, which provide that there must be no hitting below the waist, gloves must be used and there must be a referee. This is distinct from the old practice of prize fighting, where the fight occurred without rules and where, as a matter of public policy, the consent of the participants was not sufficient to negate criminal liability. That boxing is a legitimate activity was confirmed in *Brown*. It appears therefore that there is a distinction between fighting without rules, where the participants' consent is no defence, and boxing, where the consent of the parties means that no crime has been committed.

The boundary between unacceptable and acceptable fighting is difficult to draw, particularly because it has been held that conduct characterised as 'horseplay' is acceptable. This was recognised in a case called *Jones*, which involved a fight in a playground during which one boy was thrown into the air and suffered a ruptured spleen when he fell to the ground. It was held that the victim's consent was a defence because 'boys would be boys and would always engage in rough and undisciplined horseplay'. This was applied in a later case called *Aitken*, which was decided not long before the House of Lords handed down judgment in *Brown*. This was a decision of the Courts Martial Appeal Court, which is the equivalent of the Court of Appeal (Criminal Division) but which hears appeals from disciplinary decisions involving the armed forces. The case concerned a group of drunken RAF officers who celebrated the end of their exams by pouring white spirit over their fire-resistant suits and setting light to them. One officer was doused with white spirit which, once set fire, caused 35 per cent burns to his body. Aitken was found to be not guilty of inflicting grievous bodily harm, because he assumed that the victim consented to the activity and, crucially, the victim's consent could be considered legitimate because the participants were engaged in rough and undisciplined horseplay. Bearing in mind that this case was decided not long before *Brown* there appears to be an inconsistency developing, especially given that the activities in *Brown* were carefully controlled whereas those in *Aitken* were not and so were much more dangerous. It is difficult to avoid the conclusion that the context of the activities in each case played some influence in determining whether or not the conduct was considered acceptable.

The law relating to one of the other recognised situations where consent can be considered valid has in fact changed. It has been recognised that parents can use force to chastise their children. Since this exception was recognised in *Brown* it appears that parents could use force to cause actual bodily harm and the child could still be deemed to have consented to the harm, so no crime would have been committed. The law has since changed. By section 58(1) of the Children Act 2004 the defendant has no defence of chastisement if the injury caused is at least actual bodily harm. It follows that chastisement of children now falls within the principle recognised in *Brown* and so chastisement is only a defence to a battery, where no significant injury is caused, and not to assault occasioning actual bodily harm, where the injury is more than merely transient or trifling.

Bad Reasons for Consenting to Harm

Following *Brown* it is clear that the consent of the victim to actual bodily harm or worse will be relevant only if the conduct can be justified by reference to public policy. We have seen that fighting without rules and satisfaction of the sado-masochistic libido by homosexuals do not satisfy this test. What else will not satisfy it? What if, for example, the sado-masochistic activity occurs within a heterosexual relationship, for example, between husband and wife? Although the facts of *Brown* did not involve heterosexual people, does the *ratio* extend to them? It appears that the *ratio* in *Brown* is not confined to sado-masochistic activity amongst homosexuals and so all such activity would appear to be criminal, regardless of the sexuality of the participants. This is consistent with an earlier case called *Donovan* where a man caned a woman to give him sexual pleasure. It was unclear whether she had consented to this, but it was accepted that, if she had been consenting, this would have been no defence because he had caused her actual bodily harm.

A useful hypothetical example against which the application of the principle in *Brown* can be tested concerns a boyfriend and a girlfriend who are in love and the girlfriend asks her boyfriend to give her a love-bite, which he does. Assuming that the love-bite results in a bruise to the girl's neck which is painful to the touch, and so constitutes actual bodily harm, can her consent be regarded as legitimate within the *Brown* principle? It cannot be assumed that this is acceptable behaviour; a positive reason needs to be identified for such conduct. If no such reason can be identified, then giving a loved one a love-bite would be a criminal offence. This is, presumably, absurd, and we will see later that the motive of the biter may be enough to make the conduct acceptable. Similarly, what about a defendant who pierces the victim's ear to enable her to wear an ear-ring. Is that a crime? It does constitute actual bodily harm, but can a good reason for the conduct be identified? What if other parts of the body are pierced? What if the defendant is a school-friend who uses a needle to pierce the victim's ear without first sterilising it? When, if ever, should such conduct be treated as criminal within the principle recognised in *Brown*? We are forced to engage with such issues following *Brown*.

THE DISSENTING JUDGES

When you are seeking to analyse and criticise the law it is always useful to consider the judgments of dissenting judges, even though their views do not represent the law, because they can provide important arguments for criticising the decision of the majority. Both of the dissenting Law Lords in *Brown*, Lords Mustill and Slynn, shared the revulsion of the majority as to the nature of the defendants' conduct and characterised it as immoral, but they considered that this was not a sufficient reason to convict the defendants. Lord Mustill in particular sought to identify the rationale for determining when the victim's consent cannot be considered to be legitimate by reference to earlier decisions, and he concluded that no rationale existed. Rather, he considered that these cases turned on the application of vague principles of public policy and value judgments. He, with Lord Slynn, sought to identify a workable principle for such cases. Both judges accepted that there reaches a point where the nature of the injuries caused are such that public policy should treat the victim's consent as invalid, but this should only occur where the harm involves serious injury. Where lesser harm is involved, the consent of the victim should be sufficient to operate as a defence. Although the approach of the minority does not represent the state of English law, it is an approach which is arguably more principled and therefore easier to apply than that of the majority.

THEORY: AUTONOMY VERSUS WELFARE

The debate about whether the approach of the majority or the minority in *Brown* is to be preferred goes right to the heart of the criminal law since it turns on the question: what are we seeking to do when we punish? This raises some deep issues about the philosophy of law. We saw earlier that there is a tension in the criminal law between the autonomy of the individual on one side and the welfare of society on the other. This tension is illustrated best by the issues in *Brown*. An emphasis on autonomy would suggest that the defendants in *Brown* should have been acquitted, since the recognition of the autonomy principle means that the defendant should be free to do what he or she wants to do. If this involves causing harm to others then the defendant should be free to do that. This argument can be strengthened by reference to the autonomy of the victim so that, if the victim wants to be injured, then he or she should be allowed to consent to that. However, the welfare principle would appear to support the decision of the majority, on the basis that the conviction of the defendants was for the benefit of society. But where was this benefit? There was nothing to suggest that the conduct of the defendants was harmful to society since no member of the public, outside the group of sado-masochists, was in danger from this type of conduct. The welfare principle must, consequently, be interpreted in a somewhat different way so as to justify the conviction. This interpretation of welfare should encompass the morality of the defendants' conduct. This interpretation is consistent with the approach of a former member of the House of Lords, Lord Devlin, who wrote a book entitled *The Enforcement of Morals*. Lord Devlin argued that there was a need for the criminal law to exist to ensure that certain standards of morality are maintained. This approach focuses on the paternalism of criminalising this sort of conduct, namely that it is considered to be in the best interests of the defendants and society generally that sadists are convicted for causing harm. There is no doubt that Lord Devlin would have supported the approach of the majority in *Brown*.

Against the philosophical approach of Lord Devlin is the approach of other philosophers of law, especially HLA Hart and John Stuart Mill, who advocated, to varying degrees, that the criminal law should intrude only to ensure that people's interests are not adversely affected. This emphasis on adverse effects suggests that, if the victim consents to being hurt, the hurt is not adverse and so should not be criminalised. This approach clearly focuses on autonomy rather than welfare and would result in an acquittal in *Brown*. This begs the question as to whether any limit should be imposed as to the degree of harm to which the victim should be allowed to consent. Would the answer differ if the victim suffers from a rare psychiatric condition which makes him believe that one of his limbs is repulsive and needs to be amputated? What if the victim wants to die?

Brown is thus a decision which is founded on morality and the concept of paternalism. In other words, the state seeks to protect certain types of people from themselves where their conduct does not accord with what is regarded as acceptable and normal, whatever that means.

SUBSEQUENT EVENTS: MOTIVE AND RISK

Even though *Brown* is a case which suggests that the welfare principle prevails over that of individual autonomy, events subsequent to *Brown* indicate that there is a move away from this approach. This section will examine the judicial developments following *Brown*. This illustrates an important feature of the study of law, namely that it is not sufficient to focus on the principles derived from leading cases; it is also necessary to examine what has happened to those principles subsequently. It may be found that these subsequent developments have moved the law on dramatically.

One of the significant decisions following *Brown* was *Wilson*, in the Court of Appeal. Although this was a decision of a lower court, which could not overrule a decision of the House of Lords, it is possible for the Court of Appeal to interpret the principles derived from a decision of the House of Lords and apply them in such a way that we are better able to understand the rationale of those principles. That is exactly what happened in *Wilson*, which concerns a moving love story involving an elderly couple. Mr and Mrs Wilson wanted to show their love for each other by bodily adornment. After discussing the matter they agreed that Mr Wilson would brand his initials on his wife's buttocks: A (standing for Alan) on one and W (standing for Wilson) on the other. They agreed that Mr Wilson would use a heated knife to do this. The wife never complained about this conduct. Indeed, she wanted it. She went to her doctor for a medical examination; he saw the scarring and complained to the police. Mr Wilson was prosecuted for assault occasioning actual bodily harm and was convicted. He appealed to the Court of Appeal and his conviction was quashed. The decision of the House of Lords in *Brown* was distinguished for a number of reasons, including that the wife was a willing participant, that the branding was analogous to tattooing which is acceptable, and that this conduct was done in the privacy of the matrimonial home, in which it was not for the courts or the law to interfere, so that there was no public interest in prosecuting the husband for this conduct. However, there was one reason which appears to be the most significant, especially as a way of distinguishing the facts of *Brown* from those in *Wilson*. This was the motive behind the activity. In *Brown* the motive was to get pleasure from pain and this was not considered to be an acceptable reason. However, in *Wilson* the wife got no pleasure from the experience of branding; it was the consequence of the branding which she wanted. Consequently, the motive was a sign of their affection for each other. The motive was love rather than pain and love is consequently a perfectly acceptable motive for causing injury to another.

This emphasis on motive is significant. If we return to the example of a boyfriend giving his girlfriend a love-bite, although there may well be pleasure in the activity, it is not pleasure which derives from pain, but is pleasure which derives from love. Consequently, it appears that it is not a crime to give somebody a love-bite.

A further example of the retreat from *Brown* is to be seen in a series of cases involving the transmission of the HIV virus. In the first of these cases, *Dica*, the defendant, who had AIDS, had unprotected sex with two women in the course of which he transmitted the HIV virus to them. The defendant was charged with maliciously inflicting grievous bodily harm contrary to section 20 of the Offences Against the Person Act 1861. It was held that the disease constituted grievous bodily harm and that the defendant had inflicted this on the victims. He was also aware that he had the disease and that he might transmit it to the victims in the course of having unprotected sex. The crucial issue, however, concerned whether the defendant's conduct was unlawful, bearing in mind that the women had consented to have sex with him. Did it follow that the victims had consented to the disease? For, if they had consented, the defendant could not be found guilty of the offence. One argument which was adopted by the Prosecution was that, even if the victims had consented to the disease, this was not a legitimate consent within the *Brown* principle, since there was no social utility in consenting to such a disease. The Court of Appeal in *Dica* rejected this argument by distinguishing *Brown* again. The principle in *Brown* was considered to be relevant only where the harm had been deliberately inflicted and not where, as may have been the case in *Dica*, the victims had consented to the risk of the harm being inflicted. Consequently, in any case where the victim consents to the risk of harm rather than wanting the harm, the victim's consent is legitimate and the defendant would not be guilty. So, in *Dica*, if the victims had contemplated the possibility that the defendant might have a sexually transmitted disease and were prepared to take that risk by having unprotected sex, the consent to the risk would mean that the defendant would not be guilty. This raises a difficult question of policy as to whether the victim in such a case should be required to bear the burden of taking the risk of the defendant having unprotected sex with him or her. Dica was subsequently retried and was found guilty, presumably because he had falsely told the victims that he did not have the disease and so they did not in fact consent to the risk of the disease. A subsequent case, *Konzani*, has placed the burden of risk-taking squarely on the defendant by holding that the victim's consent to the risk of the disease must be a fully informed consent. So, if the defendant knew or suspected that he had the disease but did not reveal this knowledge or suspicion to the victim, that victim's consent to the risk of the disease would not be considered to be fully informed and would not therefore be relevant.

This review of the decisions following *Brown* indicates that the law has developed dramatically. Today the victim can legitimately consent to injury where the motive for the injury is regarded as acceptable or where the victim is consenting to the *risk* of injury. It is only where the defendant wants the injury to be inflicted for no acceptable motive that the victim's consent will not be considered relevant.

HUMAN RIGHTS

There is one further dimension to the decision in *Brown*, involving the application of the European Convention on Human Rights. Following the decision of the House of Lords, the defendants appealed to the European Court of Human Rights. This was on the basis that the conviction of the defendants interfered with their fundamental human rights under the European Convention. In particular, the defendants relied on Article 8, which recognises the right to respect for private and family life. They argued that this encompassed a right to express their sexuality as they wished, even if this involved sado-masochism. Article 8 does indeed protect the right to expression of sexuality, but the European Court confirmed that the conviction of the defendants by the English courts did not infringe the European Convention. This was because states which are parties to the Convention are allowed to derogate from the right under Article 8 where it is 'necessary in a democratic society' for the protection of health and morals. So even the European Court of Human Rights adopted a paternalistic approach in preference to one which respected the autonomy of the individuals to express their sexuality as they wished.

LAW REFORM

Having reviewed the decision of the House of Lords in *Brown*, its application and its implications, we should now consider whether that decision itself is justifiable. This requires students of the law to engage critically with the decision and consider whether reform of the law is necessary. You might consider that the decision of the majority in *Brown* is correct and that there is no need to reform the law. However, if you conclude that the decision is unsatisfactory, you need to consider how the law should be reformed and whether this should be left to the judiciary or should be a matter for Parliament.

The question of reforming the law in this field has been considered by the Law Commission. As we saw in chapter 1, the Law Commission was established in 1965 to review the law in certain areas and, if the law is found wanting, make recommendations for reform to the Government. The Law Commission prepares reports for consultation and, having reviewed the responses, prepares a final report. The Law Commission produced a consultation paper in 1995, soon after the decision in *Brown*, on the relevance of the victim's consent where injury has been caused. Its preliminary conclusion was that the victim's consent to personal injury should be regarded as valid save where the injury is seriously disabling or involves death, and even then the victim should be allowed to consent to the risk of injury or death where it is for a legitimate reason such as medical treatment. Unfortunately, the Law Commission did not proceed with this project to a final report to be presented to Parliament.

The Law Commission's proposals would seem to be a satisfactory compromise between the need to respect the autonomy of the individual defendant and the victim and the need to protect those parties. Where the injury is seriously disabling or worse it should be appropriate for the state to intervene through the mechanism of the criminal law to protect defendants and victims from themselves. For, in an extreme case, such as that of Armin Meiwes, a German national who advertised on the internet for a willing victim to come forward to be killed and eaten, the criminal law should make clear that such conduct is unacceptable in a civilised society. In that case a victim did come forward and allowed himself to be killed and eaten and the German court in May 2006 held that Meiwes was guilty of murder, regardless of the victim's consent. Of course, issues of consent to one's own death raise big and difficult questions concerning euthanasia, suicide and assisted suicide. These issues essentially concern the legitimacy of consent and when engaging with them the law student needs to take account not only of legal rules but also moral and ethical considerations.

CONCLUSIONS

Although *Brown* raises some issues of quite technical law, ultimately the analysis of this case raises a very simple question, namely whether it is appropriate to convict a defendant of a serious crime involving personal injury where the victim consented to that injury. The case can be analysed on a variety of different levels. First, there is the basic analysis of what the case decided and the identification of the arguments for and against the decision. Secondly, the practical implications of the decision need to be considered by reference to hypothetical examples and subsequent decisions. Thirdly, the decision needs to be considered critically by considering whether a workable principle can be identified and whether that principle is acceptable with reference to theoretical and social policy considerations. Ultimately, you need to ask, 'if I were one of the judges sitting in the House of Lords, how would I have decided the appeal in *Brown*?'.

Cases

Aitken [1992] 1 WLR 1006
Attorney-General's Reference (No 6 of 1980) [1981] 2 All ER 1057
Barnes [2004] EWCA Crim 3246; [2005] 1 WLR 910
Brown [1992] QB 491 (Court of Appeal); [1994] 1 AC 212 (House of Lords)
Coney (1882) 8 QBD 534
Dica [2004] EWCA Crim 1103; [2004] QB 1257
Donovan [1934] 2 KB 498
Emmett (1999) The Times, 15 October
Laskey, Jaggard and Brown v UK (1997) 24 EHRR 39
Jones (1986) 83 Cr App R 375
Konzani [2005] EWCA Crim 706
Wilson [1996] 2 Cr App R 241

Further Reading

Ashworth, *Principles of Criminal Law* (5th edn, Oxford University Press, Oxford 2006) 40–4
Devlin, *The Enforcement of Morals* (Oxford University Press, Oxford 1965)
Hart, *Law, Liberty and Morality* (Oxford University Press, Oxford 1963)
Law Commission Consultation Paper No 139 (1995) *Consent in the Criminal Law*
Smith and Hogan, *Criminal Law* (11th edn, Oxford University Press, Oxford 2005) 524–39

3
Law of Contract

Janet O'Sullivan

INTRODUCTION

I wonder how many contracts you have made today, before sitting down to read this chapter. Perhaps you bought a sandwich from the supermarket, travelled on public transport, opened a bank account or sold an unwanted gift on an internet auction site? You may even have bought this book today. Meanwhile, all over the world, other people are booking tickets and holidays, commissioning building work, leasing flats or signing employment contracts for new jobs, while small businesses and giant corporations are borrowing money and employing staff, acquiring premises and equipment, even taking-over other companies. The law of contract is at the heart of all these situations, the same basic principles whether it is a simple, oral contract to purchase a book or a complex financing transaction spelt out in hundreds of pages of detailed terms and conditions. (It surprises some people to discover that, with notable exceptions, most contracts can be made orally and are no less valid for not being written down.) Admittedly, you may not notice any sort of contract when you buy a book—you simply hand over your money and the shopkeeper hands over the book—but you do in fact make an invisible contract, one which, for example, obliges the shopkeeper to give you your money back if all the pages fall out of the book the first time you open it.

To a lawyer (at least one with a traditional outlook), a contract is typically an agreement between two (or sometimes more) parties who make *binding promises* to each other, each party's promise given in exchange for the other's. In this context, the adjective *binding* means that if the promise is not honoured, the law becomes involved and provides some redress for the other party (as opposed, for example, to the sorts of promise parents make to children about treats in return for good behaviour). Many simple contracts are like the book-purchase example, where the seller and the buyer don't actually spell out any promises to each other, because the goods and the money are handed over simultaneously (although the seller, whether he likes it or not, is *treated* as having made certain promises about the quality of what he is selling, because these are implied into the contract by a statute called the Sale of Goods Act). But in virtually all other sorts of contract, there is a *gap* in time between the making of the contract and its ultimate performance, ie, the date when everything is finally done as the contract requires. So the parties promise each other that they will do something in the future. For example, imagine you pre-ordered this book on the internet two months before its publication date. The moment you clicked the 'I agree' button, the internet seller promised to deliver the book, and you in turn promised to pay for it, even though both obligations would not actually be performed for a further two months.

SOME CRUCIAL ASPECTS OF CONTRACTUAL REMEDIES

The crucial point is that these promises (to deliver, to pay the price) are regarded as legally 'binding' from the moment the contract is made, not merely at the later date when performance is due. In other words, if the seller changes his mind and decides not to send you the book when it is published, you have a legal right against him and not merely a right to complain, a right to a *remedy* if your complaint doesn't persuade him to change his mind, enforceable in the civil courts. In fact, in English law, the courts rarely actually *compel* a contract-breaker like this seller to honour his contract and send you the book, but that is not usually a problem (after all, you have not paid anything yet). Imagine that the seller was offering the book for a bargain price of £5 to anyone who pre-ordered it, instead of the usual selling price of £9.99. When he failed to deliver it to you, you had to buy the book instead from your local book shop for £9.99, so the seller's *breach of contract* meant that you spent £4.99 more than you would have done if he had honoured his promise. Thus you would be entitled to *damages* of £4.99 from the seller. Identical rules apply even if the figures involved are multiplied by millions and the transaction is a complex commercial one.

All this explains why people and companies bother to make contracts at all. Imagine X is a soft drink manufacturer and Y is a commercial grower of tomatoes. X wishes to ensure a supply of tomatoes to make tomato juice, sales of which peak at Christmas time. So X makes a contract with Y in June, to purchase from Y 10,000 kilos of tomatoes to be delivered in October at an agreed price per kilo, the price to be paid on delivery of the tomatoes. Both parties, being rational, make the contract for a good reason—X to feel secure about a supply of tomatoes in October at a price it is happy with, Y because it wants to make a profit and is confident that the cost of growing and harvesting the tomatoes will be less than the price. The contract allows both forward planning and risk allocation, because the law treats it as valid and binding immediately, even before any part of the contract has been performed or any sums spent preparing to perform it. Indeed, commerce is built on the understanding that contracts create enforceable obligations and corresponding expectations *immediately*, not at some unidentifiable later date when the other party first acts, or incurs expenditure, in reliance on the contract.

Commerce also relies on the fact that Y's promise to deliver the tomatoes is a very *strict* concept, not merely a promise to take reasonable care to deliver them or only to deliver them if it has a plentiful supply. You will recall from chapter 1 that defendants are generally only liable in tort where they are at fault in some way: in contrast, liability for breach of contract does not depend on *fault*. Put another way, you can be in breach of contract merely because circumstances beyond your control prevent you from doing what you promised. So in our tomato example, the law would not allow Y to ignore its promise or to increase the contract price merely because, for example, there is an unexpected drought, tomato yields are badly affected and their market price soars accordingly. This may seem 'hard' on Y, since it is not Y's *fault* in a moral sense that it cannot honour the contract, but think back to the reasons why the parties wanted to make a contract in the first place. Y took the risk that it could perform for less than the contract price, hoping to make a profit (which it would have done if the market price had moved down instead of up). X made the contract to allow for forward planning, for the security of not having to worry about the risk of the market price moving up because of problems like a poor harvest (and was prepared to take the risk of the market price moving down to achieve this security). So it is crucial that the law holds the parties to their contract in these unexpected conditions, 'holds' not in the sense of requiring Y to deliver the tomatoes, but to pay *damages* to X instead, representing the difference between the contract price and the October market price.

At this point it is worth mentioning another important aspect of a remedy for damages, the requirement of *mitigation*, that the claimant must mitigate his or her loss. This means that claimants must act reasonably to keep their losses to a minimum; more accurately, claimants cannot claim damages for an amount in excess of what they would have lost if they had acted reasonably. So in our tomato example, X will only be entitled to the difference between the contract price and the *market* price, not between the contract price and the *highest* price of tomatoes on the date of delivery. Likewise a tort claimant who is injured by the defendant's negligent driving may claim damages if she suffers a broken arm, but if she deliberately and unreasonably refrains from seeking medical help and for this reason the arm develops gangrene, she cannot claim damages to compensate her for the gangrene—she has failed to mitigate her loss.

Now some misguided law students regard the law about contractual remedies as if it is an unimportant add-on to the legal rules about contracts, a discrete module that can safely be ignored. They think of other areas as the 'real' parts of the law of contract. It is true that the law of contract is concerned with much more than just remedies. To name just a few important issues, the law of contract determines whether a binding contract has been formed at all, what exactly the terms of the contract are and what those terms mean, whether an apparent contract is invalidated by something improper that one of the parties did (maybe he bullied the other party or made a false statement about the contractual subject matter), what happens where one or both of the parties were contracting under a mistake, whether one of the contractual promises has been breached and, if so, what effect does this have on the rest of the contract. Nonetheless, those misguided students are really missing the point. From what we have seen already, it is clear that the *remedy* for breach of contract is a crucial part of the legal regime supporting contracts—indeed, it is meaningless to envisage contractual *rights* without a legally enforceable remedy for breach of contract, meaningless to learn about the formation of contracts without understanding the law's response when a contractual obligation is breached.

For this reason, the rest of this chapter is concerned with a fascinating case called *Ruxley Electronics and Construction Ltd v Forsyth*, which is about the usual remedy for breach of contract, namely an award of damages. As you will see, it started life as a small run-of-the-mill claim in the County Court about some domestic building work, but ended up (because of a series of appeals brought by one party, then the other) being resolved by the highest court in the land, the House of Lords, whose decision is now a very important precedent shaping the law of contract for the future. This is a really satisfying feature of English law— it is not necessarily the big money cases that raise the important issues of legal principle.

THE CASE

The Pool was Too Shallow

Stephen Forsyth commissioned Ruxley Electronics, a small company run by a builder, to build a swimming pool in the garden of his house in Kent. The contract price for the pool and its enclosure, some of which was to be paid during the construction and the rest on completion of the work, totalled just over £70,000 (this simplifies the facts slightly, but not materially). The contract originally specified that the pool was to have a maximum depth of 6 feet 6 inches, but the depth specification was increased some time later, at Forsyth's request, to 7 feet 6 inches, apparently because he was a tall man and wished to feel confident that he would not hit his head when diving.

When the work was completed, Forsyth discovered that the pool had a maximum depth of only 6 feet 9 inches and that it was only 6 feet deep at the crucial entry point for dives, some distance from the end of the pool. So when he received his final bill for the reminder of the contract price (approximately £39,000), he pointed to this breach of the contractual specification and alleged a number of other defects in the work, and refused to pay. Ruxley sued him for its money (plus interest) and Forsyth *counter-claimed* for damages. This means that Forsyth didn't just defend himself against Ruxley's action for the balance of the price; he also went 'on the attack' and claimed damages from Ruxley. It also means that it is easy to get confused when reading reports of the case, because Forsyth is officially the *defendant,* even though most of the discussion concerns his counter-claim for damages and it is of course usually a *claimant* who claims damages.

Notice that, although Ruxley and Forsyth were each claiming *money* from the other, the claim and the counter-claim were for fundamentally different remedies. Ruxley's claim was for the sum of money agreed by the parties as the contract price for building the pool. In this sort of claim, sometimes also called a *debt* action, the role of the court is very simple, merely deciding whether the sum claimed is in fact due. In contrast, Forsyth's counter-claim was for *damages* for breach of contract, where the court has a further job to do once it has decided that there has been a breach of contract: it must also *calculate* those damages, work out how to convert 'loss' into 'money'. As we will see, this can be a highly complex, controversial process.

The judge at the Central London County Court examined all the evidence, listened to the witnesses and decided that there *was* a breach of the depth specification, but that the pool as constructed was nonetheless perfectly safe to dive into. He also decided, however, that Forsyth had not proved any of the other defects in the pool that he was alleging. What did these findings mean for both the claim and the counter-claim?

The straightforward part was that Ruxley's claim for the balance of its contract price succeeded. The law says that, in general, one party cannot resist paying the price unless there was a 'substantial failure' to perform the relevant contractual obligation by the other party (or, put the other way round, you must pay the price if the work was substantially performed). There are some exceptions to this rule: certain, unusual contractual obligations are said to be 'entire', in other words they must be performed entirely before the other party is obliged to pay anything at all. A good example might be a contract to paint a portrait—the painter cannot deliver a 90 per cent completed painting, lacking only ears, and demand payment of 90 per cent (or indeed any part) of his price. But this exception did not apply to our swimming pool contract. So as Ruxley's breach of the depth specification was not a 'substantial failure', Forsyth could not withhold the balance of the price.

Contractual Damages—a Brief Discussion

What about Forsyth's counter-claim for damages to *compensate* him for the fact that the pool was shallower than Ruxley had promised in the contract? This is where we need to step away from the swimming pool for a moment and introduce some basic principles about legal compensation. The rationale for any award of damages is to compensate the innocent party for what he or she has lost, but the notion of 'loss' does not mean exactly the same thing in all branches of the law. If you are the victim of a *tort* (for example, you are run over and injured by a negligent driver), you will be entitled to damages *to put you into the position you were in before the tort occurred.* Of course, money cannot literally repair broken bones, but it can compensate you for your lost wages, pain and suffering, 'lost amenity' in the sense of being able to enjoy your work and leisure activities, as well as paying for any expenditure you incurred as a result of the tort. The focus in tort is backward looking, to restore you to the pre-tort position, and is represented diagrammatically in figure 3.1.

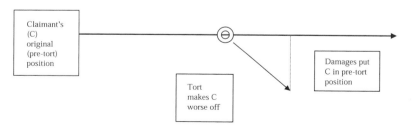

Fig. 3.1 *Damages in tort.*

In contrast, the aim of damages for breach of contract is subtly but significantly different. It was explained in an early Victorian case called *Robinson v Harman* as follows:

> The rule of common law is that where a party sustains a loss by reason of a breach of contract, he is, so far as money can do it, to be placed in the same situation, with respect to damages, *as if the contract had been performed.*

So this is forward-looking: what would your position be if the other party had performed rather than breached the contract? Sometimes a breach of contract actually causes you loss in the tort sense of the word, but very often the only adverse effect is on your expected level of profit. The significance of contractual damages is that they are paid even if you are not actually worse off than you were before you made the contract, but merely if you are not *as much better off* as you would have been if the contract had been performed (rather than breached). You may have noticed this in our earlier examples about the book ordered from the internet at a bargain price and the tomato grower that must pay its customer the difference between the contract price and the (higher) market price of tomatoes.

This contractual notion of damages is said to be compensating for the fact that you didn't get the performance you were entitled to expect

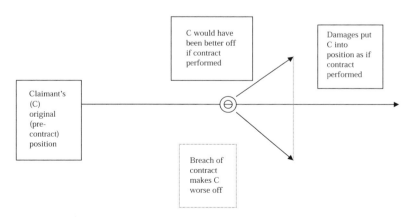

Fig. 3.2 *Damages in contract.*

from the other party, and so is commonly called the *expectation measure* of damages. All this is relatively easy in theory, but how do the courts actually put a *value* on this expectation measure?

How to Value the Contractual Expectation

Traditionally, there have been two different ways of doing this valuation exercise. The most obvious way, which works perfectly well when dealing with contracts for the sale of marketable commodities like our book and tomatoes examples, is to award the *difference in value* between (i) what, if anything, the claimant actually received and (ii) what the claimant would have received had the contract been performed. Note that the more profitable the contract would have been, the greater the amount of damages awarded to the claimant; in contrast, where the contract price is the *same* as the market price, the difference in value and thus the damages will generally be nil. So going back to our internet book example, imagine that the internet seller was not offering the book for sale at a bargain price, but only at its market price of £9.99: if the seller fails to deliver the book to you, you can simply buy it at the same price elsewhere, so your damages (assuming you have not yet paid for the book) are nil.

Sometimes, however, the difference in value approach is not appropriate, generally in the sort of case where the claimant cannot simply go to market and purchase substitute performance. For example, in *Radford v De Froberville*, Mr Radford owned a very large house in Holland Park, London, which was divided into flats let to tenants and which had a big garden (used by the tenants). He sold *part* of the garden to the defendant, Mrs De Froberville, who was planning to redevelop the plot by building a new house on it. One of the contractual terms of the sale was that she promised to build a brick boundary wall between her plot and the rest of the garden, of a thickness and height specified in the contract. But in breach of contract she did not build the wall or any other sort of boundary (having failed to redevelop the plot at all). What was the appropriate measure of damages for Mr Radford? The difference in value between his property with the boundary wall and without it was negligible, but that wasn't really the point. He *wanted* the wall and so had obtained from Mrs De Froberville a promise to build it, but he was now going to have to spend his own money if he wanted a wall. The judge explained why the difference in value measure would be inappropriate, giving an example of:

> ... a man with a garden by the sea or a river, subject to inundation on rare occasions by freak floods. He sells a part of his garden as part of the sale and stipulates that the purchaser shall erect a flood wall on the property purchased to protect both properties. If the purchaser fails to build the wall and the court is satisfied that the plaintiff intends to build on his own land what the defendant has failed to build on his, why should he be limited to the amount by which his land is diminished in value as a saleable asset by the possibility of an occasional flood? He is interested in cultivating his garden, not selling his property.

In this sort of case, the courts recognise that the difference in value measure is inadequate to value the claimant's lost expectation, so use instead another approach, namely the cost of actually putting right the breach of contract. This second approach is generally known as the '*cost of cure*'.

Often the cost of cure and the difference in value produce identical results (for example, when you can 'cure' the breach by purchasing substitute performance in the market place), but sometimes they produce dramatically different figures. This brings us back to Mr Forsyth's shallow pool, which was a striking example of the two conventional methods of assessing damages producing dramatically different figures and, more to the point, *neither* of which seemed quite right.

Back to the Poolside

The cost of cure was a staggering £21,650, since the only practical way of increasing the depth of the pool to conform to the specification would be to remove the existing pool, excavate further and construct a new pool. On the other hand, the judge's somewhat surprising conclusion was that there was *no* difference in market value between the pool as built and the pool as it should have been built (indeed it is somewhat artificial to think of built-in swimming pools as having a 'market value' at all, separate from the property in which they are constructed, so it is by no means clear precisely what the judge meant by this finding, but for the purpose of this chapter we will put these factual doubts to one side and continue).

Why is it that neither of the two conventional measures seems to fit the facts of *Ruxley*? The cost of cure 'feels' too large, because it ignores the fact that Forsyth obtained a perfectly serviceable, well-constructed pool, entirely suitable for swimming, paddling and lounging next to, but merely shallower than the depth-specification. It would over-compensate him to award the full cost of cure, particularly as Forsyth was highly unlikely to use the money to rebuild the pool. On the other hand, the difference in value (nil) 'feels' inadequate: after all, Forsyth did not get what he paid for, and it is irrelevant that what he paid for was no more valuable than what he got. After all, he did not make the contract to enhance the value of his house. In the words of Lord Mustill:

> It is a common feature of small building works performed on residential property that the cost of the work is not fully reflected by an increase in the market value of the house, and that comparatively minor deviations from specification or sound workmanship may have no direct financial effect at all. Yet the householder must surely be entitled to say that he chose to obtain from the builder a promise to produce a particular result because he wanted to make his house more comfortable, more convenient and more conformable to his own particular tastes; not because he had in mind that the work might increase the amount which he would receive if, contrary to expectation, he thought it expedient in the future to exchange his home for cash. To say that in order to escape unscathed the builder has only to show that to the mind of the average onlooker, or the average potential buyer, the results which he has produced seem just as good as those which he had promised would make a part of the promise illusory and unbalance the bargain.

The reason for the law's traditional emphasis on market value when measuring expectation damages for breach of contract is because of the historical background to the modern law of contract. The classical rules of the law of contract were first understood and conceptualised as such in the nineteenth century, in a wholly *commercial* context. To a Victorian lawyer, the ethos of the law was to interfere as little as possible in the parties' freedom of contract, while the quintessential contractual situation involved two gentlemen (note the gender!) of roughly equal bargaining-strength negotiating and then making a contract to sell a carriage or a business. This is self-evidently not the only contractual model in the twenty-first century, in particular because of the growth of contractual relationships between consumers and big businesses. Today, almost all such contracts are made on non-negotiable printed forms, often virtu-ally identical across the particular market sector; Parliament has, in turn, intervened with statutory controls on certain sorts of undesirable, one-sided contractual terms in consumer contracts.

In the area of contractual remedies, the traditional assumption that the parties were contracting merely for profit-making, commercial motives (as in our tomatoes example) does not fit comfortably in the context of consumer contracts, where it is perfectly rational to be motivated for reasons other than a desire for profit. The recognition of this in the field of building contracts led to the adoption of the 'cost of cure' measure in the first place, but *Ruxley* forced the law to confront whether more flexibility might be needed than just the two familiar approaches.

The County Court Judge's Decision and the 'Middle Ground' Award

The County Court judge refused to award the cost of cure. He said:

> Not only am I not satisfied that Mr Forsyth intends to build a new pool at a cost of £21,560, but in addition it seems to me that this cost would be wholly disproportionate to the disadvantage of having a pool whose maximum depth is 6 ft as opposed to 7 ft 6 in. In those circumstances I find that it would be unreasonable for Mr Forsyth to carry out this work at such a cost.

However, the judge did award Forsyth a small sum in damages (£2,500) as a sort of *middle-ground* award, being neither the difference in value nor the cost of cure. This, the judge said, was to reflect his *lack of amenity* in not having a pool of the correct depth, saying that it is:

> … a perfectly reasonable requirement to wish to make deeper dives or to have a greater depth of water and one can sympathise with any pool owner who makes a legitimate request for a specified depth of water and does not get the depth he contracted for. There is, accordingly, a lack of amenity brought about by the shortfall in the depth of water, but this lack of amenity is not easy to quantify.

The judge did not analyse further the theoretical basis of this lost ame-nity award, but that is unsurprising. After all, it is a commonplace, every-day matter for County Court judges to award damages for lost amenity to *tort* claimants who have suffered personal injury, reflecting their reduced ability to enjoy life as much as before the injury. As a way of valuing expectation damages for breach of contract, however, an approach based on 'lack of amenity' was new and controversial.

On Appeal to the Court of Appeal

In any event, Forsyth was unhappy with the result of the County Court decision. You will remember that Ruxley's claim for the balance of the purchase price succeeded, so Forsyth actually had to pay £39,000 plus interest, less the £2,500 damages for his counter-claim. He therefore appealed to the Court of Appeal, arguing that the judge should have awarded him the full cost of cure on his counter-claim. This time, his argument was successful. The Court of Appeal felt considerable sympathy for Forsyth, presenting him as the long-suffering, innocent victim of cowboy builders and stressing that he wanted a deeper pool because he was tall and feared diving in shallow water. With this view of the merits of the case, it is perhaps unsurprising that the Court of Appeal decided (though only by a majority of 2:1) that his damages should be the full £21,650 cost of cure (Dillon LJ agreed with the County Court judge, but his was a minority view). Staughton LJ said:

> In the present case Mr Forsyth has without question suffered a loss; he has a swimming pool which is less well suited to diving than the one he contracted for. What money will place him 'in the same situation... as if the contract had been performed?'. The answer, on the facts of this case, is the cost of replacing the pool. Otherwise, a builder of swimming pools need never perform his contract. He can always argue that 5 ft in depth is enough for diving, even if the purchaser has stipulated for 6, 7 or 8 ft, and pay no damages.

The reasonableness or unreasonableness of rebuilding the pool, and Forsyth's intentions in that regard, were not regarded by the majority of the Court of Appeal as relevant. As Mann LJ put it:

> There can be instances where the cost of rectifying a failed project is not reasonable, as, for example, where no personal preference is served or where there is no preference and the value of the estate is undiminished. In my judgment this is not such a case. The bargain was for a personal preference.

On Appeal to the House of Lords

With the score at one-all, Ruxley wanted to appeal to the House of Lords, the highest court in the land. It is worth noting that a civil litigant does not have an automatic right to appeal to the House of Lords if he or she disagrees with the Court of Appeal's decision. The litigant must obtain permission to do so, known as *leave to appeal*. Sometimes this is granted by the Court of Appeal itself, but normally the Court of Appeal refuses leave to appeal and the litigant must petition the House of Lords itself (specifically, the House's *Appeal Committee*) for permission. The Committee decides whether to allow or refuse a petition, depending on whether the case involves a point of law of general public importance that ought to be considered by the House. In our swimming pool case, the Court of Appeal refused leave (the judges naturally thought their decision was correct and should not be challenged further!), but Ruxley successfully petitioned the House of Lords for leave to appeal. This small County Court dispute had, by this stage, generated a point of law of considerable public importance and battle lines were drawn.

The appeal to the House of Lords, like many final, decisive battles in long military campaigns, was very much a *tactical* contest. It is crucial to appreciate that, in civil litigation, the loser generally pays the winner's legal costs as well as his or her own, so if Ruxley won this appeal, Forsyth would be responsible for its costs as well as his own. Bearing in mind that the dispute had already lasted seven years since Forsyth first declined to pay the final invoice for the pool, those costs were potentially astronomical. The other important tactical point was that Ruxley had always been happy with the County Court judge's middle-ground award of £2,500 and were only appealing against the Court of Appeal's decision to award the full cost of cure (concentrating only on why the cost of cure was inappropriate). More significantly, Ruxley had offered to *settle* the case on this basis (ie, to abandon the appeal and 'call it a draw' if Forsyth would accept £2,500), but Forsyth consistently refused this offer. From a costs point of view, this stubborn stance put Forsyth in a dilemma when it came to his *arguments* in the appeal, because the rules of civil procedure say that if a litigant refuses an offer to settle a case but then is *not* awarded *any more* than the other side were offering, he or she is treated as having 'lost' and must pay the other side's costs. So Forsyth was forced to argue, somewhat counter-intuitively, that the reason the House of Lords should stick with the cost of cure was because their *only* other alternative was to award him the (plainly inadequate) difference in value measure, namely nil. Only if that argument succeeded would he get his costs paid by Ruxley.

All this meant that, bizarrely, for tactical reasons *neither side* offered any argument or analysis whatsoever about the theoretical basis or practical implications of the loss of amenity 'middle-ground' award, even though this was central to the 'point of law of general public importance' which the appeal was meant to consider, namely the appropriate way of valuing Forsyth's lost expectation.

The House of Lords evidently viewed the merits of the case very differently from the Court of Appeal, presenting Forsyth as a pedantic, demanding client, trying to find technical breaches of contract to avoid paying for good work carried out by honest contractors. For example, it was revealed in the House of Lords appeal that Ruxley had already agreed to reduce Forsyth's bill because of unfounded allegations of defects and (more damning still) that Forsyth first raised the question of the depth of the pool three days after the commencement of the trial (amending his pleaded case accordingly), many years after the completion of the work!

Viewing the case in this light, it is not surprising that the House of Lords unanimously decided that the Court of Appeal had been wrong to award Forsyth the full cost of cure *and* (undeterred by the lack of submissions on the point from either side) that the *middle-ground award* for *loss of amenity* favoured by the County Court judge had indeed been a perfectly proper way to value that illusive notion of Forsyth's lost expectation from the breach of contract. As Lord Mustill said, once the possibility of a middle-ground award for loss of amenity is recognised,

> … the puzzling and paradoxical feature of this case, that it seems to involve a contest of absurdities, simply falls away. There is no need to remedy the injustice of awarding too little by unjustly awarding far too much.

So Forsyth's tactic failed and he was left paying his own legal costs as well as all of Ruxley's.

THE HOUSE OF LORDS' DECISION IN MORE DETAIL

Let us look in more detail at the House of Lords' decision. First, why was the cost of cure refused? The House (unlike the Court of Appeal) stressed that the cost of cure should not be awarded where it would be *unreasonable* for a claimant to insist on reinstatement, 'as where, for example, the expense of the work involved would be out of all proportion to the benefit to be obtained'. Their Lordships cited an old American case as an extreme example of this principle in operation, called *Jacob & Youngs v Kent*. This involved a contract for the construction of a new house, in which the (somewhat obsessive) owner had insisted in the contractual specification that the builder should install plumbing using pipes of 'Reading manufacture', but the builder had mistakenly installed practically identical pipes made by a different manufacturer. The owner's counter-claim for damages reflecting the cost of replacing the pipework was rejected: the famous American judge Cardozo J expressed the view that a claimant 'is entitled to the money which will permit him to complete, unless the cost of completion is grossly and unfairly out of proportion to the good to be attained'. In the same way, their Lordships held that it would be grossly unreasonable and disproportionate to incur the cost of demolishing the perfectly adequate existing pool just to build a new and deeper one, so Forsyth's loss should not be *valued* at the cost of reinstatement.

In addition, the House relied on the County Court judge's refusal to believe Forsyth's evidence that he intended to rebuild the pool as another factor indicating the unreasonableness of the cost of cure. Lord Lloyd said 'if, as the judge found, Mr Forsyth had no intention of rebuilding the pool, he has lost nothing except the difference in value, if any'. For tactical reasons, Forsyth was now willing to give the House an *undertaking* to rebuild the pool if they let him keep his cost of cure damages, but even this did not make any difference: it could not make the unreasonable reasonable and would not 'be allowed to create a loss, which does not exist'.

But if a cost of cure award of £21,650 was 'wholly disproportionate' to the true value of Forsyth's lost expectation, the House went on to explain why the difference in value measure (nil) was *also* inappropriate on the facts. Remember, this measure looks at the difference between

(i) the market value of the pool as constructed and (ii) its market value if it had been built to the correct specification.

The House of Lords' reasoning was very simple: it is for the particular individual making the contract, not the notional average punters who create the market value, 'to judge what performance he required in exchange for the price. The court should honour that choice'. It ought to be irrelevant that the average person would not have been bothered by the shallower pool, because Forsyth had contracted for a pool of a particular depth in the contract to satisfy *his own* preferences. Lord Mustill pointed out that, for example, contracts to install features such as:

> ... lurid bathroom tiles, or a grotesque folly... may be so discordant with general taste that in purely economic terms the builder may be said to do the employer a favour by failing to install them. But this is too narrow and materialistic a view of the transaction. Neither the contractor nor the court has the right to substitute for the employer's individual expectation of performance a criterion derived from what ordinary people would regard as sensible. As my Lords have shown, the test of reasonableness plays a central part in determining the basis of recovery, and will indeed be decisive in a case such as the present when the cost of reinstatement would be wholly disproportionate to the non-monetary loss suffered by the employer. But it would be equally unreasonable to deny all recovery for such a loss.

So, having rejected both the cost of cure and the difference in value measures, their Lordships gratefully looked back to and adopted the County Court judge's middle-ground award for *loss of amenity*. Only two members of the House made any attempt to explain the theoretical basis of the award.

Lord Mustill viewed it as reflecting the *consumer surplus*. This is an important idea that needs explanation. What it means is the amount by which the particular claimant values performance of a particular obligation, over and above the amount by which the average person would value it. In other words, it recognises that an individual can, for personal reasons, value something over and above its market value—this extra value is the consumer surplus. For example, an old gold wedding ring might be worth £100 on the market, but if that ring was a family heirloom, once your great-grandmother's wedding ring, then you will value it at much more than £100. So if you make a contract with a jeweller to repair or clean the ring, but in breach of contract he loses or destroys it, then damages of £100 will not adequately compensate you for what you have lost. The same applies to a set of wedding photographs, which have a limited market value in terms of the paper and printing costs, but are worth vastly more to the bride and groom.

Although the notion of consumer surplus had been discussed at length by academics as being an important consideration when valuing a claimant's expectation fully, Lord Mustill was the first Law Lord to acknowledge the concept. He said, 'the law must cater for those occasions where the value of the promise to the promisee exceeds the financial enhancement of his position which full performance will secure'. This is a very significant statement, forming part of the process we have already mentioned of bringing contract law into the twenty-first century and recognising that people who make contracts are not all motivated entirely by profit considerations. So, for Lord Mustill, the £2,500 loss of amenity award was best regarded as an example of the consumer surplus—the average pool purchaser placed no value on the depth of the pool, but Mr Forsyth did.

Lord Lloyd, on the other hand, explained the £2,500 award as damages for Forsyth's 'distress and disappointment'. Damages for mental distress or disappointment are not generally awarded for breach of contract: this is not surprising, bearing in mind the commercial roots of English contract law, since commercial parties are not expected to react emotionally to a breach of contract! The courts have, however, recognised for some time a couple of limited exceptions to this general rule, one of which is where the contract's *sole object* was to give pleasure, peace of mind or freedom from distress. A good example is a holiday contract: if your holiday is a complete disaster and does not accord with the promises made to you in the contract, you will be entitled to recover damages for distress and disappointment, not just a cold, financial calculation of the difference in value between the lovely holiday you were promised and the grotty one you actually had. Lord Lloyd stressed that this swimming pool contract was one to provide 'pleasurable amenity' and so was able to treat the middle-ground award *in this case* as falling within the exception.

So, although both Lords Mustill and Lloyd expressly approved of the loss of amenity award, they did not adopt the same reasoning in doing so. Lord Lloyd's approach had the advantage of being built on existing precedent, but there are strong arguments of principle for preferring Lord Mustill's consumer surplus analysis. Lord Lloyd was only able to rely on existing case law about contracts to provide 'pleasurable amenity' or 'freedom from distress' because, fortuitously, this case involved a swimming pool, something designed to give pleasure. But there may be many instances where a consumer surplus exists, and should be recognised, that do *not* fall into this exceptional category. For example, a domestic homeowner may have specified a particular heating system, roof tile or floor plan, which they value, even though failure to comply with the specification will not cause a reduction in the market value of performance. Lord Lloyd himself recognised that a 'distress' award would not be available for some defects, such as a difference in level between two rooms creating an irritating step when the customer had expressly contracted for a flat floor. There is no obvious 'pleasurable amenity' here and yet there is certainly a consumer surplus that should be compensated. So this issue was not conclusively resolved in *Ruxley,* leaving a question mark over precisely what the case decided, to be pondered by commentators and judges in the future.

In fact, some commentators felt uneasy about a more fundamental aspect of the decision in *Ruxley*, namely the court's restriction on the cost of cure measure. It has been argued that, whilst it may be right to deny the cost of cure in certain situations (for example, where the landowner died after making the contract and it is clear that his next of kin will be selling the property immediately), consumer cases where there is simply 'disproportion' between the cost of cure and the apparent value of what has been lost do not necessarily warrant the same treatment. In other words, despite the obvious lack of merits of Forsyth's own counter-claim, perhaps a general test based on whether the loss is disproportionate to the cost of cure is not sufficiently respectful of consumers' contractual expectations in domestic building cases.

For example, the 'disproportion' approach may well have unfortunate implications in the ordinary case of a domestic building contract. First, does it give the right signal to contractors? Assume, for example, a contractor doing domestic building work where, as in *Ruxley*, the client is not on site supervising his every move. If the contractor monitors the work properly, keeping the client informed at every stage, he risks spotting mistakes and defects which he will then have to spend money remedying. If, however, he ploughs on with the work, so that any defects are quickly buried in the fabric of the construction, this maximises the chances that the cost of curing such defects will be high, in comparison with the difference in market value, and thus rejected as disproportionate. Perhaps the principle encourages a culture of inefficiency and provides no incentive, indeed a positive disincentive, for builders to monitor work or keep the client informed. Secondly, the vagueness of the 'disproportion' principle makes the position of a claimant complaining of bad workmanship uncertain and risky, and (where the cost of cure is high) enables a contractor to 'hold out', offering to settle out of court for a low sum which he asserts will adequately compensate the client for his loss of amenity. As Forsyth's barrister observed after the House of Lords decision, 'many a [building owner] may well accept such sum rather than undergo the uncertainty of litigation'.

WHAT HAS HAPPENED SINCE *RUXLEY*?

Ruxley was decided over ten years ago, so for an all-round picture of the case it is important to consider how it has been applied and interpreted as a precedent in subsequent cases. In fact, it has been cited and discussed many times, in all sorts of case, but just looking at two very different examples will give you a flavour of its development and influence.

Very soon after *Ruxley* was decided, it was applied by the Court of Appeal in *Freeman v Niroomand*. Mr Niroomand commissioned a builder to carry out building work at his semi-detached house, namely constructing a porch at the front and an extension to the rear. The dispute involved the porch, which the contract specified should mirror the porch on the adjoining house and should be constructed of cavity wall brickwork (to minimise staining from the elements). When the porch was built, it did match the porch next door, but it had not been constructed with cavity walls. As is all too common, the market value of the house was not altered by the addition of the porch, *whether or not* it complied with the contractual specifications. To cure the breach, the porch either had to be demolished or have its internal dimensions considerably reduced by the addition of an inner layer of brickwork. For this reason Mr Niroomand gave evidence that he did *not* wish to rebuild the porch and thus did not *ask* for the cost of cure, but only claimed a *Ruxley* 'middle ground' award from the defendant builder, representing the value of his unfulfilled expectation (essentially, the risk of a weather-stained porch). The Court of Appeal sympathised and awarded him £130 in damages, adopting Lord Mustill's *consumer surplus* reasoning in the process. Notice that Lord Lloyd's justification would *not* have worked on the facts, as a contract to construct a porch cannot be explained as one which has 'pleasure, peace of mind and freedom from distress' as its object.

A few years later, the House of Lords had another opportunity to consider damages in the consumer contract context, although not this time concerned with a building contract. In *Farley v Skinner* the claimant, Mr Farley, was interested in purchasing a property in Sussex (near Gatwick Airport) as a quiet, relaxing house to live in once he retired. Keen to check that the house was suitable for this purpose, he employed Mr Skinner, a surveyor, to look over it and expressly asked him to report on whether aircraft noise was likely to be a problem. In breach of contract, Skinner negligently reported back that it was unlikely that the property would be noisy. Therefore, Farley bought the house, only to find to his horror that the property was seriously noisy: aircraft 'stacked' in the air just over the house at busy times (mornings, early evenings and weekends), spiralling there until a landing slot became free! Despite the fact that the trial judge found that the price Farley paid reflected the aircraft noise problem (so his *financial* loss was nil), he nevertheless awarded Farley £10,000 for his 'loss of amenity'. The House of Lords unanimously affirmed this award, although suggesting that the amount awarded was at the 'high end of what was appropriate'.

Some of the Law Lords adopted Lord Lloyd's rationalisation of the *Ruxley* middle-ground award as falling within the exceptional category of contracts (like holiday contracts) made with the object of providing pleasure, peace of mind and freedom from distress, for which damages for distress were available. It was then a simple matter merely to expand the exception very slightly to cover cases like this, where pleasure/freedom from distress was not the *sole* object of the contract, but was nonetheless an important object (after all, Farley contracted with the surveyor to check for other defects and problems with the house, not solely to consider the noise issue). Lord Scott, on the other hand, preferred

Lord Mustill's approach, unhesitatingly endorsing the concept of the consumer surplus and allowing relief on this basis: Skinner's breach of contract prevented Farley from obtaining the peace and quiet that were extremely important to him.

So, after two House of Lords cases and numerous lesser decisions, we are still not entirely certain how to rationalise 'middle-ground' awards of this kind or what the relationship is between the 'consumer surplus' and the damages for distress allowed in exceptional cases. Perhaps, by the time you study law, this issue will have been clarified, but experience suggests that, by then, new cases will have arisen with yet more factual twists, leading instead to refinement and possibly even complication of the relevant legal rules.

WHAT IF THE BUILDER HAD SAVED MONEY BY BREACHING THE CONTRACT?

One notable feature of the facts of Ruxley was that the builders did not appear to have *saved* any money by building the pool too shallow, or at least that was not mentioned in the pleaded facts. But, in other cases, a contracting party might very well save a lot of money by breaching his contract, or even make a big profit by deliberately breaching one contract in order to enter into a more favourable one with someone else. Should this be taken into account when calculating the claimant's damages for breach of contract?

The traditional answer to that question in English law has always been a resounding 'no'. Damages for breach of contract have always been purely *compensatory*, calculated (as we've seen already) to put the claimant into the position he would have been in if the contract had been properly performed—in other words, based solely on the claimant's loss, not the defendant's gain. So the rule has always been very clear—damages are not meant to strip profits away from contract-breakers or to punish contract-breakers. Their only role is to make good the claimant's loss.

There are very good reasons for contractual damages being compensatory only. For example, the requirement that claimants must mitigate their loss when suing for damages (act reasonably to keep their loss to a minimum) only makes sense in a damages regime that is loss-based. Economists offer another explanation, namely that the law should allow contract-breakers to keep any profit they make from the breach, provided they compensate the other party's losses, as this is the most 'efficient' outcome. Imagine A contracts to sell B 100 kilos of widgets for £100 when the market price is £110 (for some reason, legal examples about generic goods nearly always involve imaginary items called 'widgets'!). Then someone else, C, offers to pay £150 for the widgets (in other words, more than the market price). Economists regard it as rational for A to break his contract with B and sell to C instead, because this is said to be an *efficient* outcome. This way, A is happy because he has made £50 more than he would have done, C is happy because he has got the widgets, and B should be *neutral*, because she has got £10 damages *and* keeps the £100 price, so can mitigate her loss by buying widgets at their market value.

This economic approach looks very neat, but not everyone is happy with the idea behind it. After all, it treats A as if he had an entirely free choice between performing his contract with B or breaching it and paying damages, when he actually made a *promise* to B to sell the widgets. It seems to underplay the importance of respecting contractual promises. After all, breaching a contract is 'wrongful', although not as serious a wrong as a criminal offence or a tort. It also underplays B's expectation when making a contract: B almost certainly isn't 'neutral' about receiving £10 damages rather than the widgets she ordered, not least because of the hassle involved in finding another supplier of widgets. Finally, and more fundamentally, it just troubles many lawyers that a defendant can make a profit from a breach of contract and yet be allowed to keep that profit—surely, they argue, the law should respond to this 'unjust enrichment' of the defendant by depriving him of his profit and paying it to the innocent claimant.

These objections have led some judges and commentators to argue that damages for breach of contract should, in some circumstances, be calculated by reference to the defendant's gain and not solely the claimant's loss. This is difficult and very controversial territory. The argument generally begins by suggesting that the law already recognises 'gain-based' damages and so it is time for it to 'come clean' and admit that damages are not purely compensatory.

This is tricky because sometimes an award of damages *looks* as if it is depriving a defendant of some or all of his profit, but that profit is just being treated as a way of valuing the claimant's loss. For example, what if A sells some of his land to B for development and B promises not to build more than 20 houses on the site? If B breaches that covenant and builds 25 houses, the extra houses may have no adverse financial effect on A at all, and yet B has made more profit than he should have. English law has long recognised that B must pay damages to A in this situation and what's more those damages *will* be calculated by reference to a proportion of B's extra profit. But that approach to damages is perfectly consistent with a *compensatory* approach. B has gone ahead and built the extra houses in breach of contract without A's permission, but if B had asked A's permission to release him from the contractual restriction, A would probably have granted that permission *at a price*. So B's breach *has* deprived A of something of value—the opportunity to charge for release of the '20 houses only' restriction. And the same compensatory approach applies even if it is clear that A would not have agreed to release B from the contractual restriction at any price. Indeed, the fact that A would not have agreed at any price suggests that it is *particularly* important to him to prevent B building extra houses, so it is counter-intuitive to suggest that A has suffered no loss in such circumstances. After all, if you lose your legs as a result of someone's negligence and claim damages in tort, the fact that you would not have sold your legs for any amount of money does not mean that you have suffered no loss!

A further argument sometimes offered in favour of gain-based damages for breach of contract is that they would be a useful additional tool to help the law to protect contractual expectations properly, even where the claimant has suffered no obvious financial loss from the breach: the same sentiment, in other words, behind the decision in *Ruxley*. This is a very laudable aim, but if the real problem in the law is insufficient respect for contractual expectations (so some losses are overlooked or inadequately respected), would it not be better to attack that problem directly and concentrate on valuing contractual expectations properly, rather than turning to the defendant's gain instead?

An old American case called *City of New Orleans v Fireman's Charitable Association* provides a good example. The claimant paid the defendant to provide a fire-fighting service for five years, with the contract specifying how many men and horses should be kept available and how much hosepipe. At the end of the contract period, the claimant discovered that the defendant had failed to keep available as many men or horses as specified, or the length of hosepipe that had been promised, thereby saving itself over $40,000. However, the claimant could not show that the breach had prevented the defendant extinguishing any fires, so the Supreme Court of Louisiana held that the claimant had suffered no loss and thus was not entitled to damages.

Many commentators have argued that this is the perfect example of a case in which damages should be based on the defendant's profit, because otherwise the claimant goes under-compensated. But if you stop and think for a moment, it is obvious that the Supreme Court of Louisiana got it wrong—the claimant *has* suffered a loss, because he did not get the level of contractual performance he had bargained and paid for. This problem should be tackled directly: if the problem is failure to compensate properly, the answer is to expand the notion of loss to enable the law to compensate more fully, not concentrate on the defendant's profit instead.

However, the House of Lords in *Attorney General v Blake* have now agreed that the defendant's gain might occasionally be relevant to calculating damages for breach of contract, although only in very exceptional cases where a compensatory remedy would be inadequate. George Blake was a spy for the British intelligence services, but he was also a double agent working for the Soviet Union. He was convicted of treason and imprisoned, but later escaped from Wormwood Scrubs prison to Moscow. There in 1989 he wrote his autobiography, which contained some old information about his career in British intelligence. The information was no longer confidential by this time: if it had been, the Crown could have recovered Blake's profits in a different type of legal action for breach of confidence, but this was of course not available. Nor was its disclosure damaging to the public interest, but by releasing it Blake was in breach of his *employment contract*, in which he had promised, 'not to divulge any official information gained as a result of [his] employment' (this promise continued in effect beyond the time his employment ended). So the Crown (in the person of the Attorney General) sued for *breach of contract* to get its hands on Blake's profit from publishing the book.

The House of Lords held in 2000, by a 4:1 majority, that because the facts were so exceptional, the Crown *could* recover the profits made from Blake's breach of contract, even though it had not suffered any *loss* from that breach. The reason given by Lord Nicholls was that the traditional remedies for breach of contract were *inadequate* on the particular facts of the case:

> It will only be in exceptional cases, where those remedies are inadequate, that any question of accounting for profits will arise. No fixed rules can be prescribed. The court will have regard to all the circumstances, including the subject matter of the contract, the purpose of the contractual provision that has been breached, the circumstances in which the breach occurred, the consequences of the breach and the circumstances in which the relief is being sought. A useful general guide, although not exhaustive, is whether the [claimant] had a *legitimate interest* in preventing the defendant's profit-making activity and, hence, in depriving him of his profit. It would be difficult, and unwise, to attempt to be more specific.

He went on to explain what the Crown's *legitimate interest* was:

> The context is employment as a member of the security and intelligence services. Secret information is the lifeblood of these services. In the 1950s Blake deliberately committed repeated breaches of his undertaking not to divulge official information gained as a result of his employment. He caused untold and immeasurable damage to the public interest he had committed himself to serve.

Many lawyers have criticised this decision and its reasoning. Although it is obvious why the House of Lords disliked George Blake and wanted to find a way of making him give up his profits, it looks as if this instinct was based on a desire to punish him again for his previous treachery in the 1950s. But this was an action for Blake's *breach of contract* in publishing his memoirs in 1989, which wasn't actually a particularly serious breach of his former employment contract. So it is not obvious why the Crown's interest *is* legitimate here.

More to the point, the decision does not just affect George Blake, but (because of the doctrine of precedent) makes this sort of remedy potentially available in other cases as well. A number of judges have already struggled in subsequent cases, trying to decide whether or not their facts are sufficiently 'exceptional'. Lord Hobhouse dissented in *Attorney General v Blake*, warning of the danger of introducing an element of uncertainty into commercial transactions, which would make it hard for lawyers and their clients to predict in advance when such a remedy would be awarded. He said:

> I must also sound a further note of warning that if some more extensive principle of awarding non-compensatory damages for breach of contract is to be introduced into our commercial law the consequences will be very far reaching and disruptive.

So now if another *Ruxley*-type case came along in which the builder *had* saved money, a sharp barrister would probably try to argue that the facts fell within the *Attorney General v Blake* exception. This probably wouldn't succeed, but the law of contractual remedies is so dynamic and controversial that you never know!

CONCLUSION

I hope that this chapter has shown that there is much more to contractual remedies than just the boring mathematical bit tacked onto the end of a course on the law of contract. As a topic, it reminds us very sharply that good lawyers must be able to focus on complex arguments and make fine distinctions, whilst at the same time recognising the shared general principles and common problems that can link apparently unconnected situations like ordering books, building swimming pools, buying houses near airports and spying for the enemy.

Cases

Ruxley Electronics & Construction Ltd v Forsyth [1996] AC 344
Radford v De Froberville [1977] 1 WLR 1262
Jacob & Youngs v Kent (1921) 129 NE 889
Freeman v Niroomand (1996) 52 Con LR 116
Farley v Skinner [2002] 2 AC 732
City of New Orleans v Fireman's Charitable Association 9 So 486 (1891)
Attorney General v Blake [2001] 1 AC 268

Further Reading

Harris, Ogus and Phillips, 'Contract Remedies and the Consumer Surplus' (1979) 95 LQR 581

Hedley, '"Very much the wrong people": the House of Lords and publication of spy memoirs' [2000] Web JCLI <http://webjcli.ncl.ac.uk/2000/issue4/hedley4.html>

O'Sullivan and Hilliard, *The Law of Contract* (2nd edn, Oxford University Press Core Text Series, Oxford 2006)

4
Tort

Tony Weir

You may not be familiar with the term *tort*, but you are bound to have come across lots of tort cases in the newspapers. It derives from the French word for 'wrong' and, in English law, means a *civil wrong*. Criminal cases are pursued by the state against the wrongdoer, with punishment of that wrongdoer as the principal aim; tort cases, on the other hand, involve one individual (the claimant) *suing* another individual (the defendant) whom the claimant alleges has done him wrong in some way, principally with a view to obtaining financial compensation. The same set of facts sometimes gives rise to criminal *and* tort liability, but more often than not the wrongdoing involved in a tort case is not serious enough to attract criminal sanctions.

The case chosen here to illustrate the law of tort in operation is *McFarlane v Tayside Health Authority*. This is a case from Scotland, which is of interest in itself, because in many respects Scots law differs considerably from its English relative south of the border, yet the House of Lords is the final appeal court for Scottish cases as well as English ones. The House of Lords must therefore apply Scots law from time to time, so it helps that there are usually senior Scottish judges amongst the Law Lords. *McFarlane* is a very important case for English lawyers too, because the law of tort it considered is virtually identical north and south of the border.

McFarlane involved a bouncing baby born, owing to the fault of a doctor, to parents who had decided they had enough children already, so it could equally well figure in books on family law, or even medical law. The reason the case appears in books on tort is that the parents were suing the hospital for damages, compensation for the cost of bringing up the baby. It therefore sits in the tort books alongside other cases whose main feature is that the claimants—mainly those injured in industrial or highway accidents—are seeking damages as compensation for the harm they have suffered owing to the misconduct of the defendant or, in our case as in many others, the defendant's employee (a wrongdoer's employer is very often sued as well as, or instead of, the individual wrongdoer, because the law makes employers *vicariously liable* to pay damages wherever an employee commits a tort in the course of his or her employment; employers commonly have insurance to cover claims of this kind). Sometimes such harm is caused deliberately, but usually it is the result of carelessness, or *negligence*, as lawyers like to call it.

Just as there are a number of separate crimes (such as murder, theft and rape), similarly there are various separate torts. Of these the tort of negligence is by far the most important in practice, but you may well have heard of some of the other torts, such as defamation and nuisance. To bring a claim in negligence, the claimant must establish certain basic elements. These are first, that the defendant owed him a *duty of care* (which, as we will see later, is so self-evident in most straightforward cases that it goes without saying, but which occasionally gives rise to problems in unusual situations); secondly, that the defendant *breached* that duty by behaving unreasonably or carelessly; thirdly, that the defendant's breach of duty *caused* the claimant to suffer, fourthly, legally recognised *harm*. Lawyers tend to use the word 'negligence' in two ways: as shorthand for the second element just mentioned, careless conduct on the part of the defendant, and also (more properly) to denote the whole 'tort', the cause of action which is established if the claimant establishes all four elements.

McFarlane is a case of 'negligence' in this sense, and it is of particular interest because the outcome is not quite what one would expect in view of the accepted rules of negligence as a tort. The alleged facts were that the claimants, husband and wife, decided that four children were enough and that the husband should submit to a vasectomy, like some 8,000 other Scotsmen each year. The doctor reported that the operation, which he performed quite properly, had been successful and that normal marital relations could be resumed. Alas, the doctor was wrong in this (having misinterpreted the husband's sperm tests carried out after the operation) and the wife conceived. The pregnancy and birth, though painful as always, were quite normal, and baby Catherine McFarlane was in perfect health. But it costs a lot of money to bring up a child (an average of £165,000 has been suggested). Who was to bear this cost, the parents whose child it was, or the health service whose fault it was that the child had been born at all?

If the case had arisen in England it would never have reached the House of Lords for, in 1984, the House had declined to review a decision of the Court of Appeal which had held that there was no objection to such a claim. Although the Court of Appeal case concerned a disabled rather than a healthy child, so its decision as to a healthy child was arguably *obiter* (not binding), and although the court rendered its decision immediately after the barristers had finished their submissions, without taking any time taken to consider its implications, the decision was treated as conclusive thereafter and was followed for fifteen years. But Scottish courts are not bound by the English Court of Appeal and, unlike their English counterparts, Scots applicants such as the McFarlanes need no leave to appeal to the House. In the event, the House of Lords held unanimously that the McFarlanes' claim must fail.

THE MOST FAMOUS TORT CASE

Seventy years earlier, in 1932, Scotland had produced the most famous case in the tort of negligence—the 'snail-in-the-ginger-beer-bottle' case of *Donoghue v Stevenson*. Mrs Donoghue alleged that she had been poisoned by a foreign body, to wit a very dead snail, lurking in a bottle of Stevenson's ginger beer bought for her by a friend in a café. The Scottish court held that, even if she could show that Stevenson had been careless, her claim must fail since he owed her no duty in law to take care of her: she had not actually bought the product. The House of Lords, by a majority, held that the manufacturer did indeed owe her a duty to take such care.

Why is this case regarded as so important? After all, by 1932 there were plenty of situations in which a defendant would be liable if he caused harm negligently, but they were regarded as isolated, unconnected instances that just happened to have similar characteristics, not linked at a conceptual level to form one general tort of negligence. At the time most lawyers thought that *Donoghue v Stevenson* merely added one more such isolated pocket of liability and was no more than a small step forward for 'consumer protection', of little or no significance outside that area. But the case is as famous and important as it is today because its reasoning went beyond that narrow view, when Lord Atkin, with some aid from the Sermon on the Mount, delivered himself of a *general* statement regarding the situations in which one person would be held to owe another a duty to be careful not to injure them. There need not be a contract between the parties, it was enough if there were 'neighbourhood' between them, and one's neighbour was not just the person next door, though such persons are very close, but anyone close enough that injury to them was reasonably foreseeable if one mismanaged whatever one was doing.

As the case indicates, liability in the tort of negligence depends, among other things, on the defendant's having been under a 'duty of care'. Whether or not such a duty exists is a matter of *law*, the subject of legal argument that can be decided in principle without hearing any of the evidence. This is in sharp contrast to the question of whether or not the duty has been breached, that is, whether the defendant had actually been negligent by falling below the proper standard of conduct, which is a matter of *fact* to be proved by witnesses. This distinction was more obviously significant before 1965, when juries were still used to decide negligence cases, because questions of law remained for the judge to decide and thus it was open to the judge to hold that there was no duty of care on the facts as pleaded, however careless the defendant might have been, so that the case failed before getting as far as a jury. Nowadays negligence cases are invariably decided by a judge alone, but the distinction between questions of law and questions of fact remains a very important one in practice.

THE 'DUTY' QUESTION

Mrs Donoghue had, we suppose, suffered injury to her person, and the same was true of Mrs McFarlane, what with the pregnancy and confinement. Where the injury is physical in nature, the 'duty' question is not often discussed, at any rate where, as in both *Donoghue* and *McFarlane*, the defendant's conduct actually created the danger, as opposed to merely failing to prevent it: Stevenson actually despatched the noxious bottle into the world and the doctor in *McFarlane* said that sex was now safe (from babies anyway). So there was not much discussion of the mother's claim for the pain of pregnancy and parturition. Indeed, in cases of highway or industrial accidents the existence of the duty is never questioned—it is too obvious that road-users owe each other a duty to drive carefully, and that an employer is under a special duty to look out for the safety of his employees—but the question does arise in novel cases, especially if the judges want to exonerate the negligent defendant from liability for the foreseeable harm he has caused, for then 'no duty in law' is almost the only device they can deploy.

THE KIND OF HARM

Tort lawyers often say, somewhat illogically, that the existence of the duty, or its scope or ambit, depends on the nature of the harm that resulted from breach of the duty. In *McFarlane* there were two types of harm: the wife had suffered not only physical harm, harm to her body, as a result of the unwanted pregnancy but also financial harm, in having to pay for the baby's upkeep, while the husband had suffered only harm of the latter kind. The real issue was the cost of bringing up the child. This was problematic because our law of tort has always been less ready to award compensation for a loss which is merely financial than for damage which is physical in nature, harm to person or property. In other words, the claim 'You wounded me' has always been held stronger than 'You cost me'. Of course, where the tort has caused the claimant to suffer personal injury or property damage, its economic aspects—lost wages, cost of cure, repairs and so on—are every bit as compensable as pain and suffering and loss of amenity, but it is different if the only harm is financial, not consequent on physical damage to person or property: this is commonly called *pure* financial loss, and it is less readily compensated in tort. Some judges regarded the financial loss in *McFarlane* not as 'pure' but rather as consequential on the personal injury to the wife, and therefore compensable on normal principles, but a majority of their Lordships treated the harm to the mother as regards the pregnancy and birth as quite distinct from harm in the sense of the cost to both parents of bringing up the baby.

DAMAGE AND LOSS

This distinction between physical damage and pure economic loss makes some commentators uneasy—after all, they are both kinds of harm—but it seems perfectly justifiable, even in a society which seems to put money above all else. Consider, for example, the word 'dangerous'. It is applied only in situations where the potential harm is of a physical variety, where there is a risk of injury to person or property, and since the counterpart of 'danger' is safety, it is not too surprising if the law puts safety first. To put it another way, health is more important than wealth: we don't have a National Wealth Service—indeed, we have the very opposite, in the form of Her Majesty's Revenue and Customs.

RECOVERY FOR PURE FINANCIAL HARM

For thirty years after *Donoghue v Stevenson* it was assumed that there was no prospect of claiming in the tort of negligence for pure financial loss due to mere carelessness, as opposed to deliberate lies (deceit) or failure to do what one had been paid to do (breach of contract). Then, in 1963, the House of Lords held that such a claim might lie. In *Hedley Byrne v Heller and Partners* the claimant lost money as a result of a misleading credit-reference given, gratuitously, by the defendant bank on one of the claimant's customers. What the bank did—certifying that the customer was in a good financial position when it was anything but— was careless and negligent, but it was not *dangerous*, since the only loss that could and did result from the claimant's relying on the reference and giving credit to the customer was purely financial.

As in *McFarlane*, as we shall see, the House of Lords in the banking case was agreed as to the result—that there could be liability in negligence for causing merely financial harm—but their Lordships differed in the reasons they gave and consequently as to the circumstances in which liability would attach. The five different speeches emphasise different points. Could the defendant foresee that the recipient of the information would rely on it? Was it on a business rather than a social occasion? Was the defendant an expert on the matter in issue? Was the relationship

between the parties 'equivalent to contract'? Did the defendant undertake responsibility for the statement in question?

As the law developed, it became less important whether the defendant had spoken or acted, and more important that there be a 'special
relationship' between the parties, characterised by an 'undertaking of
responsibility' on the part of the defendant. The fact that different reasons were given for the decision made it easier for later courts to expand
its scope, to the point that in 1995 a solicitor who failed to draw up a will
as instructed by his client was held liable in *White v Jones* to the client's
daughters who would have inherited had the will been drawn up as it
should have been. The disappointed daughters won, despite the facts that
the solicitor neither spoke nor acted, and seemed to be in no very special
relationship with them, and that, even supposing that he could be said to
have assumed responsibility for drawing up the will, they surely did not
rely on his doing so, foreseeable though the harm to them was. In other
words, although he undoubtedly assumed responsibility *to his client*, the
father, it is quite another thing to say that he assumed responsibility, in
any meaningful sense, to *the daughters*. One can easily see that rather
surprising decisions may 'follow' from a previous decision, especially
one in which several different reasons are given for the same outcome.

APPLICATION IN *McFARLANE*

Now, in *McFarlane* it was plain that there was a 'special relationship'
between the parents and the doctor, that he was a specialist who under-
took responsibility and that he knew they would be relying on what he
told them. It is true that they didn't pay for the treatment, so there was no
contract, but after *Hedley Byrne* that was unimportant. It had been held
for centuries that doctors owe their patients a duty of care, and though the
cases have generally involved harm to the patient's person rather than his
pocket, Lord Devlin in *Hedley Byrne* said that that made no difference.
Since the birth of the child was the 'very thing' that the defendant was
retained to prevent, it was not easy to say that it fell outside the scope
of his duty of care; and since it is notorious that children are expensive,
the loss could not possibly be described as too 'remote'. Furthermore,

several of the judges said that it was immaterial whether the claim rested on *Donoghue* or on *Hedley Byrne*. As Lord Bingham put it in a later case, 'An orthodox application of familiar and conventional principles of the law of tort would, I think, have pointed to' imposing liability in *McFarlane*. So how was this avoided?

FAIR, JUST AND REASONABLE

The majority in the House of Lords invoked an element which their predecessors in 1990 had added to Lord Atkin's statement of the requirements for finding a duty of care. The 1990 case—*Caparo v Dickman*—was again one of pure economic loss: a shareholder interested in taking over a company was suing the auditor whose carelessly favourable statement about its profitability in its annual accounts, a publicly available document, induced him to pay too much for further shares. In rejecting his claim, their Lordships said that in addition to 'foreseeability of the harm' and 'proximity between the parties' (= neighbourhood) it must be found that it would be 'fair, just and reasonable' to impose a duty (= make the defendant liable).

The first two of these elements were plainly satisfied on the facts of *McFarlane*. The doctor could hardly have been closer to the husband in performing the operation, which he knew would, if its outcome were carelessly misreported, affect the wife. The harm was evidently foreseeable—indeed, what happened was the very thing the doctor was retained to prevent—but the majority of their Lordships held that it was not 'fair, just and reasonable' to impose liability on the careless doctor for the cost of upbringing.

THE REASONS GIVEN IN *McFARLANE*

The reasons given by their Lordships were rather varied. Some members of the House of Lords were content to rely on the formula that it was not 'fair, just and reasonable' to impose on the medical services liability for the cost of bringing up a healthy, though unwanted, child, or that to make the doctor liable to pay for the maintenance of a healthy child for eighteen years was disproportionate to his fault. Less time was

spent on justifying the decision than on dismissing arguments which had
been raised against it. These included the argument that the (provable)
harm of having to pay for the child's upbringing should be offset by the
(intangible) joy of parenthood. This was regarded as impracticable and
unprincipled: after all, a person disabled from working by a negligent
driver does not have his claim for lost earnings reduced just because he
can now relax and watch daytime television.

THE SPEECH OF LORD STEYN

Lord Steyn did not care much for the reasons given by his colleagues:

> To explain decisions denying a remedy for the cost of bringing up an unwanted
> child by saying that there is no loss, no foreseeable loss, no causative link or
> no ground [for] reasonable restitution is to resort to unrealistic and formalistic
> propositions which mask the real reasons for the decisions. And judges ought
> to strive to give the real reasons for their decision.

He held that when there were thousands of people in the kingdom who
desperately wanted a family and paid good money in the vain hope of
achieving it, it would be contrary to the principle of distributive justice
to give damages to the parents of a healthy child they did not want (but
kept). Furthermore, he said:

> Instinctively, the traveller on the Underground would consider that the law of
> tort has no business to provide legal remedies consequent upon the birth of a
> healthy child, which all of us regard as a valuable and good thing.

Lord Millett said much the same. He said that 'plaintiffs are not allowed,
by a process of subjective devaluation, to make a detriment out of a benefit' and that 'it is morally offensive to regard a normal, healthy baby as
more trouble and expense than it is worth.'

DISTRIBUTIVE JUSTICE

Lord Steyn referred to 'distributive justice', a rather unattractive term
often attributed to Aristotle's distinction between what is fair between
claimant and defendant on the one hand and what is fair between different
classes of claimant or potential claimant on the other. Thus Lord Steyn

suggested that when deciding on a claim made by parents who didn't want a child one should bear in mind the many other people who do want a child and can't have one. He might also have mentioned another constituency, namely sick children who would be deprived of proper treatment if the limited resources of the health service were deployed to pay for the upbringing of children in perfect health.

PSYCHIATRIC HARM

The term 'distributive justice' had surfaced in the House of Lords a few years previously in one of the cases arising out of the Hillsborough disaster in Sheffield when 95 football fans were crushed to death when the police negligently allowed too many of them to enter the stadium. Many claims were brought by relatives of the deceased victims, who had been shocked by what they witnessed, with their own eyes or on television, but almost all their claims were dismissed. The harm here was psychiatric, not physical: to the mind, not the body. Harm of this kind might well seem at the other extreme from pure economic loss, but it, too, is subject to restrictive rules: in particular, the claimant, unless himself physically endangered, must have been physically close to the shocking event and emotionally close to the person primarily affected. But there was some authority that the second restriction did not apply to those who went to the rescue of those actually injured, and clear authority that employers owe their employees a special duty not to cause them injury, so there was a problem when claims were brought by members of the police force, shocked by having to deal with the dead and dying, since they were rescuers suing their employer, the negligent police authority. Could the courts really bring themselves to award damages to the police when they had refused to compensate relatives of the deceased victims, members of the public whom the police are supposed to protect? To award damages might be fair as between the policemen and their employers, but it wouldn't seem right as between policemen and the relatives. Likewise, in the *McFarlane* case, it didn't seem right to award damages to parents of a child they didn't want (though now dearly loved) when so many parents wanted children they couldn't have, however much they paid.

EFFECT ON THIRD PARTIES

That the courts do and should consider the effect of their decisions on third parties is shown by another recent case. In *Tomlinson* a young man ignored signs prohibiting swimming in a reservoir in a public park and was badly injured in the water. The Court of Appeal held the occupier liable because, knowing that the prohibitions were ineffective, it had failed to erect a physical barrier which would have prevented all access to the water. A unanimous House of Lords, in unusually vigorous judgments, reversed the Court of Appeal's decision: to block access in this way was not fair to innocent holiday-makers who wished to sit beside the water, and the local authority had, in deciding to effect a physical barrier, overreacted to the fear of being held liable to injured trespassers.

TORT AS DETERRENCE

To be held liable is unpleasant, even if one has insurance against such liability (as is required of employers and motorists, among many others), so the risk of being held liable may act as a deterrent. Indeed, it follows from the doctrine of precedent that decisions which impose liability are apt to affect third parties: court decisions may affect the behaviour of the public, or a relevant section of it, just as much as statutory prohibitions. Given that tort liability is commonly imposed for conduct which is dangerous, it may well be conducive to safety if third parties, especially public bodies and firms conscious of risk management, respond to the decision. So tort law certainly has *some* deterrent effect. But there may be better devices, in particular those enforced by the criminal law. A statute or regulation can state precisely what must be done on pain of penalty—for example, that a guardrail must be provided where persons work more than two metres above the ground, but all a judge can say—and that after the event—is that the employer or occupier must take reasonable care of the safety of his employees or visitors. Indeed, the existence of sanctions other than damages was one reason why the House of Lords recently reversed a decision of the Court of Appeal which had held that where a claimant's 'constitutional right' had been infringed by malicious conduct on the part of a public officer (in the case, a prison officer who insisted on reading the prisoner's privileged mail), there was no need to prove any damage at all.

DETERRENCE AND COMPENSATION

If the primary, though by no means the sole, function of tort law is to award compensation for harm due to culpable conduct, there are dangers in overemphasising its deterrent aspects: since compensation looks to the harm suffered by the claimant and deterrence looks to the conduct of the defendant, compensation and deterrence do not quite go hand in hand. Accordingly, to focus on deterrence may lead one to downplay the importance of the harm in relation to the conduct: one might be tempted to impose liability on those who have acted negligently so as to deter others from doing likewise, even if the harm in the case is not obviously attributable to their negligence. After all, the defendant's carelessness might well have caused harm even if it did not obviously do so in the particular case, and might, unless repressed now, do so the next time. Does some such idea lie behind the fact that the common law seems to treat damage to property very much like injury to the person, although people are surely more important than their property and should have greater protection? After all, anything which can damage a thing could have injured a person. Again, one might think that *unless* we hold people liable for breaching their duty of care, even if it is not clear that the breach caused any harm, people similarly situated might be able to ignore their duty with impunity.

TWO RECENT CASES

Two cases from the start of the twenty-first century are indicative. In *Chester v Afshar* a doctor failed to inform his patient, as he was duty-bound to do, of the risk of paralysis inherent in the proposed operation, which tragically materialised even though the operation was performed impeccably. Had she been informed, the patient would *still* have had the operation, though not then and there because she would have wanted to go away first to consider and research the possible risk, and that risk would have been the same on whatever day she eventually had the surgery. The minority in the House of Lords would have absolved the doctor on the ground that his breach of duty did not increase the risk of harm, but the majority gave judgment for the patient, even though they said that this was inconsistent with the conventional principles of causation, because otherwise doctors could ignore their duty with impunity. Similar considerations led to a unanimous decision in *Fairchild v Glenhaven Funeral Services* to impose liability on all the successive employers who had carelessly exposed the claimant to asbestos fibres, although only one of them could possibly have triggered his cancer: in certain circumstances, especially where it is impossible to identify the precise cause, you are taken to have caused harm if your misconduct increased the risk of its occurrence, for otherwise your breach of duty would have no legal consequences at all.

Analogous are cases where a defendant who had acted in a manner apt to cause physical harm has been held liable for harm of a different kind not otherwise compensable. In *Page v Smith*, for instance, the defendant was held liable when his slightly bad driving caused a minor accident in which the claimant, though not physically injured at all, was (unforeseeably) shocked enough to take to his bed. Again, it was held in *Anns v Merton LBC* that the buyer of a badly built house was entitled to damages, but only if the house was 'imminently dangerous' so that it could have collapsed and injured him physically, though it didn't, and all he lost was some money. That decision also held that if the house was dangerous the local authority was liable for negligently permitting it to be built. The risk of such liability was later felt to induce planning authorities to be overcareful and unduly scrupulous, thereby delaying the construction of buildings in an unacceptable manner. *Anns* has since been overruled. One reason for the overruling was that there was a statute on the books which provided the purchaser of a jerry-built dwelling with a claim against the builder.

STATUTES AND JUDGE-MADE LAW

That statute (the Defective Premises Act 1972) applied only to *dwellings*, homes for people; *Anns*, had it not been overruled, would have applied to all buildings, including office-blocks. This indicates a distinction between statutory and judge-made rules which deserves a moment's notice. In *McFarlane* itself no statute was involved, and our choice of it to illustrate the law of tort might lead one to suppose that tort law is largely judge-made. The supposition is quite false: almost all tort suits involve, and frequently turn on, a statute. This is true not only of those cases where a workman sues for breach of a safety regulation and his claim is based explicitly on the statutory rule, but also of cases where statute has intervened to reverse or modify rules laid down by judges. Thus in every case involving death or more than one defendant or injury to which the claimant's fault has contributed or which occurred on the defendant's premises or which is due to a defective product or the act of an animal—and that is a lot of cases!—the outcome depends on some statute or other.

Statutory rules and those laid down by the judges are very different in nature and operation. Judge-made rules are applied *by analogy*—a decision involving a dog may well be applied in a case concerning a cat, since cats and dogs are analogous (in some ways), but a statute which refers to a dog could never be applied to a cat, for a statute applies only to what is covered by its wording, whatever the courts hold the words to mean. Again, while both Parliament and the courts speak by a majority, often a very slim one, Parliament speaks with one voice, and its very words are law. One cannot imagine five different versions of a statute, but a court may speak with five different voices, and while it is the actual holding which is binding rather than the words the judges use, it is the reasons they give which will be ventilated in subsequent cases.

THE EFFECT OF *McFARLANE*

We have seen that the decision in the case of the misleading banker's reference, in which there were five different speeches, has been applied in situations very far from the facts of *Hedley Byrne* itself. There were five different speeches in *McFarlane* also, and though it can hardly prove equally seminal, it has left some unanswered questions. Thus while we know that a doctor whose fault is responsible for the birth of a healthy baby need not pay for its upbringing, what if the child is born because of a defect in a contraceptive device carelessly manufactured, or sold, by the defendant? What if the child is not healthy, but handicapped? Are these also situations in which it would not be fair just and reasonable to make the defendant pay?

The actual decision in *McFarlane* displeased two classes of critic— those who objected to the displacement of the normal rules of tort law, and those who thought it was unfair on the parents. Two years after *McFarlane*, the Court of Appeal held in *Parkinson v St James and Seacroft University Hospital NHS Trust* that if the child was disabled the extra cost of upbringing attributable to the disability could be claimed, and shortly after that the same court held in *Rees v Darlington Memorial Hospital NHS Trust* that where the extra cost was due not to any disability in the child but to the disability of the mother, that too was compensable. Both parties in *Rees* appealed to the House of Lords so, less than four years after *McFarlane*, the House, with seven judges instead of the usual five, was invited to change its mind about its original decision. All seven judges held that *McFarlane* should not be overruled, and allowed the defendant's appeal. But then four of them did something very remarkable: they held that though, under *McFarlane*, the parents of the unwanted child could not claim *damages*, that is, full compensation for their loss, they should nonetheless receive a *lump sum* of £15,000.

DAMAGE AND THE INVASION OF RIGHTS

This decision to award £15,000 is simply extraordinary, as the minority emphasised with great vigour. The only explanation is that the claimants had suffered a wrong in that their right to organise their life and plan their family had been negligently infringed, and that while *McFarlane* had declined to award compensation for the consequent harm (the standard consequence of wrongful conduct), still something should be done about it. It is true that in recent years we have become increasingly used to people claiming that their rights have been infringed. In fact, however, the common law always did award money when certain basic rights had been infringed (even without negligence or consequent harm): the right to freedom of movement, to physical integrity and to undisturbed possession of property were protected by the tort of trespass, and the right to one's reputation was (over)protected by the tort of defamation (libel and slander).

Now, since the enactment by the Human Rights Act 1998 of the European Convention of Human Rights, the number of protected rights has been greatly increased, but the person complaining of infringement of one of the new rights (including the right to 'respect for family life') may have to forgo damages and be content with a declaration that his grievance is justified. Future McFarlanes will do better than that—they will get £15,000. The £15,000 was said (but not held) to be payable whether the child is healthy or disabled, with the implication that (contrary to *Parkinson*) even where the child is disabled, only the £15,000 is payable. But *McFarlane* and *Rees,* which endorsed it, were concerned only with the healthy child, so there are some untidy ends, as well as an unprecedented precedent.

THE UNWANTED BABY ABROAD

There seem to be unwanted babies and claimant parents all over the world, and in *McFarlane* the House of Lords considered a few decisions from abroad. Subsequently the High Court of Australia, after very full argument, declined (by a majority) to follow *McFarlane* and awarded full damages in the case of a healthy child. In Germany the Constitutional Court split on the question whether to treat a child as harm was consistent with the constitutional requirement of respect for the human being, but now it is accepted that the harm is not the existence of the child but the cost of maintaining it, and the courts, treating the doctor's negligence as a breach of contract, award damages to the mother, though not the full amount where the child is healthy. France is different, as usual, for it holds that to have a healthy child is not damage at all, which is a very sensible view. But then the French court did something remarkable, not possible in England: it held that the *child itself* could sue if (a) the doctors had failed to recognise that it would probably be handicapped and (b) the mother, if informed of this, would have proceeded to a lawful abortion. Now there is certainly something odd and unpalatable about letting a person claim on the basis that if the defendants had done their duty he would not have been born at all, but be that as it may, the decision caused public outrage and legislation was passed in great haste: it was the *state's* job to provide for disabled persons, regardless of the reason for their disability, and doctors were to be liable for the parents' personal harm only, ignoring the extra cost of the child. Subsequently, however, the High Court in the Netherlands has held that the disabled child can indeed claim for being born if the doctors carelessly failed to inform his mother that he was likely to be born disabled, and she would, if so informed, have proceeded to an abortion. Whether this approach enhances or reduces the dignity of the disabled claimant, and how it affects the perception of disabled people in society, are impossibly difficult questions to answer, indeed even to address in civil legal proceedings.

CONCLUSION

It is hardly surprising that courts in different countries, faced with the same problem, reach different conclusions. Nor is this entirely due to the fact that they may be operating in different social and legal contexts and traditions. After all, even in a single system such as ours, quite cogent decisions of trial judges may be reversed by a divided Court of Appeal, and unanimous decisions of the Court of Appeal, seemingly the last word, may be overturned by three members of the House of Lords, unpersuaded by the very plausible speeches of two determined dissentients. There is therefore no point in pretending that the ultimate holding in any debated case is at all inevitable or obviously 'right'. But disputes must be resolved and cases decided: there must be a decision one way or the other so that citizens can be advised where they stand (and perhaps press for remedial legislation). Meanwhile, the ultimate decision is authoritative, however minoritarian or objectionable. It is necessary, therefore, to know what the law is (for the time being), but it is also very desirable to know how it comes to be the way it is and how easily it might have been otherwise. And that is one of the things that makes the study of law as interesting as it is.

Cases

Alcock v Chief Constable [1992] 1 AC 310
Anns v Merton London Borough Council [1978] AC 728
Caparo Industries v Dickman [1990] 2 AC 605
Chester v Afshar [2004] UKHL 41
Donoghue v Stevenson [1932] AC 562
Fairchild v Glenhaven Funeral Services [2002] UKHL 22
Hedley Byrne & Co v Heller and Partners [1964] AC 465
McFarlane v Tayside Health Board [2000] 2 AC 59
Page v Smith [1996] AC 155
Parkinson v St James and Seacroft University Hospital NHS Trust [2001] EWCA
    Civ 530
Rees v Darlington Memorial Hospital NHS Trust [2003] UKHL 52
Tomlinson v Congleton BC [2003] UKHL 47
White (or Frost) v Chief Constable [1999] 2 AC 455
White v Jones [1995] 2 AC 207

Further Reading

Atiyah, *The Damages Lottery* (Hart Publishing, Oxford 1997)
Cane and Atiyah, *Atiyah's Accidents, Compensation and the Law* (7th edn,
    Cambridge University Press, Cambridge 2006)
Weir, *An Introduction to Tort Law* (2nd edn, Oxford University Press, Oxford
    2006)

5

Land Law

Kevin Gray

INTRODUCTION

William Blackstone was the first ever Professor of English Law, being
appointed to the newly established Vinerian Chair in Oxford in 1758.
He wrote four monumental volumes of *Commentaries on the Laws of
England*, a work which still ranks as one of the most remarkable attempts
to rationalise and expound the law for the benefit of university students
and, more generally, for an intelligent citizenry. However, Blackstone
concluded the second volume of his *Commentaries* (which was devoted
to the law of property) on an extremely gloomy note, recording his fear
that this volume 'has afforded the student less amusement and pleasure
in the pursuit, than the matters discussed in the preceding volume' (*Bl
Comm*, Vol II (1766), p 382). Blackstone's evident disenchantment with
the law of property—and particularly with the law of land—inaugurated
a myth which has since coloured the perceptions of entire generations
of students as they embark on their exploration of land law. Many have
approached the encounter with a weary resignation born of some appre-
hension that the law of realty (as it is often known) will be dry, dusty and
dull in comparison with the more vivid entertainment offered by, say, the
law of crime or tort.

How wrong such perceptions turn out to be! True it is that property
matters are, at least initially, more technical than many other areas of
law. It is also fair to say that the land law of Blackstone's day was deeply

marked by the mind-numbing complexities of a rapidly disintegrating feudal order. But the reality of realty—so to speak—is that 'all human life is here' (if we may borrow a phrase once employed by the *News of the World*). If you want sex, lies, violence and vitality—the full gamut of human strengths and frailties—it is all here. Moreover, there is something for everyone: something for the theorist, the technician, the pragmatist, the romantic and the cynic alike. The reason is not hard to search out. The law of property is not ultimately about land or things. It is about ourselves; it is about the way in which we perceive our relationship with the external world; it is about the rapaciousness with which we choose to seize the resources and opportunities offered by that world. Here is an arena in which the agony and ecstasy of life are played out against a backdrop of abstract proprietary concepts.

THE PROBLEM OF PROPERTY

For the student, the challenge of property is deeply internal. Property law is, effectively, a kind of applied psychology. The law of property poses fundamental questions to which the answers lie not outside, but inside, oneself. How absolute or sacrosanct should property entitlements be? How much room is there for notions of fairness in the allocation of property rights? What is the proper balance between justice, certainty and efficiency? Is property law simply about excluding other people from resources which one values or is it more about a sharing of socially valued resources with others? How do human rights and property rights interact? On what grounds can one's property be taken away or confiscated? What is property anyway? The answers to such questions depend upon the private, latent, barely conscious assumptions and perceptions which each of us brings to the study of property. Yet our responses to these ancient questions have implications which go far beyond the immediate resolution of property disputes. Our conclusions impinge upon a whole range of modern debates—about personal privacy, civil liberty, distributive justice, social exclusion and environmental welfare—debates which are central to the way in which we live our lives. Property questions are profound; their reach is universal; their power to engage is immense. Small wonder that even Blackstone, in one of his more cheerful moments, recognised that there is 'nothing which so generally strikes the imagination, and engages the affections of mankind, as the right of property' (*Bl Comm*, Vol II, p 2).

In the case of land, the factor which intensifies the explosive cocktail of proprietary emotion is the truism that there is a strictly limited supply of the commodity. Particularly in the context of land, property becomes the obsessive concern of a lifetime: ask anyone with a mortgage or, for that matter, anyone who sleeps in a doorway. Indeed you, the reader, are already a fully fledged expert on property, for you have spent most of your life engaged in the constant and instinctive—often subconscious—identification of things as being either your own or someone else's. Nor will you ever escape the long reach of land law, for this body of rules has something to say about every aspect of your daily life. What right, for example, do you have to be in the place where you are reading this book? Do you own the space in which you are sitting? Are you a tenant? Are you a licensee (or permitted visitor)? Are your parents entitled to throw you out of the family home? Or are you, perhaps, a squatter or trespasser in someone else's premises? You are never, in fact, immune from classification in land law terms. As the American jurist, Max Radin, once said, '[t]o go to sleep in one's bed is as much and as little of a legal act... as signing a deed'. Even when you rest six feet under, land law can still tell us your precise legal status in relation to realty.

THE CASE (*CHHOKAR v CHHOKAR*)

An Ordinary Family Home

But let me transport you far away from these musings to a street in West London and to an everyday story of ordinary people living in Southall. The central characters in this drama are a husband and wife, Mr and Mrs Chhokar. The beguiling normality of the suburban context should never, of course, blind us to the volatility of emotion, the duplicitous scheming and the bizarre twists of fate which often flourish in such settings: always expect the unexpected! The tangled narrative of the Chhokars' life together was to end up in the Court of Appeal in the 1980s and to lead to a ruling which, somewhat improbably, invoked the authority of an unreported decision of a Venetian court some four centuries earlier.

Two years after their marriage in 1975 the Chhokars bought a house in Clarence Street in Southall for a price (in today's values) of £92,000. The deposit of £7,000 came from their joint savings and the remaining £85,000 was borrowed by Mr Chhokar from a building society. The Chhokars were typical participants in what soon became Thatcher's 'property-owning democracy' or, as Lord Diplock more accurately described it in *Pettitt v Pettitt* (1970), 'a real-property-mortgaged-to-a-building-society-owning democracy'. The Chhokars' purchase was doubtless founded on hard work; their aspirations were upwardly mobile; they had a young child for whom they were striving to create a better life.

Legal title to the Chhokars' home was registered at the Land Registry in Mr Chhokar's name alone (although, in the confusion of the purchase, his wife initially believed that it had been registered in their joint names). The rights of the building society were, incidentally, merely those of a secured creditor. This meant that, although the money which it had lent to Mr Chhokar ranked immediately as *his* money for the purpose of the purchase, the building society was entitled, in the event of any default, to recover the outstanding loan money by forcing a sale of the home. Herein lies the essence of mortgage-fuelled house-purchase. The borrower is enabled to acquire a major capital asset (usually by means of instalment payments over a mortgage term of some 20 or 25 years), whilst the lender's rights are confined to the eventual return of the loan principal plus any interest which has accrued on this sum. Of course, land (together with any house which is part of the land) tends to inflate in value over time, with the result that the modern mortgage operates as a very remarkable engine of wealth creation for the borrower. By purchasing a house with externally sourced funds, the borrower is allowed to ride up on the steadily increasing capital value of the land, thereby achieving a tax-free windfall in which the lender takes no share beyond the contracted return of loan money with interest.

Legal and Equitable Ownership

Right at the outset we meet our first difficulty in the Chhokar saga—where exactly did Mrs Chhokar fit into the ownership picture? So far as the Land Registry was concerned, Mr Chhokar was quite plainly the sole registered proprietor of the matrimonial home. There was not a scrap of documentation anywhere to suggest that his wife owned *any* share in that home. Yet it was beyond dispute that at all relevant times Mrs Chhokar had handed her wages over to her husband, with the result that both the initial deposit on the house and the subsequent mortgage payments had been generated by the earnings of both. No matter how the registered (or 'legal') title is held, it seems intuitively *unfair* that joint contributory effort should not be recognised in some form of shared ownership. But here the legal ownership of the Chhokars' home had already crystallised definitively in the husband's name alone.

At this point an extraordinarily significant branch of English jurisprudential doctrine comes into play. For centuries the courts have recognised that ownership can sometimes exist on two parallel planes. In such cases, 'legal' ownership (or ownership 'at common law') comprises merely the superficial documentary record of ownership (usually as evidenced by title deeds or by the proprietorship entered in the Land Register). Viewed in this way, 'legal' ownership is only the external face of proprietary entitlement. It is, in many ways, a nominal kind of ownership, signifying simply that someone is the *caretaker* or *custodian* of the land. 'Legal' ownership is not even that important, since it does little more than reflect the fact that the name of a particular transferee has been inscribed (sometimes quite fortuitously) on a deed of transfer. More vital by far is the 'equitable' (or 'beneficial') ownership of the asset in question. The jurisdiction of equity—originating in the court of the king's Chancellor in medieval times and later exercised by the Court of Chancery—came to recognise that 'legal' ownership is not necessarily conclusive of the allocation of proprietary entitlement (see chapter 6). Equity's central contribution to English jurisprudence has always been the idea that conscience-based obligation takes priority over strict legal right. Unlike the common law (which is moved by the sheer outer form of documentary titles), equity looks to the inner reality of transactions. Accordingly, in appropriate circumstances, equity answers its primary call of conscience by engrafting a corrective image of entitlement—a species of 'equitable' ownership—upon the ownership which exists at common law.

In this way equity is able to supplement the common law by responding more flexibly and sensitively to the need for fair dealing and just outcomes. It would be wrong, however, to suggest that equity intervenes in *every* circumstance in which a person in the street might identify a particular outcome as unfair. To go down this path would simply lead to chaos. But one of the standard cases where equity *does* interpose its own view of ownership occurs where a legal title to property is purchased using money contributed by some person or persons who are omitted from the legal ownership. In a world where money talks loudly, it is intrinsically unlikely that money contributors will have intended to part with substantial amounts of cash otherwise than in the expectation of some form of ownership. In these circumstances it seems 'inequitable' for the purchaser of a legal title to deny the ownership rights of the very persons who made his acquisition possible. Accordingly, in the absence of any proven contrary intention, equity regards the purchaser as a mere 'trustee' (or custodian) who holds his legal title 'on trust' for those who directly funded his purchase (each in proportion to their respective money contributions). The fair return expected by the money contributors takes the form of shares of 'equitable' (or 'beneficial') ownership under the 'trust'. In effect, 'legal' ownership is reserved for the person nominally entitled to the property, whilst a parallel form of 'equitable' ownership—ultimately the more important kind of ownership—is recognised in those whose efforts, in reality, facilitated the purchase. So forceful is equity's mandate of conscience that the trust which arises here requires no documentary existence. It subsists as an 'implied trust', hovering—as it were—in mid-air, but in no sense diminished or weakened by its lack of visible paper form.

When this doctrine of trusts is applied to the facts of the *Chhokar* case, it readily yields the conclusion—undisputed by all parties concerned— that whilst Mr Chhokar owned the matrimonial home 'at law', ownership 'in equity' was divided between husband and wife in equal shares by virtue of their joint contributions of money (see Fig. 5.1). (Ongoing mortgage payments are effectively treated as a discharge by instalments of the initial purchase price.) The overall effect was therefore that, whilst Mr Chhokar (as 'legal' owner) retained the bare right to sell or otherwise dispose of the home, the money value inherent in that home was shared equally between husband and wife as co-owners of the 'equitable' (or 'beneficial') interest. These parallel versions of ownership can be expressed in the following graphic form:

Fig. 5.1 *Ownership in law and equity by Mr and Mrs Chhokar.*

A Dreadful Deed

So far so good. You have just survived a first (and not entirely easy) encounter with the technicalities of the law of property. But the same cannot be said for the Chhokar family, because from here on storm clouds begin to gather over their heads. Tolstoy wrote famously that 'all happy families are alike but an unhappy family is unhappy after its own fashion'. Domestic discord struck the Chhokars in an inimitable sequence of events. In 1978, just as their second child was on the way, Mr Chhokar suspected his wife of infidelity, although no evidence was ever found to support such an assertion. Nevertheless, Mr Chhokar devoted himself single-mindedly to a strategy which was designed to rid himself of his wife. He took her to India for a short holiday and, while there, he confiscated her return ticket and came home alone, leaving her destitute. Somehow Mrs Chhokar, heavily pregnant, managed to borrow enough money to make her way back to London: we are told that her husband was 'surprised to see her'. Mr Chhokar then embarked upon a scheme which he hoped would not only disembarrass himself permanently of his wife, but also siphon-off a sufficiently substantial portion of the value of the matrimonial home to enable him to start a new life elsewhere without her. To this end he met a Mr Parmar in a bar somewhere in London. There, as Ewbank J was later to say, he had 'a discussion that might take place in similar circumstances in relation to property ... asserted to have fallen off the back of a lorry'.

The upshot of this conversation was an agreement to sell the Chhokars' home to Parmar for £127,000, a sum which was patently a gross undervalue. The transaction was planned behind the back of Mrs Chhokar, who was led to believe that Parmar, during his inspection of the premises, was merely a prospective lodger. Parmar was fully aware of Mr Chhokar's fraudulent intent and together they agreed that completion of the house transfer should occur while Mrs Chhokar was in hospital having her next baby. Such plans never, of course, run smoothly. Mrs Chhokar's baby was tardy in making its appearance and completion of the transfer had to be postponed for some four days after the expected date of delivery. Notwithstanding this inconvenience, the duplicitous transfer eventually took place while Mrs Chhokar was still in the maternity ward. Mr Chhokar immediately repaid his outstanding mortgage debt and set off for India with a cash windfall of over £40,000. Two days after completion Parmar put the house on the market for £185,000—almost £60,000 more than the price he had paid to Mr Chhokar. When, a day later, Mrs Chhokar emerged from hospital clutching her new-born child, she found the locks changed at her home and, on trying to gain access, was beaten up by Parmar's heavies. Parmar threatened to throw the baby out of a window and he and his thugs proceeded to break every window in the house and vandalise the lavatory in an attempt to render the house uninhabitable by Mrs Chhokar.

An Unforeseen Outcome

At this stage the scoreline could not but register the fact that some of the participants in this story had fared rather better than others. Parmar had got the house and the prospect of a massive profit on resale; Mr Chhokar had got no wife, a large cash bonus, a new life incognito, and probably a new woman; whereas Mrs Chhokar had got two small children and no home and was therefore compelled to live in a hostel. But how fundamentally the circumstances of life can alter! As the Bard of the North once put it, 'the best laid plans of mice and men gang aft agley'. Two entirely unforeseen developments occurred which were to confound the expectations of Parmar and his feckless accomplice. A few months after the fraudulent transfer Mrs Chhokar—a brave and resourceful woman—managed to move back into her former home in Southall, still unoccupied, and to reinstate there a semblance of family life with her two children. Then somewhat less predictably—and after an absence of two years—Mr Chhokar reappeared on the scene. The prodigal husband, it turned out, had wasted his substance in riotous living, had secretly returned to England, and had been working on the buses in Leicester. He now sought a reconciliation with his wife and children—to which, amazingly, Mrs Chhokar eventually agreed—with the consequence that things had now come full circle. Mr Chhokar resumed residence in the original matrimonial home. The Chhokars were once again living *en famille* under the same roof. One suspects, nonetheless, that the balance of power in the Chhokar household had altered for ever and that Mr Chhokar was made keenly aware that his whole domestic existence rested on the leave and licence of his incredibly long-suffering wife.

The only trouble was that the roof under which the Chhokars were living now belonged at law to someone else, ie, Parmar. However wrongful the actions of Mr Chhokar—and no matter how complicit Parmar was in Chhokar's dishonest design—the transfer of the matrimonial home had indeed been effective to pass the registered (ie, the 'legal' or 'paper') title to Parmar. This consequence followed from the fact that, unlike equity, the common law focuses simply on the outer form of transactions. Here there had been a duly executed transfer of title perfected by the registration of Parmar as the new proprietor. And Parmar, on becoming aware that the Chhokars had been restored to a state of family life within his own house, was inevitably concerned to terminate what he perceived as a trespass upon his property. The newly reconstituted Chhokar family was equally determined to resist Parmar's attempts to deprive them of their home. These competing concerns translated themselves into a number of legal questions which eventually required to be decided by the Court of Appeal.

Some Legal Realism

Now it is highly likely that you have already reached some preliminary view of the intrinsic merits of the *Chhokar* case. Anyone who engages seriously with this miserable narrative of treachery and double-dealing has probably decided that the scales of justice tilt rather more heavily in favour of Mrs Chhokar than of Parmar. But this, of course, is to state merely a moral preference as distinct from a reasoned legal conclusion. Yet there has long been a branch of jurisprudential theory (promoted largely by the 'American Realists' of the 1930s and 1940s) which tends towards the view that instinctive ethical assessments of given fact-situations play a hugely formative role in the process of judicial decision. Much has been written about the function of the judicial 'hunch' in the determination of legal outcomes; and there may well be a residual truth in the idea that legal decisions are governed, in some degree or other, by the judge's perception of the relative moral merits of the opposing parties. In effect, the judge first decides which party he or she wants to win and then crafts a judgment (ie, manipulates the legal 'rules') so as to bring about precisely this result. On this basis, a judge's ruling in any particular case is little more than a semantic ploy aimed at achieving the desired conclusion; the ruling is simply an *ex post facto* rationalisation of an intuitively preconceived solution. In the words of one of the Realists, court judgments should be seen, not as mirroring the actual process of deciding cases, but 'rather as trained lawyers' arguments made by the judges (after the decision has been reached), intended to make the decision seem plausible, legally decent, legally right, to make it seem, indeed, legally inevitable' (Karl N Llewellyn, 'Some Realism about Realism' (1931) 44 Harvard Law Review 1222 at 1238–39). The student of the law is always well advised to look closely at what judges are *really* doing, rather than merely at what judges *say* they are doing.

Let us bear this injunction in mind as we examine the various questions posed in the *Chhokar* case and the responses made by the court. The case was heard first by Ewbank J as a single judge in the High Court and then, on appeal, by Cumming-Bruce LJ and Reeve J in the Court of Appeal.

Did Mrs Chhokar still Own any Share in the Home?

In *Chhokar* an initial question obviously arose as to whether, in the aftermath of the dishonest transfer of the house to Parmar, Mrs Chhokar retained any *equitable* entitlement in the property. In other words, had her beneficial half-share in the matrimonial home been destroyed by the sale of that home to a stranger? If that were so, not only would

Mrs Chhokar have lost any right to live in the house, but she would also have lost the money value of her substantial investment in its acquisition. Her sole remedy would have been a futile action in damages against her indigent husband for breach of trust. Accordingly, it was vital for Mrs Chhokar to be able to show that her beneficial half-share had survived the transfer of the registered title to Parmar. But there arises here a technical difficulty which originates in a much more general principle of land transfer under English law.

It is a major objective of English law to ensure that, in so far as possible, the transferee of a registered title (such as Parmar) takes the land free of all pre-existing interests. The transferee thus starts, as it were, with a clean sheet. He or she is unencumbered by adverse entitlements belonging to others which might impede the enjoyment or profitable exploitation of the land or might act as a disincentive to long-term planning, strategic investment and future marketability. Fundamental economic motivations underpin this concern to liberate the new registered proprietor from interests which could otherwise operate as a drag (or, in more old-fashioned terminology, a 'clog') upon his or her title. A healthily functioning economy requires that land should remain open to efficient processes of sale or other disposition. It is important, so to speak, that land is kept on the move: the fewer the burdens which inhibit market transfer, the better.

It follows that the statute law which governs registered transfers has always placed strict limits on the interests which are allowed to continue to affect a registered title after its transfer. A few kinds of entitlement survive the transfer precisely because they are recorded very obviously on the face of the transferor's register of title and are therefore deemed to have been perfectly apparent to any potential transferee. Otherwise, however, the basic rule is that every new registered proprietor is immediately released—in all but a small number of specially defined circumstances—from the burden of pre-existing rights belonging to other persons. In the *Chhokar* case the normal expectation would therefore have been that the new legal owner, Parmar, took his title free of any adverse claims made by others (including the claim by Mrs Chhokar to a 50 per cent beneficial share in the home by way of implied trust). However, such an outcome would have spelt complete disaster for Mrs Chhokar and her vulnerable family.

The Protection of Actual Occupation

At this point we look more closely at the text of the Land Registration Act, which carefully details the exceptional cases where preexisting entitlements continue to bind the transferee of a registered title. One such exceptional case relates specifically to the proprietary rights of anyone who, at the time of the transfer, was a 'person in actual occupation' of the land concerned. It has long been clear that the proprietary rights of actual occupiers—albeit unrecorded on the face of the Land Register—are protected on a transfer of the legal title. These rights are said to 'override' the transfer and to fetter the land in the hands of the transferee (Land Registration Act 1925, s 70(1)(g); Land Registration Act 2002, s 29, Schedule 3, para 2). This significant exception to the normal rule reflects the enormous respect which English law has traditionally accorded to the entitlements of those who, at any given time, have established a physical presence on the ground. Precisely the same impulse underlies the ancient maxim that 'an Englishman's home is his castle', as also the longstanding distaste of the common law for any form of violent seizure or forcible eviction. Moreover, the statutory protection of those 'in actual occupation' of registered land is widely viewed as striking a fair balance between all parties concerned. Even though their rights are not apparent from the Land Register itself, actual occupiers can justifiably claim that the sheer fact of their physical occupancy sends a powerful signal to any potential transferee that they may own proprietary rights in the land which merit further investigation. It seems not entirely unfair that an intending purchaser who fails to inquire into the possibility of their entitlement should therefore take the land subject to any interests held by persons whose presence was so blatantly obvious.

Herein, of course, lay a significant difficulty for Mrs Chhokar. It was painfully apparent that, although she had undoubtedly held proprietary 'rights' in the land (ie, her beneficial half-share), she was absent from that land at the precise moment of the transfer of the legal title to Parmar. She had been in the maternity ward of the local hospital. Could it really be said that, for the purpose of the statutory exception, she was a 'person in actual occupation' of the land?

Some Statutory Interpretation

Here we must learn something about the art of statutory interpretation. By virtue of the sheer indeterminacy of language, words can convey only a crude approximation of meaning: they are the distorted echoes of ideas. Words, declared Oliver Wendell Holmes, are not transparent crystals: they are merely 'the skin of a living thought' and they may 'vary greatly in color and content' according to the context in which they are used. In particular, statutory words have a flexibility of application (or plasticity) which almost always enables the judge to work towards an ethically satisfying solution of the legal problem before the court. Thus, in the *Chhokar* case, the first instance judge adopted an expansive interpretation of the phrase 'actual occupation'. True it was that Mrs Chhokar had not been physically present in the home at the date of transfer. But what, on closer analysis, does 'actual occupation' really mean anyway? The phrase surely cannot be interpreted in such an arbitrary or quixotic fashion that people forfeit their rights simply because, on some vital date, they are rushed off to hospital with a broken leg or happen to go away on holiday or even—come to that—pop out of the house for five minutes to buy a pint of milk. Lord Wilberforce once claimed, slightly incautiously, that the phrase 'actual occupation' comprises 'ordinary words of plain English' (*Williams & Glyn's Bank Ltd v Boland* (1981)). It became readily apparent, however, that these innocuous words conceal some rather difficult questions relating to the required substantiality or continuity of the presence concerned. In this example—as in so many others—the intrinsic frailty of legislative language is rapidly exposed. Statutory words are indeed blunt instruments in the communicative process and it is hardly surprising that the angle, force and range of their impact often need to be controlled by an actor somewhat closer to the scene than the legislator. The process of statutory communication cannot be allowed to be erratic—and indeed it is not. The statutory bludgeon becomes the judge's chisel; the dull blow of the parliamentary draftsman is converted into the judicial craftsman's more finely fashioned legal solution.

Thus, at first instance in the *Chhokar* case, Ewbank J found no difficulty in construing the relevant statutory formula so as to catch circumstances where—as in the present case—the home still contained furniture and other items belonging to the absent Mrs Chhokar. The statutory requirement of 'actual occupation' could not (and did not) exclude occupation which was symbolised, or established vicariously, by the presence of personal paraphernalia associated with the claimant 'occupier'. In this way statutory language can be seen as the tool of the judge, rather than the judge as a mere tool of the legislative process. And the end result—not contested before the Court of Appeal—was that Mrs Chhokar's beneficial half-share in the matrimonial home was held to 'override' the transfer of the registered title to Parmar. He effectively took that title subject to an implied trust under which he now shared the beneficial ownership on equal terms with Mrs Chhokar (see Fig. 5.2). In reality, Parmar had simply stepped into the shoes of his vendor, Mr Chhokar. In graphic form, the history of the entire transaction now appears as follows:

Fig. 5.2 *The transaction between Mr Chhokar and Parmar.*

Could Parmar Force a Sale of the Home?

Of course, the conclusion that Mrs Chhokar still held an equitable interest did not necessarily foreclose a number of other claims which Parmar wished to advance in respect of the house. Having grudgingly accepted that Mrs Chhokar's beneficial rights had survived the transfer, Parmar predictably sought to salvage what he could from the *débacle* by requesting the court to order a sale of the home in which the Chhokar family were now residing. (The court has a discretionary power, now formalised in the Trusts of Land and Appointment of Trustees Act 1996, to order the sale of land which is the subject of a trust.) Such an order would have involved a mandatory disposal of Parmar's registered title on the open market, Mrs Chhokar's beneficial share in the home being compulsorily converted into a half-share of the sale proceeds. At least in this way

Parmar could recoup the value of his own beneficial half-share in the property.

At first instance Ewbank J ordered that a sale of the Chhokars' home be effected within nine months and that the sale proceeds be divided between Parmar and Mrs Chhokar. Ewbank J's decision was based on his belief that it was 'quite wrong' that Parmar should provide the Chhokars, free of charge, with a relatively valuable house as their home for the indefinite future. This conclusion was consistent with a long line of cases in which the courts had tended to order the sale of a co-owned home where sale was being pressed for by some complete stranger to the family relationship (such as a creditor who had lent money which he now wished to recover from the sale proceeds).

Ewbank J's ruling in favour of sale was, however, reversed on appeal. In giving the principal judgment in the Court of Appeal, Cumming-Bruce LJ indicated that, although the 'scoundrel Parmar' had no 'matrimonial privity' with Mrs Chhokar, he had sought by his 'monstrous fraud' to 'intermeddle in the wife's interests in the family home'. Parmar was not therefore truly a 'stranger to the marriage'. Accordingly, the discretion to order sale fell to be exercised with reference to the criteria normally applicable where, no 'stranger' being involved, a family home is held on trust for a number of co-owners who cannot agree between themselves whether a sale should occur. These criteria have always placed a heavy emphasis on the question whether the original underlying purpose of the trust remains capable of substantial fulfilment. Ironically, in view of the extraordinary reconciliation achieved between the Chhokars, this original purpose—ie, the provision of a home for the Chhokar family—still seemed eminently capable of fulfilment. Nor could the Court of Appeal now see any reason for frustrating the Chhokars' initial intention to use the property as their matrimonial home. But it is also interesting to note that the refusal of the sale so desperately sought by Parmar was explicitly linked to the Court's perception that '[e]verything that [Parmar] did from first to last in connection with the transaction is stamped with immoral stigma'. Cumming-Bruce LJ declared it difficult to 'find language which, with becoming moderation, describes the moral turpitude of every step taken by Parmar throughout'. To the judge it seemed quite plain that, on the question of sale, the voice of the 'innocent' Mrs Chhokar should 'prevail over the voice of the scoundrel who, as the accomplice of [Mr Chhokar], attempted by fraud and diverse devices to frustrate and destroy the wife's overriding interest'. Parmar had been 'caught' in his 'deceit' and could not therefore succeed.

The Court of Appeal accordingly declined to order any sale of the family home. Cumming-Bruce LJ observed that Mrs Chhokar might 'very well be entitled' to 'enjoy her beneficial interest in the matrimonial home, in consortium with her husband or otherwise, for the rest of her life'. Of course, it always remained open to Parmar to re-apply to the court for an order for sale in the event of some substantial change in the parties' circumstances, but Cumming-Bruce LJ (with whom Reeve J expressly agreed) thought it unlikely that such an application could or should be made for 'many years ahead'.

Could Parmar Insist on Sharing Residence in the Home?

If an immediate sale of the Chhokars' home was no longer an option available to Parmar, there arose some question as to whether Parmar could at least insist on sharing residence in that home alongside the entire Chhokar family. In English law, after all, a co-owner is presumed to be equally entitled—together with any other co-owner—to enjoy physical possession of each and every part of the co-owned land. However, when the *Chhokar* case reached the Court of Appeal, even Parmar's counsel shrank from pressing such a claim on his behalf. As Cumming-Bruce LJ pointed out, Parmar was a married man himself and 'no court would allow him to try to occupy the matrimonial home in common with Mrs Chhokar'. Indeed, said the judge, 'Mrs Parmar might have something to say about it too, if he tried to do so'.

Could Parmar Exact any Payment of Rent?

Deprived of the possibility of either sale or shared residence, Parmar then argued before the Court of Appeal that Mrs Chhokar should be required to pay him a money rent by virtue of the Chhokar family's exclusive occupancy of the house. Parmar was, after all, a beneficial co-owner and he plainly thought it not improper to extract some rental income in recognition of his equitable half-share in the property. There is, however, a general principle of English law that no rent obligation arises between co-owners merely on the ground that one of these co-owners happens to enjoy sole possession of the co-owned land. This rent immunity flows from the intrinsic entitlement of all the co-owners to share simultaneous physical possession of the land. In effect, no rent can be demanded by a co-owner whose absence from the premises is simply the result of his own voluntary choice. Over the years the courts have been compelled to recognise certain exceptions to this principle, as for example where one co-owner's absence is precipitated by a wrongful act of forcible eviction or domestic violence committed by a co-owner now in possession. Indeed, in modern times it is highly likely that the question whether an occupation rent is due from a co-owner in sole possession has come to rest on a simple test of 'fairness'. Would it be 'fair' to impose such an obligation in all the circumstances of the case?

In *Chhokar* it could, of course, be said that Parmar's absence from the co-owned premises was not immediately a matter of his own choosing: the courts had explicitly denied him any chance of shared occupancy. The historic rationale for rent immunity between co-owners supposedly rests on the freedom of each to occupy the co-owned property at will. Yet the Court of Appeal showed no detectible sign of regret that this freedom was presently unavailable to Parmar. In view of Parmar's 'crooked deceptions' and 'fraudulent conspiracy', the Court considered that it was now wholly *unfair* to cast any rental burden on Mrs Chhokar. In the result Parmar was condemned to stand idly by while the Chhokars enjoyed, for the indefinite future, rent-free occupation of his property. It was quite irrelevant, said Cumming-Bruce LJ, that Mrs Chhokar had currently decided to share this rent-free accommodation with her 'unsatisfactory' husband.

CONCLUSION

All in all, the *Chhokar* case provides a superb cautionary tale couched in the improbable language of the law of realty. It comprises a modern *conte morale*, in which human weakness is countered and ultimately redeemed by the magnanimity of a courageous and determined woman.

Powerful forces of lust and cupidity are brought low. There is an eventual triumph of good over ill. There is an ethically satisfying conclusion. A confused and feckless husband is rescued by an act of forgiveness and reconciliation; an avaricious and unscrupulous intermeddler suffers a reversal of his fortunes. Indeed, by the conclusion of the Court of Appeal hearing in the *Chhokar* case, the wrongdoer Parmar began to cut a rather woebegone figure—but the Court seemed disinclined to temper justice with much mercy. Parmar ended up owning a half-share in a house which he could neither occupy nor sell and from which he could derive no rental income. He still owed £50,000 to an estate agent who had lent money towards his conspiratorial purchase. He was ordered to pay a further £16,500 to Mrs Chhokar and her children by way of damages for their wrongful eviction. For Parmar the only morsel of comfort lay in the fact that when the house finally came to be sold at some (as yet unknown) future date, he would receive credit for the original mortgage debt which had been discharged by Mr Chhokar out of the proceeds of their conspiratorial transaction.

By contrast Mrs Chhokar (with the help of legal aid) had vindicated her original entitlement to a half-share in her family's home. Furthermore she was guaranteed rent- and mortgage-free accommodation in that home for the indefinite future, together with the possibly more dubious benefits of continued cohabitation with her reconciled husband. It would have required the skill of a consummate playwright to craft so ironic a conclusion to this remarkable human drama. But, as the Court of Appeal observed, there was no room for 'crocodile tears' on behalf of Parmar merely because his unlawful enterprise did not succeed. Indeed, Cumming-Bruce LJ professed himself able to see 'no reason for giving him anything more than the court in an unreported case gave to the money-lender who had rights over a debtor'. The proceedings, said the judge, 'are recorded in a play of Shakespeare'.

Cases

Chhokar v Chhokar [1984] 5 FLR 313
Pettitt v Pettitt [1970] AC 777
Towne v Eisner 245 US 418, 62 L Ed 372 (1918) (Holmes J)
Williams & Glyn's Bank Ltd v Boland [1981] AC 487

Further Reading

Gray and Gray, *Land Law* (5th edn, Oxford University Press, Oxford 2007)

Anne Bottomley and Hilary Lim, 'Feminist perambulations: Taking the law for a walk in land', in H Lim and A Bottomley (ed), *Feminist Perspectives on Land Law* (Routledge-Cavendish, Abingdon 2007), 1–30

John Dewar, 'Land, Law, and The Family Home', in S Bright and J Dewar (ed), *Land Law: Themes and Perspectives* (Oxford University Press, Oxford 1998), 327–55

Louise Tee, 'Co-ownership and trusts', in L Tee (ed), *Land Law: Issues, debates, policy* (Willan Publishing, Devon 2002) 132–68

Max Radin, 'The Permanent Problems of the Law' (1929–30) 15 Cornell LQ 1–24

6
Equity

Graham Virgo

Charles Dickens' *Bleak House*, first published in 1852, contains this description of equity as practised in the courts of the time:

> On such an afternoon, some score of members of the High Court of Chancery bar ought to be—as here they are—mistily engaged in one of the ten thousand stages of an endless cause, tripping one another up on slippery precedents, groping knee-deep in technicalities, running their goat-hair and horse-hair warded heads against walls of words, and making a pretence of equity with serious faces, as players might.

Dickens adds that all the people in the court are yawning 'for no crumb of amusement ever falls from JARNDYCE AND JARNDYCE (the cause in hand), which was squeezed dry years upon years ago'. That case involved a disputed inheritance and, as Dickens says: 'this scarecrow of a suit has, in course of time, become so complicated, that no man alive knows what it means'. By the end of the novel, judgment is given but the legal costs which have been incurred are so great that they devour most of the estate which was disputed in the first place.

This is the equity of the nineteenth century, which was concerned with death and succession, taxes and debts. This is dry and technical law. But equity today is very different. Although the modern subject is built on the old cases, the principles which underpin those cases have been refined over the years and are of real significance today, often in contexts very different from inheritance disputes. For example, a lot of modern commercial law, especially company law, has been dramatically influenced by equity. Equity is a subject which is intellectually challenging but provides solutions to some important and difficult current problems. This is shown by the case on which this chapter will focus: *Foskett v McKeown*, a case which arose from a father's greed and stupidity. At its heart the House of Lords was concerned with the question: 'should the sins of the father be visited on his children?'. This raises difficult questions about what justice demands, especially when all the parties before the court are innocent of any wrongdoing. But the case raises even bigger questions than this, involving the very nature of legal reasoning and legal method. When judges, especially judges in the appeal courts, have to decide a case, they are faced with a dilemma. Should they be concerned primarily with the merits of the case and focus on the facts, or should they have regard to the bigger picture, by ensuring that the rules and principles of law are clear and coherent to resolve both the present dispute and also future cases? This dilemma can be caricatured as being a choice between a just and fair result (colloquially called an equitable result), which might be uncertain, and a clear and principled result, which might be unjust on the facts. It is a dilemma which underpins much legal decision-making, but it was particularly marked in *Foskett v McKeown*.

But before that case is considered we need to examine what this body of law known as equity actually involves.

WHAT IS EQUITY?

Much of the law which you have been reading about in this book so far is called the common law. It has been developed by the judges in the courts over hundreds of years. But there is another stream of judge-made law known as equity. To understand why we have two different streams of judge-made law we need to go back in time to the medieval age. This was the period when judge-made law started to develop rapidly. Legal principles, some of which are still relevant today, started to emerge. However, the general attitude of the judges was strict and inflexible. Although there was room for judicial creativity, the judges tended to interpret the law rigidly and developed it through the elaboration of ever more complicated rules. In particular, claims brought by individual litigants had to fall within clearly established categories and, if they did not, they would fail. If no remedy was awarded or was even available, it was possible to petition the King to seek justice. The King delegated this function to his principal minister, the Chancellor, who exercised his judgment according to his conscience. Equity in this period was discretionary and vague, as was famously described by John Selden, a legal author in the seventeenth century:

> Equity is a roguish thing: for law we have a measure, know what to trust to; equity is according to the conscience of him that is chancellor, and as that is larger or narrower, so is equity. [It is] as if they should make the standard for the measure we call a foot a chancellor's foot; what an uncertain measure would this be! One chancellor has a long foot, another a short foot, a third an indifferent foot. 'Tis the same in the chancellor's conscience.

Eventually a separate court was established, known as the Court of Chancery, to deal with petitions to the Chancellor and it was the law which was developed and applied in this court which became known as equity. The purpose of this body of law was to temper the rigidity in the application of the law by common law judges. From the seventeenth century onwards this body of law became more systematic.

Equity is still sometimes described as operating to modify the rigidity of the common law. But, to the extent that this indicates that equity is vague and unprincipled, it is untrue, for much of equity today is rule-based and certain. But it does not follow that equity is, as it is sometimes quaintly put, 'past the age of child-bearing'. Equity can still be used to create new doctrines and to develop existing ones to provide solutions to problems which are ignored by the common law.

THE CONTRIBUTION OF EQUITY

Equity has had a profound contribution in many areas of the law, especially as regards the identification of rights and the development of important remedies, such as the order of *specific performance* to make the defendant perform his or her obligations under a contract, or *injunctions* to stop the defendant from committing a wrong. The creative function of equity is particularly well illustrated by an important remedy developed in the 1970s to deal with the problem of a defendant who seeks to hide his or her assets or take them out of the jurisdiction to prevent the claimant from enforcing a judgment for damages against him or her. To avoid this problem equity was relied on to create a new form of injunction, known then as a *Mareva* injunction (after the case which first recognised it, which concerned a ship of that name) and now known as a freezing order. This is an injunction which can be used by judges to freeze some or all of the defendant's assets to ensure that any judgment can be enforced against the defendant. For example, the order might mean that the defendant would not be able to gain access to money which has been credited to his or her bank account. This is an injunction which has proved to be a significant feature of the English law of civil procedure.

Equity has been influential in many other ways. For example, there is a body of law where equity can be used to regulate exploitative transactions, such as where one party unduly influences another to enter into a disadvantageous contract or to make a gift. Equity is also responsible for the recognition and regulation of certain types of relationship which are called fiduciary relationships. A fiduciary is somebody who is in a relationship of trust and confidence with somebody else, known as the principal. The fiduciary is expected to be loyal to the principal and to maintain the highest standards of behaviour in looking after the principal's interests. Typical fiduciary relationships are those of company directors who are in a fiduciary relationship with their company, and solicitors who are in a fiduciary relationship with their clients. The importance of fiduciary law is illustrated by *Attorney-General of Hong Kong v Reid*, a decision of the Privy Council. Reid was a public prosecutor in Hong Kong. Having been bribed by a gang to obstruct the prosecution of members of the gang, he invested the bribe money in land in New Zealand. The Hong Kong government sought to recover this land. The Privy Council held that Reid was a fiduciary, because he was in a relationship of trust and confidence with the state; that he had breached his fiduciary duties in accepting the bribe money; and this money should be treated as belonging to the state, which therefore owned the land in New Zealand because it had been bought with the bribe money.

Despite the significant contribution of these different equitable remedies and doctrines to English law, the most important contribution of equity is undoubtedly the *trust*. The crucial feature of the trust is that property is held by one person for the benefit of another. This is recognised through the division of property rights. One person holds the legal title to the property. This is the *trustee*. As far as the common law is concerned that person is the sole owner. But equity can see that the legal owner holds the property for the benefit of somebody else, the *beneficiary*. That beneficiary therefore has an equitable interest in the property. The trustee is obliged to look after the property for the benefit of the beneficiary. If the trustee fails to do this, he or she will have breached the trust and will be liable to the beneficiary.

TYPES OF TRUST

English law recognises a variety of different trusts. The main form is the express trust, which is created intentionally by the settlor (if the trust is created by somebody, while he or she is alive, who 'settles' property on trust) or the testator (if the trust is created by somebody in a will). The express trust can either be fixed or discretionary. In a *fixed* trust the interests of the beneficiaries are established at the time the trust is created. For example, a father may put in his will that, if he dies before his three children attain the age of 18, his property should be transferred to trustees for the benefit of the children. If the father died before the children were 18 the trustees would have legal title to the property, but they would not be able to benefit from it since they would have to manage the property for the children until they attained 18. Each child would have a fixed equitable interest in one-third of the property until they became 18, when the legal interest in their share of the property would be transferred to them. Alternatively, in an express *discretionary* trust the trustees own the property at law but no beneficiary has an existing defined interest in the property. Rather, the trustees have a discretion to distribute the property as they see fit to people from a particular class of potential beneficiaries. So, for example, the trust may give the trustees a discretion to use the trust property to pay for the education of children of employees from a particular business. The trustees would be free to decide how they could allocate trust funds to such children in such amounts as they consider to be appropriate.

There are a number of reasons why a settlor or testator might wish to establish an express trust. There may be a particular advantage in having trustees managing and administering the property. This might be because the beneficiaries are too young to do so or cannot be trusted with the property. Or the trust might be a convenient way of holding the property for the mutual benefit of a group of people. This is one of the main reasons why the trust is used in the commercial world. For example, it is used as a mechanism for managing pension funds for the benefit of many employees, or as a mechanism for a group of people investing their funds by means of a unit or investment trust. Another purpose of the trust is that it can provide a means for avoiding tax, by transferring property to somebody whose tax liability might be smaller. But here the trust might be open to abuse and there is a lot of complex law to ensure that the trust is not used as an illegitimate method of tax evasion.

Another type of trust is known as the *constructive trust*. This arises through the application of legal rules rather than being expressly created by a settlor or testator. It is relevant, for example, where a defendant has obtained property by fraud. Even though the common law might say that the property belongs to the fraudster, equity will say that the property is held on constructive trust by the fraudster for the victim of the fraud.

Normally the trust works well, but sometimes the temptation of the trustee to benefit personally from the property is too great and there is an abuse or breach of trust. It was a breach of an express fixed trust which triggered the litigation in *Foskett v McKeown*.

THE FACTS OF *FOSKETT v McKEOWN*

A group of businessmen decided that they wished to invest in property on the Algarve in Portugal, which they wanted to develop as a golf course. They agreed that their money should be held on trust for them, so that the money was managed by somebody else on their behalf. The money was therefore transferred to a trustee. He had legal title to the property but, because he held it on an express trust for the businessmen, they had an equitable interest in the money.

Some time earlier the trustee had set up a life insurance policy on his own life. The terms of the policy were such that, when he died, the sum of £1 million would be paid to his children. He was required to pay annual insurance premiums of about £10,000. These premiums were invested to obtain units and it was the value of these units which was used to pay for the maintenance of the policy. The trustee paid the first three premiums from his own money. He then stole £10,000 from the trust to pay for the fourth premium and did the same the following year. This constituted a breach of trust. He then committed suicide. The fact that he died at his own hand did not invalidate the policy. It followed that his children were eligible to receive a lump sum payment of £1 million from the insurance company (see Fig. 6.1).

Year		1	2	3	4	5				
Trustee's own money		X	X	X			→	suicide	→	£1m.
Beneficiaries' Money					X	X				

Fig. 6.1 *Sources of payments of the insurance premiums.*

However, the beneficiaries of the trust discovered that the trustee had stolen £20,000 from the trust and that he had used this money to pay two of the premiums. The beneficiaries argued that, since their money had been used to pay two of the five premiums which had contributed to the payment of £1 million, it followed that they should have two-fifths of that sum, amounting to £400,000. The children contested this on the basis that the money belonged to them and either they should keep the whole £1 million or they should simply reimburse the beneficiaries for what they had lost.

THE POSSIBLE SOLUTIONS

Despite the somewhat complicated facts of *Foskett v McKeown*, the basic issue was straightforward: should the businessmen beneficiaries recover a proportionate share of the £1 million? There were essentially four solutions to this dispute:

1. As the beneficiaries argued, since the money which had been used to pay the fourth and the fifth premiums belonged to them in equity, they should get a two-fifths share of the £1 million.
2. Since the beneficiaries had only contributed £20,000, that is what the children should be required to reimburse, plus interest to compensate the beneficiaries because they had not been able to use their money for a period of time.

3. The beneficiaries should recover nothing. This argument, which was also made by the children, was dependent on the peculiar nature of the insurance policy. The premiums which were paid were not automatically used to maintain the policy. Rather, the premiums were used to purchase units. The first three premiums had purchased sufficient units to mean that, even if the fourth and the fifth premium had not been paid, the insurance policy would not have lapsed and the £1 million would still have been paid. Consequently, it was argued that the beneficiaries' money had not contributed to the receipt of the £1 million in any way.

4. There is a further solution which was not argued in the case, namely that, because the fourth and the fifth premiums had been stolen from the trust, which was a criminal offence, it followed that the £1 million was the proceeds of crime. English law has long recognised that recipients of the proceeds of crime should be required to give up those proceeds to the victim and cannot be seen to benefit from them. Consequently, even though the children were innocent of the crime themselves, they could not be seen to benefit from their father's crime in any way and so the beneficiaries should recover the whole of the £1 million.

IDENTIFICATION AND APPLICATION OF RULES AND PRINCIPLES

Although the five judges in the House of Lords were divided by three to two as to the appropriate result, there was a great deal of consensus amongst them as to the proper mode of analysing a problem such as this. The judges identified the following principles and steps in their reasoning.

Principle and Not Discretion

In determining whether the businessmen beneficiaries or the children should win, one approach is to determine what is the just and fair result by reference to the facts of the case. This is a discretionary approach. Such an approach may have a variety of benefits, but it is subject to the drawback that it results in uncertain and unpredictable law. Where there is a dispute between parties it is preferable to resolve that dispute outside the courts through a settlement between the parties, if only because it is quicker and cheaper to do so. If the law is certain and predictable it makes it much easier for a settlement to be reached because the parties can predict how a judge might decide the case. Even where a settlement may not be possible, perhaps because there is a dispute as to the facts and the case goes to trial, there are major advantages in having law which is certain and predictable. This is because it enables the judge to apply the law more easily and ensures that there is consistency in that application, for otherwise the result of the case may become a lottery, depending on which judge hears the case.

In *Foskett* the majority recognised that vague notions of justice and equity, in the sense of fairness, were not appropriate when considering who had an interest in the £1 million. That should be resolved through the application of established principles. The relevance of principles was identified by one of the judges as follows:

> This case does not depend on whether it is fair, just and reasonable to give the purchasers an interest as a result of which the court in its discretion provides a remedy. It is a case of hard-nosed property rights.

Certainty and clarity in the law were considered to be more important than the application of judicial discretion.

The Proprietary Base

It was therefore necessary for the judges to consider what the applicable principles were. For the beneficiaries to show that some, if not all, of the £1 million received by the children belonged to them, they needed to show that the money which was stolen from the trust was their money. This has been called the *proprietary base* on which the claim is built. This proprietary base was very easy to establish on the facts of the case because it was clear that the money was stolen from an express fixed trust. This trust was significant for two reasons. First, because it showed that the beneficiaries had a property interest in the money. Secondly, because it meant that this interest was equitable. The nature of the interest is very important for a number of reasons. Legal property interests are governed by the common law, whereas equitable proprietary interests are governed by equity. The source of the interest will be particularly important as regards the nature of the remedy which is awarded. This is because, where somebody has taken your property, the common law's response is almost always to require the defendant to pay the claimant the value which that property had when it was stolen. This is called a 'personal' remedy. However, equity is much more prepared to require the defendant to transfer the property itself back to the claimant by means of a proprietary remedy. This is often a much more attractive remedy, especially where the value of the property has increased, as it had in *Foskett*.

Following and Tracing

Once the beneficiaries could show that money which belonged to them in equity had been used to pay two of the premiums, they then needed to be able to link this money to the eventual payment of the £1 million. This involved the application of a complex body of law known as the *following* and *tracing* rules. The application of these rules can be illustrated by the following examples. First, imagine that your car has been stolen by a thief who gives it to the defendant. In order to make a claim to the car you need to be able to show that the car which was stolen from you was the same car which was received by the defendant. You would establish this by following the car from you to the thief to the defendant. Following involves identifying the original property in somebody else's hands. This is easy. But things become a lot more difficult where the car was stolen by a thief who sold it and used the proceeds to buy a motorbike which he gave to the defendant. Let us also assume that the car has been destroyed. In those circumstances you cannot follow the car because it no longer exists. But you can show that the value which was within the car has been used to purchase the bike. You should then be able to make a claim to the bike on the basis that the bike now represents your car. To make such a claim you need to trace the value which was within the car into the bike. The application of tracing rules enables the owner of property to claim a substitute for that property or its product.

The reason why the law in this area is so complex is because the rules relating to tracing are interpreted differently depending on whether you are tracing property at law, where the claimant has a proprietary base recognised by the common law, or in equity, where the proprietary base is equitable. The common law adopts a restrictive approach to its tracing rules, especially because the common law says that where the claimant's property is mixed with other property it is no longer possible to identify the claimant's property and so tracing fails. The equitable tracing rules are different, since equity is willing to trace property into and through a mixture. This difference between tracing at law and in equity is most important as regards money credited to a bank account. This can be illustrated by the following example. Imagine that the claimant has two bags, one containing £1,000 and the other containing £2,000. The first bag belongs to the claimant at law; but the second bag is held on trust for the claimant, so that she has an equitable but not a legal interest in it. Both of the bags are then stolen by the defendant who takes them to a bank where the money is credited to the defendant's existing bank account. When you pay money into a bank account, those particular notes and coins are not paid physically into a particular account. Rather, the money is credited to that account. This means that the bank owns the actual notes and coins, but the credit to the account means that the bank owes the account-holder the amount of money which was credited. In other words, the relationship between the account-holder and the bank is one of creditor and debtor. Even though there is no physical money in the account, the debt which is owed by the bank is itself a piece of property which can be owned and transferred. This debt is sometimes known as a 'thing in action' or a 'chose in action'. Whatever it is called, it is a piece of property in its own right which is distinct from the original cash.

Returning to our example (see Fig. 6.2), when the defendant took the two bags to the bank, let us assume that he already had £500 credited to his account. So when the money in the two bags is deposited it will mean that the defendant has £3,500 credited to his bank account, as follows:

Fig. 6.2 *Tracing and Following.*

Can the claimant trace his money in such circumstances? As regards the £1,000 which belongs to the claimant at law, tracing is not possible because that money is transformed into a debt worth £1,000 but this has become mixed with the existing £500 which was already credited to the account, so that it is no longer possible to say which money belongs to the claimant and which to the defendant. It is like mixing the claimant's bag of peas in a saucepan with the defendant's bag of peas; it is no longer possible to say which peas belong to the claimant and which to the defendant. Consequently, the common law throws up its hands and says 'we cannot unpack this mixture because the peas all look the same' and so tracing into the mixture will fail. It follows that all the peas will belong to the defendant. Of course, the answer would be different if the claimant's peas were green and the defendant's peas were yellow, because they could be easily distinguished. Even if the peas were the same colour, however, equity, which is more creative than the common law, is willing to separate the mixture into its constituent parts. So, if the claimant knew that his bag contained 1,000 peas he would be able to recover any 1,000 peas from the mixture, even though some of the peas may actually have been contributed by the defendant. Equity is able to do exactly the same as regards money credited to a bank account. In our example there will be £3,500 credited to the defendant's bank account. £500 of this will belong to the defendant, since that was the amount which was already credited to the account. £1,000 will represent the money which belonged to the claimant at law, and which will have lost its identity because it was paid into a mixture. But the remaining £2,000 will represent the money in which the claimant had an equitable interest and which will not have lost its identity because equity can see it represented within the mixture. So the claimant will be able to recover this amount in equity. This example shows how important it is to distinguish between interests in property which exist at law and those which exist in equity, because different rules apply.

Although these examples are very basic, they form the foundation for the intervention of equity in cases involving millions of pounds. Some of these cases may involve massive corporate fraud or money laundering where it is important to show that the value of money which belonged to the claimant can be identified in different property which is now in the hands of the defendant money-launderer.

The importance of the tracing rules is especially well illustrated by the facts of *Foskett v McKeown*. Once the claimants had established that the money which had been taken from the trust belonged to them in equity they needed to show that this money existed in the £1 million. They could not follow their money into the £1 million, because it was clearly not the same money as that which had been stolen from the trust, so they had to rely on the tracing rules and, because they had an equitable proprietary interest in the trust fund, they relied on the equitable tracing rules.

The judges in the majority clarified what the function of the tracing rules was, by emphasising that tracing was concerned with identifying the value which was originally in the trust fund and locating it in the £1 million. This involved two different steps. First, it was necessary to establish that the money which had been taken from the trust could be traced through various bank accounts and into the fourth and fifth premiums which were paid to the insurance company. Equity was willing to do this even though the money had been mixed in various bank accounts.

Secondly, and this was the most difficult part of the claim, it was necessary to show that the value of the money which had been taken from the trust could be traced from the premiums into the £1 million. This was difficult to establish because of the peculiar nature of the insurance policy which meant that, even had the fourth and fifth premiums not been paid, sufficient value had been contributed by the first three premiums to mean that the £1 million would have been paid anyway. How then could it be shown that the fourth and five premiums contributed to the £1 million? For one of the dissenting judges this was the reason why the beneficiaries' claim failed, because it was not possible to show that the payment of the fourth and the fifth premiums had caused the £1 million to be paid. But, for the majority, it was possible to trace into the £1 million despite this feature of the insurance policy. This was because it was sufficient that the value of the money which had been taken from the trust could be attributed to the £1 million, even though this value had not caused the £1 million to be obtained. This attribution was established by reference to a very technical argument which derived from the terms of the insurance policy. That policy said that the death benefit would be paid 'in consideration for' all of the premiums which had been paid. What this meant was that, in return for the payment of the premiums, £1 million would be paid once the person whose life had been insured died. In other words, although £1 million would have been paid even had the fourth and fifth premiums not been paid, the £1 million was paid with explicit reference to all the premiums, which included the contribution from the beneficiaries.

The consequence of the approach of the majority was that the value which was recognised by equity as belonging to the beneficiaries in the trust fund could be traced from that fund, through various bank accounts, into the fourth and fifth premiums and from there into the £1 million.

Identification of the Remedy

Even though the beneficiaries could show that they had an equitable proprietary interest in the £1 million, it certainly did not follow that they could recover the whole amount. This was because the beneficiaries had only contributed two-fifths of the premiums which had been paid, with the remaining three-fifths being contributed by the trustee himself. It was therefore necessary for the court to determine what the appropriate remedy should be. This was the crucial part of the case and the part which proved to be most controversial.

Once a claim or cause of action has been established this means that the claimant has a right which needs to be protected or remedied in some way. In *Foskett v McKeown* the businessmen beneficiaries were able to show that they had a property right which needed protecting. There are two general types of remedy which can be used to protect property rights. The first is called a *personal* remedy. This requires the defendant to pay to the claimant the value of the property which has been received. In other words, it creates a debt. The other type is a *proprietary* remedy. This can operate in a number of ways, but the simplest is to require the defendant to transfer the actual property received to the defendant. Personal and proprietary remedies have different advantages and disadvantages.

The main advantage of personal remedies is that, if the property is lost or falls in value, the defendant is still liable to pay money to the claimant which represents the value of the property at the time it was received. However, if the property still exists and has increased in value, it is preferable to get a proprietary remedy, because the claimant will get the benefit of that increase in value. Proprietary remedies have another advantage which is relevant where the defendant has few, if any, assets. Such a defendant may be declared bankrupt, if they are an individual, or insolvent, if they are a company. The defendant will typically owe money to a number of creditors and there may not be enough to go around, so with a personal remedy the claimant may end up with nothing. However, if the claimant is awarded a proprietary remedy he or she would rank above other creditors and would be able to claim the relevant property in priority to their claims. This might prove to be highly significant, depending on the defendant's financial circumstances.

We have already seen that one of the key differences between legal and equitable remedies is that the common law, for the most part, awards only personal remedies, to restore the value of the property received, whereas equity can award both personal and proprietary remedies. In *Foskett v McKeown* the beneficiaries sought a proprietary remedy to recover a proportionate share of the £1 million, amounting to £400,000. This remedy was not awarded in the Court of Appeal. Rather, that court held that the children were liable to repay only £20,000 because the beneficiaries' contribution was not used to acquire the £1 million, but operated only to maintain the insurance policy. An analogy can be drawn with money being spent on a house. If the claimant's money was used to acquire the house, either completely or partially, the claimant should have a property interest in the house to the extent of that contribution. If, however, the money was used simply to maintain the house which already belonged to the defendant, for example by enabling the defendant to paint the external walls, it would not be appropriate to say that the claimant had a property interest in the house itself because the value in the claimant's property had not been used to acquire the house. Rather, the claimant should only be reimbursed the cost of maintaining the house. The cost of maintaining the policy was held by the Court of Appeal to be £20,000, representing the value of the fourth and fifth premiums.

The House of Lords accepted this distinction between acquiring and maintaining property, but reached the opposite conclusion when applying this distinction to the facts. The majority in the House of Lords concluded that the beneficiaries' money was used to acquire the £1 million rather than simply to maintain the policy and so it was held that the children were liable to pay £400,000 of the £1 million to the beneficiaries.

This conclusion needs to be considered carefully. Is it really fair that the beneficiaries should have recovered such a large amount of money? This may have been appropriate had the fourth and fifth premiums actually been necessary to obtain the £1 million. But that was not the case on the facts. It was one thing to conclude that the beneficiaries had a property interest in the £1 million. It is a very different matter to conclude that this interest should be valued at two-fifths of the fund where the beneficiaries had not actually contributed to that amount being obtained. Against this you might wish to argue that it is not fair that the children should get £1 million minus £20,000, when their father had stolen money from the beneficiaries and when that money would have been necessary to obtain the £1 million had the father lived a bit longer. When it comes to criticising a decision such as this it is difficult to avoid introducing questions of justice and fairness—and even to ask, 'what would be the equitable result?'

Defences

Some of the judges went on to consider one other matter relating to property claims in equity, even though this was not relevant on the facts. Once it has been concluded that a claim had a proprietary base, that the value in this property could be traced into the property held by the defendant and that the appropriate remedy was a proprietary one, it may also be necessary to consider whether the defendant should be given a defence to protect him or herself from the claim. The most important defence which might be available is one which has been called the defence of change of position. At its most basic this defence is relevant where, for example, the claimant paid £1,000 to the defendant by mistake but the defendant, without knowing or suspecting that there had been a mistake, spent £800 of it on a holiday. When the claimant sues the defendant for the £1,000, the defendant is not liable to pay back £800 because his or her position has changed. It follows that, if the defendant had spent all the money, he or she would not be liable to pay anything to the claimant.

The issue which was canvassed in *Foskett v McKeown* was whether this defence of change of position should be available even where the claimant wishes to recover his or her property. The issues of principle

and policy which this raises can be illustrated by the following hypothetical problems:

- A trustee steals £1,000 from a trust and gives this money to the
defendant. The defendant is a poor student who, thinking that the
money belonged absolutely to the trustee, uses it to go out to various pubs and clubs and spends all of it. The beneficiaries of the trust
would not be able to bring a claim against the defendant to recover
the money. But this is not because of the application of the defence
of change of position as such. It is simply because, if the defendant
no longer has assets in which the claimant has an equitable proprietary interest, the claimant cannot recover any property since the
defendant does not have any property which belongs to the claimant. In such a case the claimant would have to sue the trustee for
breach of trust in stealing the money in the first place. This is the
easy case. The following scenario is more difficult.
- Again, the trustee steals £1,000 from the trust, which he gives to the
defendant. But this time money is credited to the defendant's bank
account. Since the defendant is richer than he was before, he decides
to sell some shares which had been left to him by his grandmother.
He sells them for £1,000 and uses this to pay for a holiday to the
Caribbean. In this situation the defendant still has assets in which the
claimant has a proprietary interest, in the form of the money which
is credited to his bank account. But the defendant has changed his
position in good faith as a result of receiving this money, since he
sold the shares and spent the proceeds. In this situation whose interests should prevail? Should it be the claimant, who can show that the
defendant still has property which belongs to the claimant in equity?
Or should it be the defendant, who is now in no better position after
having sold the shares, which would not have been sold had the
defendant not received the money from the trustee?

Lord Millett in *Foskett v McKeown* indicated, in part of his judgment
which did not relate to the issues arising in the case and so is called *obiter
dicta*, that the defence of change of position should not be available where
the claimant wishes to recover his or her property and where that property
or its substitute or product remains identifiable. Whether you like such a
result will depend, to some extent at least, on the general approach which

you want to adopt to the structure and operation of the law. If you would prefer the legal system to operate to obtain a just result at all costs you might prefer the defence of change of position to operate in such a scenario. For the defendant did nothing wrong in selling the shares and we can show that those shares would not have been sold had the £1,000 not been received. Against this, a stricter, more principled, approach would focus on the fact that the claimant's property is still in the defendant's hands. Property rights are particularly strong rights in English law and perhaps they should not be defeated by changes in the defendant's circumstances, save where that change has the effect of destroying the property in which the claimant has the right. The rejection of the defence of change of position is consistent with this idea that property rights are strong, or, as Lord Browne-Wilkinson described them in *Foskett v McKeown*, they are 'hard-nosed' rights. According to this approach it is tough luck that the defendant changed his or her position and, anyway, the defendant did at least have the benefit of the holiday in the Caribbean.

CONCLUSIONS

The analysis of *Foskett v McKeown* tells us a lot about the nature of that body of law known as equity, but also forces us to think rather more deeply about out approach to legal method. It can be seen that this body of law is technical, but it is a vital part of being a law student that you are able to apply legal rules and principles logically and go on to consider whether the interpretation of the law is acceptable and workable.

But this case raises some bigger questions. First, is the fundamental distinction between the common law and equity defensible today? We have seen that equity developed as a distinct stream of law hundreds of years ago for reasons which are no longer relevant today. We have seen that the maintenance of two distinct streams of judge-made law makes for very complex exposition of that law. This is especially well illustrated by the fact that we have different tracing rules at law and in equity. Is this defensible today? Indeed, a number of the judges in *Foskett v McKeown* suggested that these two sets of tracing rules should be merged. But if such merger did occur, where should it stop? Should we get rid of equity completely? If so, we would lose many vital mechanisms in the law, especially the trust. Perhaps we need closer co-operation between law and equity, but this should not extend to total assimilation.

Finally, we are left with the big theme which runs throughout *Foskett v McKeown*. Should our approach to law and legal method be principled or discretionary? Justice, equity and common sense are vital attributes of any coherent legal system, but the importance of principles must not be forgotten. This was expressed most eloquently by Lord Goff in a lecture called *The Search for Principle*:

> When we talk about the desired result, or the merits, of any particular case, we can do so at more than one level. There is the crude, purely factual level—the plaintiff is a poor widow, who has lost her money, and such like. At another level there is the gut reaction, often most influential. But there is a more sophisticated, lawyerly level, which often consists of the perception of the just solution on legal terms, satisfying both the gut and the intellect... The judgment so exercised should not be, and is not, a purely personal judgment. It is an informed and educated judgment, formulated in public discussion and founded not merely upon a shared experience of the practical administration of justice, but also upon an accepted basis of systematic legal principle.

There is a role for the gut reaction in our approach to the law, but it is the identification of principles which is at the heart of the study of law as an intellectual discipline.

Cases

Attorney-General of Hong Kong v Reid [1994] 1 AC 324
Foskett v McKeown [1998] Ch 265(CA); [2001] 1 AC 102 (HL)
Lipkin Gorman (a firm) v Karpnale Ltd [1991] 2 AC 548
Mareva Compania Naveira SA v International Bulk Carriers SA [1975] 2 Lloyd's Rep 509

Additional Reading

Dickens, *Bleak House* (1852)
Lord Goff of Chieveley, *The Search for Principle: Essays in Honour of Lord Goff of Chieveley* (Swadling and Jones, eds) (Oxford University Press, Oxford 1999) 313–29
Virgo, *The Principles of the Law of Restitution* (2nd edn, Oxford University Press, Oxford 2006) Part V
Worthington, *Equity* (2nd edn, Oxford University Press, Oxford 2006) chapter 1

7

Constitutional Law

David Feldman

INTRODUCTION

Constitutional law deals with the allocation of power, responsibility and accountability within the state: matters which go to the heart of democratic government. Previous chapters have dealt with rules which lay down standards of behaviour to be observed by people who want to achieve a particular goal (such as the right to live in their house or to make a contract) or to avoid various legal consequences (such as being prosecuted or sued). Constitutional law is different. A *constitution* establishes the structure of the state; the functions of its institutions such as Parliament, government, civil service and judiciary; and their relationships with each other and, sometimes, with ordinary people. Principles of *constitutional law* do not usually identify what makes people's behaviour good or bad, but are concerned with the creation of a framework of rules and procedures which govern state action, including how, by whom and under what circumstances laws can be made, unmade and implemented. They also determine who sits in Parliament and who decides whether the country should make war or peace. Most of us do not spend much time thinking about such relatively abstract matters and do not have much experience of the workings of state institutions. But for lawyers and public officials this subject is of vital importance.

This chapter examines a case about the power to make an Act of Parliament, which is the highest form of law which can be made by any body in the UK. The case is *R (on the application of Jackson and others) v Attorney General*, in which the House of Lords had to decide whether the Hunting Act 2004, making it a criminal offence to hunt a wild mammal with dogs or to engage in hare coursing, was a valid Act of Parliament.

The passing of the Hunting Bill through Parliament was highly controversial and raised fierce passions. Those in favour of it argued that hunting with dogs was cruel. Opponents, amongst whom the Countryside Alliance was prominent, argued that hunting was an effective way of controlling the fox population, and that the Bill was an improper restriction of liberty and damaging to the rural economy and way of life. Hunt supporters used a variety of stunts to persuade MPs and the public that hunting should not be banned including, on one occasion, taking the unprecedented step of getting on to the floor of the House of Commons during a debate.

Despite this, the Hunting Bill was passed on 18 November 2004 and the only avenue left for the opponents of the Act was to challenge it through the courts. They did this in two separate claims. In one, *Countryside Alliance v Attorney-General*, the opponents argued that the Hunting Act contravened both European Community law and the European Convention on Human Rights. This case is of little constitutional significance, because it was not a challenge to any major constitutional principle, but we shall return briefly to it at the end of the chapter. In the other case, *Jackson*, on which this chapter concentrates because of its considerable constitutional significance, the opponents sought *judicial review* of the Act. Judicial review is a procedure in which a court scrutinises an act or decision of a public body to determine, for example, whether that body had the power to do what it did.

However, the opponents of the Act faced a problem with their action for judicial review: there is nothing in the UK's constitution to prevent an Act of Parliament from introducing ill-advised or illiberal measures. To attack the lawfulness of the ban, the opponents had to find grounds for arguing that the Hunting Act was *legally* flawed, so they challenged the lawfulness of the special and controversial *procedure* used to enact the legislation rather than the content of the rules contained in the Act. The procedure, laid down in the Parliament

Acts 1911 and 1949, allows the monarch and the House of Commons to make an Act of Parliament without the consent of the House of Lords in certain circumstances. In *Jackson* the claimants argued that the procedure used to pass the Hunting Act 2004 had not been authorised by the Parliament Acts on a correct interpretation of the Parliament Act 1911. Thus the constitutional validity of a prohibition on hunting with dogs depended not on the merits of hunting, which were hardly mentioned in the judgments, but on rules about the structures, powers and procedures of the Queen in Parliament, the law-making body.

You might have expected such a central issue of constitutional law—the roles of different bodies in the process of legislating—to have been settled long ago. However, *Jackson* shows that there is a surprising level of disagreement about such fundamental questions. We shall see that the three courts which considered the case at different levels in the legal system agreed on the outcome, yet disagreed about significant aspects of their reasoning. What is more, in the House of Lords, the highest court, the judges' arguments differed significantly from each other. One of the reasons for this is that the Law Lords were concerned about the implications of their decision for future statutes which might be passed according to the special procedure which had been used to enact the Hunting Act 2004. A desire to limit the future effect of a decision may lead one judge to adopt different reasoning to support the decision from that used by another judge, who would be happy for the decision to have a wider impact in the future. This aspect of common-law decision-making can be seen in many areas of law, and *Jackson* is just one example.

This chapter begins with an outline of some important features of constitutional law in the UK, including the structure of the United Kingdom, the constitution and the legislative role of Parliament. It then explains the special procedure under the Parliament Acts 1911 and 1949 which was used to enact the Hunting Act 2004. The chapter then looks at the grounds on which pro-hunting campaigners challenged the Act's validity, the approaches adopted by the judges who decided the case, and some of the developments after the House of Lords' decision.

SETTING THE SCENE: SOME IMPORTANT FEATURES OF CONSTITUTIONAL LAW IN THE UK

The UK's 'Constitution'

The UK's constitutional system is unusual. Since a short-lived experiment with republicanism after the English Civil War in the 1640s, it has never been codified in a single document. Unlike the more or less codified constitutions of many other countries, such as the United States, constitutional rules and principles in the UK are scattered through legislation, case law, conventions and political and legal literature, and cannot be found in a single legal document. But there is no authoritative method of determining whether a given rule or principle should be regarded as having constitutional status. Usually this does not matter too much because, at least until recently, nobody considered that whether a rule or principle was considered to be 'constitutional' would affect its validity or the way it would be applied in *legal* proceedings, although it might affect its weight in *political* discussion.

Furthermore, lawyers in the UK, unlike those in many other countries, have not generally regarded the constitution as a special type of law, superior to ordinary laws. One of the greatest English constitutional lawyers, Professor A V Dicey, writing in 1885, regarded it as one of the hallmarks of our constitution that it emerged from ordinary law and was not separate from or above it. One example of the lack of a distinction between ordinary law and constitutional law is the traditional view that any Act of Parliament is superior to judge-made (common) law, even if the common law embodies an important constitutional principle such as freedom from arbitrary arrest and detention or from unauthorised interference with a person by a public official and the Act deals with a relatively commonplace matter such as the regulation of the financial services industry. Until recently all Acts of Parliament have been equal, and no court has been able to hold that one Act is invalid or ineffective on the ground that it is inconsistent with an earlier Act or with a constitutional principle. There has been little incentive to identify some rules as 'constitutional', because it has made no practical difference to their legal effects (although, as we shall see, the position may now be changing).

You might wonder whether such a curious and apparently chaotic arrangement could be called a 'constitution' at all. Nevertheless, as we have already seen, this country does have laws—statutes, common law rules and conventions—that perform the functions which other countries expect their constitutions to perform. These functions are, as a minimum, the following:

- to establish the structure of the state and some key state institutions, such as Parliament, the executive and the courts;
- to allocate responsibilities and powers to each institution; and
- to confer legitimacy on the governmental system as a whole by making provision for bodies which exercise public power to be accountable for that exercise.

In this last category are two important principles:

1. *The rule of law*
   This is a complex concept, the core of which is hard to pin down. At the very least it requires that people who exercise public powers and who bear public responsibilities must be able to point to legal authority for what they do. They must also act within the scope of that authority. In short, government must be conducted according to the law. In addition, the rule of law requires that ordinary people must be able to challenge the legality of any exercise of public power before an independent judicial tribunal.

2. *Democratically accountable, responsible and representative government*
   This requires that Parliament, as the primary political institution of the state, should represent the whole nation and should, at least to some degree, be electorally accountable to it. In addition, the executive (which includes government ministers and civil servants who form, and try to implement, government policy) should accept that it is accountable to Parliament for its policies, decisions and actions. The democratic accountability of the House of Commons to the electorate

is one reason why it has been regarded as legitimate to give immense legislative power to the monarch-in-Parliamentand, within Parliament, to give primacy to the Commons.

The Structures of the State

The structures of the UK are complex. The United Kingdom is just that: a union of several elements (Scotland, Wales, Northern Ireland and England) each of which had a previous existence independent of the others but which were gradually brought together by conquest, ties of feudal loyalty and treaties, although they have been effectively governed to a great extent separately. They have now achieved a significant degree of self-government through the devolution settlement of 1998, with legislative ('law-making') and executive ('decision-making') powers being devolved to Northern Ireland (although they were suspended for much of the intervening period) and Scotland, and executive power being devolved to Wales. The Government of Wales Act 2006 extended the legislative power of the Welsh Assembly. Only England has no devolved powers so far.

The main national institutions of the UK 'state', apart from those of the European Community and Union (on which see chapter 8), are:

- the monarch, as Head of State;
- Parliament in Westminster, with responsibility for creating a government and holding it to account;
- the Queen in Parliament (ie, the monarch giving formal approval to a Bill previously approved by Parliament), as the legislature with the highest law-making capacity apart from the European Community's legislative machinery;
- the government, headed by a prime minister; and
- the armed forces, which are institutions in their own right and which are centrally organised and managed.

There are then a number of more locally organised institutions. The judiciaries of England and Wales, Scotland and Northern Ireland are separate, as are their three legal systems, despite sharing some common rules and features. For some purposes, since devolution, Wales should also be regarded as having a separate legal system. Following the implementation of the Constitutional Reform Act 2005, there is a clear separation between the judiciary and the political (executive and legislative) institutions of the state. The Welsh Assembly acts as an executive body, but (as mentioned earlier) also increasingly as a legislature for Wales in respect of devolved matters. In Scotland, there are a Scottish Parliament and a Scottish Executive, which deal with matters devolved to Scotland. Northern Ireland has a Legislative Assembly and an executive formed by a First Minister and Deputy First Minister dealing with devolved matters in Northern Ireland. Then there is local government, now largely funded by grants from Parliament but still electorally accountable to local people. Police forces are predominantly county-based, although an increasing number of special agencies operate regionally or nationally, such as the Serious Organised Crime Agency and the Criminal Records Bureau.

This is the constitutional context in which the doctrine of the legislative supremacy or sovereignty of the Queen in Parliament, the main focus of this chapter, operates.

The Two Houses of Parliament and the Making and Effect of Acts of Parliament

Houses of Parliament

There are two Houses of Parliament. The lower House, the House of Commons, consists of 646 Members of Parliament (MPs) each of whom represents, and is elected directly from, a constituency. In this sense it is a representative body. Nearly all MPs have a party affiliation, and by convention the monarch invites the person who leads the party with most MPs following a general election to form a government. The upper House, the House of Lords, now consists of life peers who are appointed by the monarch on the advice of the Prime Minister (there were 606 on 30 November 2006), together with 92 hereditary peers elected by the other hereditary peers to sit in the House under the House of Lords Act 1991, 26 Law Lords and retired Law Lords (judges who sit or have sat in the Appellate Committee of the House of Lords, which exercises the judicial functions of the House of Lords as the highest court in England and, for some purposes, Wales, Scotland and Northern Ireland), and 26 bishops and archbishops of the Church of England. The House of Lords had 750 members in all on 30 November 2006. Members of the House of Lords are not accountable to geographical constituencies, but individually and collectively they have a wealth of expertise and experience which makes the House a very good consultative chamber and revising chamber for legislation.

Reform of the House of Lords is a contentious political issue. There have been plans to change its powers and membership for almost a century, and some progress has been made. In 2006 the then Prime Minister, Tony Blair, wanted to finish the process of reform by moving to an entirely appointed House of Lords, but in 2007 the House of Commons voted for an entirely elected House of Lords. Whatever change may occur, it will be just the latest step in a long process of restricting the powers and changing the composition of the second chamber. But until relatively recently, and certainly when the Parliament Acts 1911 and 1949 were passed, the House of Lords consisted entirely of hereditary peers, Law Lords and Anglican bishops and archbishops.

The Doctrine of Parliamentary Sovereignty

When the text of a Bill (a draft of an Act of Parliament) has been agreed by both Houses of Parliament and received royal assent, it becomes an Act of Parliament, which is the highest source of law in the UK, apart from European Community law. We know this not because any statute tells us so, but because the officials of the system (politicians, judges, civil servants and others) have long treated such a text as a uniquely authoritative source of law in the UK. Professor A V Dicey, writing in 1885, regarded this so-called *legislative sovereignty* of the Queen in Parliament, also known as *parliamentary sovereignty,* as a central feature of the UK's constitution, and many lawyers still take that view. Parliamentary sovereignty has a number of elements.

First, an Act of Parliament can be made in respect of any matter whatsoever.

Secondly, Parliament can impose legal obligations outside the territory of the UK, although these obligations may not be enforceable outside the territory.

Thirdly, it is often said that there is no limit to the measures that an Act of Parliament may include or do: it may make and unmake any law whatever, and until recently no court has been able to hold an Act of Parliament invalid or ineffective on account of its being inconsistent with any other rule or principle. On the traditional approach, if an Act of Parliament requires that all blue-eyed babies be slaughtered, the courts would have to enforce it; its validity could not be challenged as a matter of law.

However, in reality there are limits to this absolute notion of parliamentary sovereignty. It is well established that an Act which makes provisions which are inconsistent with directly effective European Community law is ineffective (although strictly not invalid: it will merely be 'disapplied' by the national courts) to the extent of the inconsistency: see further chapter 8. More recently, the Human Rights Act 1998 has introduced a procedure whereby the higher courts can assess whether a provision in an Act of Parliament is compatible with those rights under the European Convention on Human Rights ('Convention rights') that the Human Rights Act has made part of our national law. If the provision is incompatible with the right, the higher courts (including the High Court, the Court of Appeal and the House of Lords, the Courts-Martial Appeal Court, and in Scotland the Court of Session and the High Court of Justiciary) are allowed to make a 'declaration of incompatibility'. This does not make the incompatible provisions invalid or ineffective; they must still be applied, despite the fact that this will inevitably violate people's fundamental rights. The Human Rights Act therefore does not affect parliamentary sovereignty as a constitutional principle; in fact it was drafted carefully to avoid doing so. Nevertheless, a declaration of incompatibility has some influence on future legislation: so far, every such declaration has led to legislation being introduced to amend or repeal the incompatible provisions. Finally, some argue that there are limitations deriving from common law, political morality or both which constrain the freedom of Parliament to do what it likes, so that there are fundamental constitutional rights or constitutional Acts of Parliament which cannot be abrogated, amended or repealed (save, perhaps, by clear words in an Act of Parliament). We shall see examples of such arguments later in this chapter.

Fourthly, it is usually said that no Parliament can bind its successors. In other words, one Parliament cannot prevent later Parliaments from amending or repealing its legislation. If there is a conflict between two Acts of Parliament the doctrine of *implied repeal* applies. According to this doctrine, where a later Act of Parliament is inconsistent with an earlier Act the courts will apply the *latest* Act and any earlier Act will, by implication, be repealed or amended if the later Act contains different rules. However, some legislation, such as the European Communities Act 1972, by which the UK acceded to what is now called the European Union, and the Human Rights Act 1998, through which the UK incorporated the European Convention on Human Rights into national law, may have special ('constitutional') status. According to some lawyers, such legislation could not be repealed except by the use of clear and explicit words which achieve that result. If this is correct, the doctrine of implied repeal would not apply to such 'constitutional' statutes. This view marks a departure from the traditional view that all statutes are of equal status.

Others argue that the idea that no Parliament can bind its successors does not apply to so-called 'manner and form' rules. In other words, it might be possible to change the way in which an Act of Parliament can be made or the form it must take in such a way as to make it either more difficult or easier to legislate on some matters, even if the content of the legislation cannot be limited in advance. We shall see more of this later, as parliamentary sovereignty was put under scrutiny when opponents of the Hunting Act 2004 challenged the validity of a legislative procedure laid down in the Parliament Acts 1911 and 1949.

House of Commons v House of Lords

According to orthodox legal theory, in most situations the two Houses of Parliament have equal authority when legislating. However, in practice the House of Commons has for some time been regarded as having greater legitimacy and greater authority than the House of Lords, particularly since the right to vote was extended to more and more people after 1832, making the lower House more representative of, and accountable to, a wider electorate. There was a 'convention' (ie, a shared understanding among the members of both Houses) that the House of Lords would not prevent the House of Commons from getting its way on legislation for government spending and taxation. However, the attempts by Conservative peers with a majority in the Lords to block the Liberal Party government's budget legislation in 1909 breached this convention. Mr Asquith's Liberal government called a general election on the issue and won. The Lords then passed the budget legislation.

Asquith's government subsequently decided to try to reform the Lords by turning it into a representative chamber, but, until it could formulate the necessary plans, it wanted to put the convention of the superiority of the Commons on a legal footing to ensure that the government could get its legislative business through the Lords. It therefore brought forward a Parliament Bill to remove the power of the Lords to delay so-called Money Bills (involving the use or management of public money, public borrowing or taxation) and to limit the Lords' power to delay or reject other Bills. This Parliament Bill was rejected by the Lords. The Prime Minister called and won another general election on the issue, and the Conservative majority in the Lords gave way, approving the enactment of the Parliament Act 1911 to give legal force to the supremacy of the Commons over the Lords in legislative matters (although only after the Prime Minister had threatened to advise the King to create a large number of Liberal peers to give the government a majority in the Lords).

The Parliament Acts 1911 and 1949

The main effect of the Parliament Act 1911 was to allow the disagreement of the House of Lords to any Bill to be ignored, and an Act of Parliament to be made by the monarch and the House of Commons alone, in certain circumstances. First, section 1 of the Act dealt with the issue of Money Bills which had precipitated the political crisis of 1909 and 1910. If the Speaker of the House of Commons certifies that a Bill deals only with taxation, the use or management of public money or public borrowing, and has been passed by the Commons and presented to the Lords at least a month before the end of a parliamentary session and not passed by the Lords without amendment (or with only such amendments as have been agreed by the Commons) by the end of the session, it may be submitted for royal assent without approval by the Lords. This deprived the

Lords of power to reject a Money Bill or to delay it beyond the end of the session in which it was first introduced to the House of Commons. (A session normally lasts about a year, beginning in November. At the end of each session Parliament is 'prorogued', or suspended; Bills which have not been passed are normally lost. Parliament then reassembles for a new session, traditionally opened by the monarch with a speech from the throne setting out the government's main policies and legislative plans for the coming session.)

Section 2(1) of the Act went on to restrict the power of the Lords to reject or delay Bills which are not Money Bills. It provided:

> If any Public Bill (other than a Money Bill or a Bill to extend the maximum duration of Parliament beyond five years) is passed by the House of Commons in three successive sessions (whether of the same Parliament or not), and, having been sent up to the House of Lords at least one month before the end of the session, is rejected by the House of Lords in each of those sessions, that Bill shall, on its rejection for the third time by the House of Lords, unless the House of Commons direct to the contrary, be presented to His Majesty and become an Act of Parliament on the Royal Assent being signified thereto, notwithstanding that the House of Lords have not consented to the Bill...

This meant that the House of Lords could merely delay a Bill (other than a Money Bill or a Bill to extend the life of Parliament beyond five years) for between two and three years after the first debate on it in the House of Commons, and could not block it permanently if the House of Commons insisted on it.

The Parliament Act 1911 was soon used to pass two major pieces of constitutional legislation: the controversial Government of Ireland Act 1914, which extended home rule to Ireland, and the Welsh Church Act 1914, which dis-established the Anglican Church in Wales; but it was not deployed otherwise. However, the Lords conducted their business in the knowledge that it might be used if they pressed their objections to Bills too far. After the 1945 general election, the Labour government commanded an overall majority in the House of Commons but, like its Liberal predecessor in 1910, had only a minority in the Lords. This was important because the Labour government expected its programme of social and economic reform, including extensive nationalisation, to face strong opposition in the Lords. Looking forward to the end of the Parliament, due at the latest in July 1950, Mr Attlee's Labour government wanted to ensure that controversial Bills, including those to nationalise the iron and steel industries, could be enacted before the general election. The government therefore introduced a Bill to the Commons to reduce the power of the Lords to delay passing a Bill from three years to a maximum of two years. The Conservatives in both Houses opposed this, and the Lords rejected the proposal, so the government used the procedure laid down in the Parliament Act 1911 to pass the Parliament Act 1949, amending the 1911 Act and requiring the two Acts to be read together. This meant that the Parliament Act 1949 was itself passed without the approval of the Lords, using the 1911 procedure. In other words, the 1911 Act procedure was used to amend the 1911 Act itself. As you will discover, this is a crucial point: the legality, or otherwise, of this manoeuvre was at the heart of the arguments in *Jackson*.

As it turned out, it was not necessary to use the revised procedure with the shortened period for delay by the Lords until 1991, when the Conservative government relied on it to overcome the Lords' opposition to the War Crimes Act 1991, which retrospectively made it a criminal offence which could be prosecuted in the UK to commit a war crime abroad. This permitted the prosecution of Nazi war criminals in the UK, even though their crimes had been committed abroad. The Labour government, too, used the Parliament Acts of 1911 and 1949 to pass, first, the European Parliamentary Elections Act 1999 (changing the method of election of UK members of the European Parliament from a 'first past the post' system based on single-member constituencies to a system of proportional representation of regional, multi-member constituencies) and, secondly, the Sexual Offences (Amendment) Act 2000 (reducing to 16 the age at which people could consent to homosexual activities, in line with the age of consent for heterosexual activity). However, the Bill which provoked the most widespread and continuing public controversy and protests in relation to both its content and the manner of its enactment using the Parliament Acts was the statute, as Lord Steyn was to say in *Jackson*'s case, enacted to 'abolish the ancient liberty of the British people, regularly exercised by a great many individuals up and down the land, to take part in fox hunting.'

THE HUNTING ACT 2004

The Hunting Act 2004 prohibits both the hunting of wild mammals with dogs and hare coursing. There are certain exemptions, but these do not affect the constitutional issues. The debates about the Bill within and outside Parliament were intense and protracted. Supporters of the Bill regarded it as a measure to advance animal welfare and protect mammals against cruelty. Opponents considered that it interfered with people's liberty, was an attack on country pursuits, and was damaging to the rural economy and to the ability of farmers to protect livestock against pests. They also drew attention to what they regarded as discrimination between pastimes, in that, while hunting with dogs was prohibited, fishing and shooting were unaffected by the Bill.

Police seek to restrain Hunting Bill protestor.
© Getty Images.

Over a number of years there had been various attempts by MPs who were not government ministers to introduce legislation (so-called 'Private Members' Bills') to ban hunting. After the 1997 general election produced a large Labour majority in the House of Commons, there were three such Private Members' Bills, two (in 1997 and 2000) to prohibit hunting of mammals with dogs, and one (in 1998) to prohibit hare coursing. The 1997 Bill made some progress but ran out of time, and the 2000 Bill was withdrawn when the government announced that it would bring forward its own proposals.

The government initially introduced a Bill in a form that took the almost unprecedented step of allowing the two Houses to choose between (a) prohibiting hunting and hare coursing subject to specified exceptions, (b) a scheme for licensing hunting and hare coursing, and (c) a light-touch supervision of hunting and coursing which would have left hunts largely self-regulating. The Commons selected option (a), prohibition subject to exceptions, but the Lords preferred (c), the supervision option. The Bill failed when the Prime Minister called a general election for June 2001 and Parliament was dissolved. The Labour Party's election manifesto contained a commitment to allow Parliament to consider the matter again. After the Labour Party's victory, the government conducted consultations and introduced a new Bill in 2002. Meanwhile, the Scottish Parliament prohibited the hunting of wild mammals with dogs in Scotland.

The Bill introduced in Westminster in 2002 was therefore to apply to England and Wales only. It essentially proposed option (b), a licensing scheme, but the Commons amended it to prohibit almost all hunting with dogs. This Bill did not become law, because it ran out of time at the end of the parliamentary session in November 2003. The government re-introduced the Bill to the Commons in the 2003–04 session in the form in which the Commons had passed it in the previous session. It was rushed through the Commons in one day on 15 September 2004, despite interruption by a group of pro-hunting protesters who infiltrated the Palace of Westminster and disrupted proceedings for a time.

The Lords amended the Bill to replace the outright prohibition option with a licensing scheme. There followed a kind of legislative ping-pong, in which the Bill passed back and forth between the

Lords and the Commons, being amended each time to reflect the preferences of the House in question, with each House insisting on its own amendments and the other House rejecting them. This continued until 18 November 2004, the last day of the 2003–04 session, when the Bill would have been lost if not passed. The Speaker of the House of Commons then announced that the conditions for passing the Bill without the approval of the House of Lords had been satisfied, in accordance with the procedure laid down in the Parliament Acts. The Bill was immediately presented for royal assent with the approval of the House of Commons alone, and became the Hunting Act 2004.

The next day pro-hunting campaigners launched judicial review proceedings which sought declarations against the Attorney-General (representing the Crown, the government and the House of Commons) that the Hunting Act 2004 was not a valid Act of Parliament and had no legal effect. The only way of doing this was to show that the use of the Parliament Acts to pass the Hunting Act 2004 had been improper. (As we have already seen, it is not possible under English law to challenge the content or 'substance' of an Act of Parliament.) The claimants pointed out that the Hunting Act 2004 had been passed using the procedure set out in section 2(1) of the Parliament Act 1911, but with the shorter time limits on the power of the House of Lords to delay legislation which had been substituted for the original time limits by the Parliament Act 1949. But they argued that the 1949 Act was invalid because it had been passed using the procedure in the 1911 Act which, the claimants said, could not be used to amend the 1911 Act itself. The 1911 Act, they argued, could be amended only with the approval of *both* Houses of Parliament under the usual rules, not by the special Parliament Act procedure. If the amendments made by the 1949 Act to the 1911 Act were not valid, it followed that the Hunting Act 2004 itself was not valid, as it had not been introduced to the Lords in three successive sessions as the 1911 Act had originally required.

The nature of these arguments put in issue not only the rules governing conflicts between the House of Commons and the House of Lords, but also a further constitutional issue: could the *courts* decide what was, or was not, an Act of Parliament, and thus by implication place some limits on the legislative activities of the monarch, Lords and Commons?

THE *JACKSON* CASE

The Issues in the Litigation

The claimants argued that the Parliament Act 1949 was invalid on two main grounds. First, they said that the 1911 Act had been a political settlement which had conferred additional legislative power on the Commons in certain circumstances. The Act contained a Preamble (introductory words explaining why the Act was passed) stating that it had been 'expedient that provision should be made for regulating the relations between the two Houses of Parliament', and 'provision will require hereafter to be made by Parliament' to substitute a popular for an hereditary House of Lords. The claimants argued that, seen in this light, section 2(1) of the 1911 Act, which allowed certain Bills to become Acts without the approval of the House of Lords in some circumstances, must have been drafted with a view to ensuring that further changes to the constitution of Parliament should be made by the monarch in Parliament as a whole (ie, monarch, Lords and Commons), not the monarch and the House of Commons alone. The claimants argued that the 1911 Act was therefore impliedly limited so that changes to the procedure laid down by section 2(1) of the Act could not be made using the 1911 Act's procedure itself, but required instead the approval of both the Commons and the Lords. It would follow that the 1911 Act should not be interpreted as allowing the monarch and Commons alone to amend the conditions on which their power to legislate without the Lords had been conferred, and that the 1949 Act, amending section 2(1), could not have been validly passed using the procedure provided by section 2(1) itself.

Against this, the Attorney-General argued that the express terms of the 1911 Act were very wide, and quite wide enough to authorise the procedure to be used to amend the 1911 Act itself: as we have already seen, section 2(1) of the 1911 Act spoke of 'any Public Bill (other than a Money Bill or a Bill containing any provision to extend the maximum duration of Parliament beyond five years)', and contained no other express or implied limitation as to the kind of provision that could be contained in a Bill enacted under the procedure which it laid down.

The claimants' second main argument was that a statute passed under the 1911 Act's procedure was not a full Act of Parliament, because the Queen and the Commons alone could not have equal authority to the Queen in Parliament. This was a different argument from the previous one concerning implied limitations in the 1911 Act, since the claimants were now arguing that any Act passed under the 1911 Act procedure had a lesser status than Acts which were passed under the normal procedure with the approval of both the House of Commons and the House of Lords. The 1949 Act was passed without the consent of the House of Lords, and was therefore subordinate to a normal Act of Parliament such as the 1911 Act. It is possible for subordinate legislation to amend an Act of Parliament, but only if the power to make such an amendment is expressly granted by an Act of Parliament. Nothing in the 1911 Act expressly authorised the Queen and the Commons to amend the 1911 Act by using the procedures set out in it. The 1949 Act therefore could not amend the 1911 Act by making it easier or quicker to make legislation under the procedure laid down in the 1911 Act.

In reply, the Attorney-General argued that the purpose behind the 1911 Act was not to confer extra power on the Commons but to remove certain powers from the Lords, allowing the Queen and Commons to override the disagreement of the Lords if, after an appropriate period for reflection, the Commons considered it expedient to do so. A Bill passed under that procedure was not to be regarded as subordinate to an Act of Parliament, because section 2(1) expressly stated that, following the giving of Royal Assent such a Bill 'shall ... become an Act of Parliament'.

The Decision of the High Court

Having heard the arguments, the Administrative Court, which is part of the High Court, held that the Parliament Act 1949 and the Hunting Act 2004 were both valid Acts of Parliament. Section 2(1) of the 1911 Act referred to 'any' public Bill, and this was wide enough to allow it to be used to pass any Bill other than one of a kind expressly excluded by the sub-section, so no limitations were implied into the Act. The Preamble was ambiguous: the 1911 Act sometimes referred to 'Parliament' in a context that could make it mean 'the Commons'. Given the political context in which the 1911 Act was passed Maurice Kay LJ did not believe 'that the Preamble can be read as a self-denying ordinance which put out of reach resort to section 2 in the event of the House of Lords itself subsequently rejecting such a reform—a possibility which must have been considered'.

Next, the Court rejected the argument that an Act passed using the procedure laid down in the Parliament Act 1911 is subordinate or delegated legislation, ie, made by a body inferior to the Queen in Parliament, and so of lesser authority than a normal Act of Parliament. Section 2(1) of the 1911 Act made it clear that a Bill passed under its procedure becomes an Act of Parliament and one cannot call any Act of Parliament subordinate or delegated legislation. Maurice Kay LJ considered that the 1911 Act had remodelled Parliament, so that there were now two ways of enacting an Act of Parliament instead of just one, and both ways produced Acts of equal status. Collins J agreed, but added an important gloss. He thought that Parliament:

> … can, if it wishes, put constraints on the extent of its own sovereignty. What it did in the 1911 Act was to provide for a new procedure whereby an Act of Parliament could be enacted and to limit to a small degree what an Act which came into existence by means of that procedure could deal with. That is not to say that the Act that results is to be regarded as delegated legislation, but merely that the sovereignty is, by decree of Parliament, subject to a limitation which must be followed. It is only if that limitation is on the face of the Act not complied with that a court can intervene; otherwise the Act is unimpeachable.

This is highly contentious, because the idea that the 1911 Act had introduced even a small limitation on what could be enacted by an Act of Parliament (by whatever procedure it was passed) seems inconsistent with the idea of 'continuing' sovereignty, namely the inability of one Parliament to bind its successors. If it is now possible for an Act of Parliament to impose limits on the legislative sovereignty of the monarch in Parliament, it could mean that an Act of Parliament could require a two-thirds majority in each House before a later Act could pass or amend certain Acts, and that this might bind future Parliaments.

The claimants appealed to the Court of Appeal.

The Decision of the Court of Appeal

The Court of Appeal gave judgment in February 2005, two days before the Hunting Act 2004 was due to come into force. The Court of Appeal reached the same result as the Administrative Court, but approached the arguments in a very different way.

The Court considered that an Act of Parliament like the Parliament Act 1949, which was made under the procedure laid down in the 1911 Act, could not be regarded as a normal Act of Parliament. This is because the courts are able to decide whether or not an Act passed under the Parliament Acts procedure (unlike an ordinary Act) is valid. By contrast, when an Act is passed by the normal procedure courts refuse to investigate whether parliamentary procedures have been followed properly.

There were some restrictions on the uses to which the procedure under the 1911 Act could be put. While some amendments to the 1911 Act would be possible using its own procedure, the Court of Appeal held that the 1911 Act could not be used to make fundamental constitutional changes. Abolishing the House of Lords would be such a change, but changing the number of sessions in which a Bill had to be introduced before using the Parliament Acts procedure was not. As the 1949 Act made the latter, rather than the former, kind of change, it was a valid use of the 1911 Act's procedure.

The Court of Appeal clearly wanted to limit the implications of its decision for the future use of the procedure under the Parliament Acts, being guided by the concern for constitutional theory and what was desirable rather than rigorous statutory interpretation.

Next, the Court of Appeal examined the debates on the 1911 Bill, and decided that they showed that both Houses had understood that the procedure under the Bill which became the 1911 Act could potentially be used to amend the 1911 Act itself by reducing the number of sessions in which a Bill would have to be introduced from three to two. It was therefore unnecessary to interpret section 2(1) of the 1911 Act as impliedly excluding its use to amend the Act itself by speeding up the process of enacting legislation without the approval of the House of Lords.

Thirdly, the Court of Appeal took account of the fact that the monarch and Commons had passed the 1949 Act on the assumption that they had

had the power to do so, and had also passed other Acts on the basis that the 1949 Act was valid. The Court of Appeal thought that this was relevant to the interpretation of the 1911 Act, because the 1911 Act was not just an ordinary piece of legislation. As the Court recognised:

> What is in issue is a consensual constitutional change in the manner in which sovereign power is exercised. The nature of that change depends not simply on the words used in the legislation by which that change was brought about. It depends on general recognition of the nature of the change, as demonstrated particularly by those who brought about the change, but additionally by all affected by it.

Finally, the Court of Appeal did not consider that the 1911 Act had redefined Parliament. Instead, a sovereign parliament had exercised its power to make relatively modest alterations to its legislative powers and procedures, which could then be further altered by legislation made under the new procedures.

In its way, this conclusion is just as controversial as the comments of Collins J in the High Court: the Court of Appeal's conclusion suggests that a change to the constitutional position with regard to the legislative sovereignty of Parliament can be brought about 'consensually' and that this consensual change would bind future Parliaments. But this could not occur by the simple process of Parliament enacting a statute which asserted that Parliament had decreed that the change had occurred. Rather, it required that the change must also be 'recognised' by 'all affected by it', which presumably must include the courts as well.

In the end, the Court of Appeal held that there were limits to the extent of constitutional changes which could be introduced under the 1911 Act's procedure, but that the changes actually made by the 1949 Act were not so fundamental as to be outside the proper scope of the 1911 Act. Accordingly, both the 1949 Act and the Hunting Act 2004 were valid Acts of Parliament.

The Hunting Act 2004 accordingly came into force, but the claimants successfully applied to the House of Lords for leave to appeal. The Attorney-General did not oppose the application, partly because he wanted to contest the reasoning, though not the conclusion, of the Court of Appeal, which would have imposed limits additional to those expressly set out in section 2(1) of the 1911 Act as to the circumstances in which that section's procedure could be used.

The Decision of the House of Lords

The appeal to the House was heard by the Appellate Committee of the House sitting with nine Law Lords instead of the usual five, a recognition of the constitutional importance of the case. The House unanimously dismissed the claimants' appeal and held that the Hunting Act was validly passed. The Act is therefore still in force. Yet despite what Lord Walker called a 'striking unanimity' on the crucial points to be decided, in their opinions the Law Lords took a variety of views on some of the incidental issues, and canvassed an interesting range of constitutional assumptions and opinions which were thought to be relevant to the way the Parliament Acts might be used in the future, rather than confining themselves to the validity of the Hunting Act 2004. For example, eight of the Law Lords (Lord Bingham, Lord Nicholls, Lord Steyn, Lord Hope, Lord Rodger, Lord Walker, Baroness Hale and Lord Brown) rejected the view of the Court of Appeal that the 1911 Act was calculated to allow the monarch and House of Commons without the Lords to effect only relatively modest but not significant or fundamental constitutional change.

On the other hand, they were divided on other key points. For example, the starting point for Lord Bingham, the Senior Law Lord, was that the supremacy of Parliament, with unconstrained ability to make or unmake any law whatever, was the 'bedrock of the British constitution' both in 1911 and today. For Lord Steyn, on the other hand, this wide view of parliamentary supremacy was mistaken. It was implausible, he thought, to say that the UK has an uncontrolled constitution. It is subject to constraints derived from EC law; sovereignty was divided by the devolution settlement of 1998; and the Human Rights Act 1998 created a new 'legal order in which the United Kingdom assumes obligations to protect fundamental rights, not in relation to other states, but towards all individuals within its jurisdiction'. His Lordship continued:

> The classic account given by Dicey of the doctrine of the supremacy of Parliament, pure and absolute as it was, can now be seen to be out of place in the modern United Kingdom. Nevertheless, the supremacy of Parliament is still the *general* principle of our constitution. It is a construct of the common law. The judges created this principle. If that is so, it is not unthinkable that circumstances could arise where the courts may have to qualify a principle established on a different hypothesis of constitutionalism. In exceptional

circumstances involving an attempt to abolish judicial review or the ordinary role of the courts, the Appellate Committee of the House of Lords or a new Supreme Court may have to consider whether this is [a] constitutional fundamental which even a sovereign Parliament acting at the behest of a complaisant House of Commons cannot abolish.

This view of the constitution made Lord Steyn reluctant to accept that the 1911 Act should be interpreted as allowing its procedures to be used to abolish the House of Lords, although none of these questions arose in *Jackson* itself. Lord Steyn also drew a distinction between the static concept of Parliament as its constituent elements (monarch, Lords and Commons) and the dynamic concept of Parliament, the elements of which functioned together as a law-making body. Acting dynamically, he thought, Parliament could redefine Parliament for particular purposes, for example by requiring that certain legislation could pass only with a two-thirds majority in each House, and the Parliament Acts had indeed redefined Parliament for particular purposes. Courts would enforce that requirement, and might also enforce other such constitutional principles or values against Parliament in extreme circumstances. Baroness Hale also accepted that courts might not accept that Parliament has power to 'subvert the rule of law by removing governmental action affecting the rights of the individual from all judicial scrutiny'. She considered that European Community law (and, more controversially, the Human Rights Act 1998) had limited Parliament's power, at least temporarily, and that other constraints might emerge in due course. However, generally she thought that 'the constraints upon what Parliament can do are political and diplomatic rather than constitutional'.

Lord Hope said that, although parliamentary sovereignty dominates the constitution, it 'is no longer, if it ever was, absolute'. As a Scottish judge he was especially conscious of the protection offered to some Scottish institutions by provisions of the English and Scottish Acts of Union of 1707, as well as limits imposed through EC law; but he also referred to the rule of law (the requirement that public bodies must act only within the scope of their lawful powers, to protect people against arbitrary government), rather than parliamentary sovereignty, as 'the ultimate controlling factor on which our constitution is based'. Finally, he noted that the principle of parliamentary sovereignty 'which[,] in the absence of higher authority, has been created by the common law is based upon the assumption that Parliament represents the people whom it exists to serve'. The implication is that the principle might be rethought if Parliament ceased to represent the people in some sense or other.

Lord Steyn's suggestion that Parliament's power might be subject to substantive limits, and Lord Hope's and Baroness Hale's emphasis on the rule of law, have important implications. If the monarch in Parliament were to pass an Act which explicitly allowed officials to lock people up in prison without any opportunity to test the grounds for their detention before a court, the courts might not enforce the Act. This represents a possible departure from the traditional understanding of parliamentary sovereignty and suggests that there may be some things which are beyond the reach of even a sovereign legislature under our constitution.

THE AFTERMATH OF THE CHALLENGE TO THE HUNTING ACT 2004

The outcome of *Jackson* was a unanimous decision of the House of Lords that the 1949 Parliament Act was authorised by section 2(1) of the 1911 Parliament Act, so the Hunting Act 2004, enacted by way of the procedure laid down in the Parliament Acts, was a valid Act of Parliament. As a result, the Hunting Act is in force and, to a limited extent, enforced. There have been a few successful prosecutions brought under the Act, but the organised hunts have generally been able to avoid liability by a variety of strategies. For example, it is still permissible for dogs to be used to flush foxes out of cover to allow the hunters to shoot them, as long as the dogs do not kill the fox. Tony Wright, the Master of the Exmoor Fox Hounds, was convicted in Somerset in August 2006 of breaching the Act because, it was alleged, the dogs killed the fox instead of leaving it to be shot, but an appeal to the Crown Court is under way. Other people convicted under the Act, such as Paul McMullen of Bootle, Merseyside, have not been fox hunters, but people who were (or said they were) out with terriers digging for other animals such as rabbits and killed a fox disturbed by their activities. The typical fine for such activities has been between £500 and £750, but few people have been charged and even fewer convicted.

The pro-hunting campaigners didn't give up. Having failed to persuade the courts that the Hunting Act was invalid, they subsequently brought three further legal challenges to the Hunting Act, albeit in cases of far less constitutional significance than *Jackson*. These three cases were heard together by the Divisional Court and, on appeal, the Court of Appeal. In *R (Derwin and others) v Attorney General* the claimants tried to establish that the Act violated their rights under European Community law, which would have led to the Act being ineffective to the extent that it did so (but otherwise fully effective). The claimants argued that the Act was an improper interference with the right to free movement of goods between Member States of the Community under Article 28 of the EC Treaty (because hunts in England and Wales import many horses and hounds from Ireland), and with the right to free movement of services between Member States under Article 49 of the Treaty (because people in England and Wales offer hunting holidays to visitors from other Member States who ride with hunts in England and Wales). The Divisional Court and the Court of Appeal rejected these claims. The Act was not consciously aimed at restricting interstate trade in horses and hounds, and did not discriminate between goods from different Member States. The Act therefore did not engage Article 28 at all. The Court of Appeal, differing from the Divisional Court, also held that the Act did not engage the freedom to provide services under Article 49 either, but agreed with the lower court that, in any case, any interference was justified on public morality grounds as being proportionate to a legitimate state aim under Articles 30 and 46 of the EC Treaty.

In *Countryside Alliance v Attorney General* and *R (Friend and another) v Attorney General* the claimants argued that the Act violated Convention rights under the Human Rights Act 1998. This could not make the Act ineffective, but might have led the courts to make a declaration of incompatibility which, in turn, might have influenced the government and Parliament to reconsider the Hunting Act. In *Countryside Alliance* the claimants relied on the right to respect for private life and home (including autonomy, lifestyle, and use of private land) under ECHR Article 8, the right to freedom of assembly under Article 11, and the right to peaceful enjoyment of possessions under Article 1 of Protocol No 1 to the ECHR. The courts rejected these claims, holding that an attachment to hunting and the use of private property for hunting were not protected under Article 8, and that there was no infringement of Article 11 because people remained free to assemble as long as they did not then hunt wild mammals with dogs. There was an infringement of the right to peaceful enjoyment of possessions, but it was justified by the aim of the Hunting Act to reduce suffering of animals and was proportionate to that aim. Future earnings or livelihoods of those who worked in the hunting industry were not possessions within the meaning of Article 1.

In *Friend* the courts held that a commitment to hunting did not constitute a religion or belief such as Article 9 of the ECHR protected, and that the hunting community was not an 'ethnic group' and so was not protected against discrimination by the Race Relations Act 1976 or any international human rights treaty which had effect in English law.

The result is that the pro-hunting campaigners were denied even the limited moral satisfaction of a declaration of incompatibility.

Despite having been upheld comprehensively against legal challenges, the Act continues to be extremely controversial, with the Countryside Alliance and the Conservative Party seeking its repeal. A poll carried out by the *Today* programme on BBC Radio 4 in 2006 concluded that more people would like to repeal the Hunting Act than any other, although the BBC later admitted that its poll had been skewed by an organised campaign by pro-hunting campaigners.

CONCLUSIONS

The *Jackson* case was the really significant constitutional challenge to the Hunting Act 2004, and as we have seen all the judges decided that the Act was valid and effective as a matter of law. But behind this unanimity as to the validity of the Parliament Act 1949 and the Hunting Act 2004 the opinions of the judges revealed significant differences of opinion about fundamental questions in relation to parliamentary sovereignty. Whilst these differences did not in the end affect the decision in that case, they were significant because of their implications for the use of the Parliament Acts in other contexts. Two examples will illustrate this.

First, suppose a government wants to abolish the House of Lords, or even to alter its membership significantly, overcoming opposition in the House of Lords itself by using the Parliament Acts. Would such a major change be within the powers of the monarch and Commons under the Parliament Acts, or are there limits to section 2(1) of the 1911 Act which would make this a judicially preventable abuse of the procedure? This could easily happen in the course of the current round of the battle to reform the House of Lords, for instance if the Commons and Lords disagree about whether to turn the Lords into an all-elected second chamber. The approach of the Court of Appeal in *Jackson* would suggest that the Parliament Acts could not be used for this purpose, while the opinions of the majority in the House of Lords suggest that it could.

Secondly, suppose a government introduces a Bill to Parliament to deprive individuals of the right to apply for judicial review of immigration and asylum decisions, and that this Bill is blocked by the House of Lords. Access to judicial review of decisions of public officials is one of the central principles of the constitution. Could the Parliament Acts be used to force the legislation through without the consent of the Lords, or are there judicially enforceable limits to the legislative power of the Queen in Parliament or the monarch and Commons to legislate in a way that is inconsistent with the principle of the rule of law? This scenario came close to being realised in 2004, had the government not backed down in the face of opposition to provisions in the Asylum and Immigration (Treatment of Claimants, etc) Bill. The judiciary then made it clear that, were the Bill to become an Act, courts would have to decide whether or not to apply those provisions. This would have been a major challenge to an important plank in parliamentary sovereignty, because the courts would have had to decide whether some rule or principle had a higher legal status than parliamentary sovereignty, allowing courts to override an Act of Parliament. In *Jackson*, Lord Steyn suggested that such a challenge might work at some point; Lord Bingham gave a contrary indication; while the other Law Lords seem to be strung along a spectrum between them.

Behind these issues lies a further question, one of political morality rather than law. If the fundamental reason for accepting parliamentary supremacy and the primacy of the Commons in the law-making process within Parliament is to uphold representative democracy, would it be appropriate for judges to change their attitude to those matters should Parliament seek to enact legislation inconsistent with a fundamental feature of democracy (or, perhaps, other constitutional fundamentals), as Lord Steyn suggested? For example, democracy might be considered to require protection against abuse of power by the representatives of the people, or the rule of law might be regarded as an intrinsic element in any worthwhile democracy. Should the courts be able to disregard legislation which threatens such models of democracy, or are such matters only remediable by political means? If the latter, are there now sufficient checks against abuse or subversion of democratic processes, particularly having regard to the operation of the Parliament Acts 1911 and 1949, a matter about which Baroness Hale expressed doubts?

The fact that these are live questions following the decision of the House of Lords in *Jackson*'s case illustrates the essentially contested and dynamic nature of constitutional law. It is not a system of settled rules, but a process of debate by reference to arguments based on legal materials in the light of political as well as legal principles. Constitutional law embodies arguments about the fundamental design of the good state, and continuously reflects on and reshapes itself and the state. The outcomes of cases for the parties are in a sense less important for constitutional law than the way the constitutional principles are developed and applied.

Cases

R (Countryside Alliance and others) v Attorney-General; R (Derwin and others) v Attorney General; R (Friend and another) v Attorney General [2006] EWCA Civ 817, [2006] 3 WLR 1017

R (on the application of Jackson and others) v Attorney General
Divisional Court: [2005] EWHC 94 (Admin)
Court of Appeal: [2005] EWCA Civ 126, [2005] QB 579
House of Lords: [2005] UKHL 56, [2006] 1 AC 262

Websites

For Parliament's own website: <http://www.parliament.uk>.
For details of the background: <http://www.supportfoxhunting.co.uk/the_hunting_ bill.shtml> (last visited 26 July 2007)

Further Reading

Good general introductions to constitutional law, both of which pre-date *Jackson*'s case, include:
Eric Barendt, *An Introduction to Constitutional Law* (Oxford: Oxford University Press, 1998)
Adam Tomkins, *Public Law* (Oxford: Oxford University Press, 2003)
A thought-provoking and up-to-date volume is:
Colin Turpin and Adam Tomkins, *British Government and the Constitution: Text and Materials* (Cambridge: Cambridge University Press, 2007)

8

European Union Law

Catherine Barnard

INTRODUCTION

I bet you aren't neutral about the European Union: you are bound to be either (strongly) for or against it. And perhaps 'against' is more likely, given the often hostile media coverage in this country about the EU. You might have heard that the EU has tried to ban prawn-cocktail crisps, home-made jam, round cheese, donkeys from beaches, and darts from pubs—none of which is true. You might also have heard that the EU lets foreigners claim social security benefits and receive free healthcare when they come to the UK— some of which is true. And you might have heard that the institutions of the EU (the Commission, the Council, the European Parliament, the European Court of Justice) are full of people feathering their own nests but who are incapable of organising a party in a brewery let alone a major international organisation which affects the lives of nearly half a billion people.

But what you do not often hear about are the EU success stories: that we can travel (and live) in the 27 different countries of the EU with virtu- ally no restrictions, that we can get there cheaply thanks to the low-cost airlines such as Ryan Air and EasyJet, and that pasta and café latte have become the standard fare of the British high street. Most importantly, thanks in part to this free trade facilitated by the European Union, states like France, Germany, Spain and the UK, which have been enemies for much of the previous 1,000 years and fought two world wars in the last century, have not been to war with each other since the EU was founded.

Love it or loathe it, the EU is a fundamental part of our daily existence and European Community (EC) law has a profound effect on every aspect of national law, since EC law is part of our law and takes precedence over our law. This so-called *doctrine of supremacy* of EC law is what Eurosceptics rail against. For example, the Referendum Party, campaigning to secure Britain's withdrawal from the European Union, took out a full page advert in a national newspaper filled with the words 'John Major is impotent'. This referred not to the sexual health of the then British Prime Minister but to the fact that he was 'completely powerless in the face of diktats from unelected European bureaucrats'. The advert continued: 'Yet again it demonstrates that Brussels [the seat of most of the Community institutions], not Westminster [the seat of the British Parliament], now decides how we must lead our lives'. A similar point is made in the cartoon on page 173. It is an issue which has bedevilled the British relationship with the EU.

But EC law is not just about economics, high politics and constitutional issues. Like contract, tort, and equity, it is also about individuals who have suffered some harm and want the courts to give them a remedy. But what makes EC law exciting for lawyers is the fact that the doctrine of supremacy of EC law, so mistrusted by Eurosceptics, gives lawyers a trump card to help them win their case. If a point of EC law is successfully raised it will defeat arguments based on *national* law, where the two conflict. This is exactly what the lawyers did in *Bosman,* the case discussed in this chapter. Jean-Marc Bosman was a Belgian footballer, not a very good one, but a footballer with the sense to hire good lawyers to challenge the rules of the Belgian football association and UEFA which prevented him from playing for a French club. The legal case he fought—which ended up before the European Court of Justice (ECJ)—tells us much, not only about the rather murky world of professional football but also about the nature of European Community law, its relationship with national law, the legal reasoning of the Court of Justice and the broader political context in which the ECJ operates. These issues form the heart of this chapter. But first the facts of *Bosman*.

THE DISPUTE

Bosman was a Belgian national employed by the Belgian first division club RC Liège. When his contract expired he wanted to play for the French second division club, US Dunkerque (see diagram, below). However, UEFA (the Union of European Football Associations) and the Belgian football association (URBSA) had two rules which stood in the way of Bosman playing for US Dunkerque.

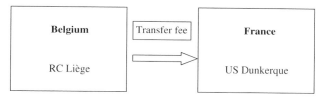

Fig. 8.1 *The transfer fees in Bosman.*

The first, the so-called '3+2 rule', said that national football associations could allow each first division team to field up to three foreign players and two 'acclimatised' foreigners (players who have played in the country for an uninterrupted period of five years) in domestic league matches, but no more than five foreign players in total.

The second concerned transfer fees. According to these rules, on the expiry of a contract with club A (RC Liège), a professional footballer could not play for club B (US Dunkerque) until club A (RC Liège) had released his registration. This would be done only on the payment of a transfer fee. Since RC Liège did not think that US Dunkerque would be able to pay the (high) transfer fee it had put on Bosman's head, Bosman found himself without a club for the following season. He did eventually manage to sign two short contracts with French clubs before ending up at Olympic de Charleroi, a Belgian third division club. There was strong circumstantial evidence that Bosman was being boycotted by all the European clubs that might have engaged him because, as a result of the litigation he brought, he was seen as a trouble-maker.

INTRODUCTION TO KEY PRINCIPLES OF EUROPEAN COMMUNITY LAW

The Relevant Rules

But what did European Community law have to do with Bosman's tale of woe? Well, quite a lot. He argued before his national court that UEFA's rules contravened Article 39 of the European Community (EC) Treaty, giving workers the right to move freely around the EU, and Article 81 of the EC Treaty prohibiting *anti-competitive* agreements (these are agreements between companies and/or individuals which restrict the free operation of the market in some way).

Article 39 on the free movement of workers is one of the 'four freedoms' at the heart of the European Union. The others are the free movement of goods, services and capital. Together, these freedoms form the core of the 'common' or 'single' market project, begun by the European Economic Community (EEC) Treaty in 1957. This Treaty, which has been amended a number of times, is to all intents and purposes the 'Constitution' of the European Community. And, as with any 'federal' constitution, state laws can be checked against the constitution to see if they are compatible with it.

The four freedoms share a common feature—that goods, persons, services or capital moving from one Member State of the European Union to another should not suffer discrimination simply because they are foreign. In other words, it should be as easy to trade or move between London and Budapest as it is between London and Birmingham. So, the big idea behind the single market is market integration: the removal of barriers to trade and to migration between states. But what are the advantages of market integration? Well, in the case of free movement of persons, there are benefits for both individual migrant workers and the 'host' state where they go to work. Workers coming from other Member States often take up jobs which cannot be filled by national workers. Migrants might also bring new talents and skills which the national workforce cannot offer. For the individual migrants, moving to a new job in another Member State means escaping from possible unemployment at home, bettering their personal circumstances and broadening their range of experience.

So far, so win-win. When times are good, workers from other Member States do help to fill a skills gap, as we have seen in the UK with the arrival of hundreds of thousands of Polish, Hungarian and other Eastern European workers since 2004. But when times are bad, migrant workers are seen to threaten jobs for nationals (see, eg: Milland, 'Jobless up 92,000 as Poles flood in', *Daily Express*, 17 August 2006, 1; Whitehead, '92,000 East Europeans Milk Our Benefits', *Daily Express*, 23 May 2007, 1) and it is then that host governments, bowing to domestic political pressure, may decide to make life more difficult for migrant workers. They might, for example, limit the number of foreigners who can do a particular job (as with the 3+2 rule in *Bosman*) or they might ban foreigners from working in the host state altogether. This is where Community law comes into play: Article 39 can be invoked by the migrant worker to challenge such unjustified barriers created by laws and practices of the host Member State.

But removing barriers (sometimes referred to as *negative integration*) may not be enough to get the job done. Sometimes additional rights are needed to achieve free movement (referred to as *positive integration*). These additional rights take the form of legislative measures adopted by the institutions of the European Community to help facilitate free movement. Most commonly, these measures take the form of *Regulations*, which automatically form part of domestic law, or *Directives*, which must be implemented by Member States by passing legislation in their own national systems. These measures are proposed by the European Commission, the executive arm of the European Community (the officials in Brussels who run the Community day to day), and then adopted (usually) by a combination of the Council of Ministers (meetings of Ministers from each of the Member States) and the European Parliament.

One such legislative measure, the Workers' Regulation 1612/68, was agreed as early as 1968 to allow workers to move freely *with* their families. The Regulation says that workers have to enjoy an equal chance with nationals of getting a job and to benefit from equal treatment once employed. It also said that the worker's family members should be able to join the worker in the host state and work there themselves. These latter provisions have been replaced by the Citizens' Rights Directive 2004/38 which has, more fundamentally, overhauled the system of free movement rights. We shall return to this Directive later. For now remember that, as he began to challenge the 3+2 nationality rules, Bosman relied on not only Article 39 of the EC Treaty but also the provisions of Regulation 1612/68.

The Principles of Supremacy and Direct Effect

The Principles

But how can these *EC* rules be raised in a *national* court given that you might expect that national courts would apply national law only? The

European Court of Justice (ECJ) answered this question in two seminal cases decided in the 1960s, *Van Gend en Loos* and *Costa v ENEL*. In these cases the Court of Justice, adopting a *teleological* approach to interpretation (looking at the purpose of the Treaty rather than its literal meaning), developed two key principles: direct effect and supremacy. *Direct effect* means that unconditional and precise Community law rules, including provisions of the Treaty, can be enforced by litigants in the national court. *Supremacy* or *primacy* of Community law means, as we have already seen, that Community law takes precedence over any conflicting national law. The two principles go hand in hand: without supremacy there is no point in having direct effect (otherwise national law would trump Community law) and, conversely, without direct effect there is no point in having supremacy (otherwise supreme Community law could not actually be enforced in national courts).

Criticism of the Principles

The upshot of the principles of direct effect and supremacy is that Bosman could rely on the provisions of the EC Treaty to make his case against UEFA and URBSA in his local (Belgian) court and, if the local court found in his favour, Community law would prevail over the conflicting UEFA/URBSA rules. This is what makes the Eurosceptics angry: why should national rules give way to European Community law? Different Member States respond to this question differently. For the UK the answer is reasonably clear. In 1973 the British government signed up to the European Economic Community (EEC) Treaty and that Treaty, as interpreted by the European Court of Justice, implicitly included the principles of supremacy and direct effect. The UK incorporated these principles, together with the rest of EC law, into British law by the European Communities Act (ECA) 1972. In principle, this Act, like any other Act of Parliament, is subject to the doctrine of parliamentary sovereignty considered in chapter 7. This means that it can be repealed (ie, reversed) by the British Parliament at any stage, thereby freeing the UK of its obligations under European Community law. The doctrine of parliamentary sovereignty should have helped to put the Eurosceptics' minds at rest. In practice, however, as we saw in chapter 7, the ECA 1972, like the Human Rights Act 1998 incorporating the European Convention on Human Rights into UK law, has assumed a special constitutional status, and will not be repealed lightly. So perhaps the Eurosceptics have a point.

This cartoon by Gaskill illustrates the concerns expressed by Eurosceptics about the loss of (UK) parliamentary sovereignty to 'Brussels'.
© David Gaskill, *The Sun.*

Critics of the EU also complain about the ECJ's activism. What right did the Court have to 'invent' principles, such as direct effect and supremacy, which are not actually written down in the Treaty? The ECJ argues that it is empowered by the EC Treaty to ensure that 'the law is observed' which, to the Court of Justice, means making sure that Community law is *effective* in practice and that Member States comply with their Treaty obligations. Other federal systems where power is divided between the central (federal) and local (state) levels have equivalent rules to ensure their systems can operate; the ECJ has introduced these principles to make sure that the European Community system, while not a federal system in the German or American sense, can function effectively too. There is no point in individuals (ie, people and companies) seeing Community law as remote and inaccessible. For it to work they must be able to rely on it before their local courts: in Riga, Rimini and Rotherham.

Express reference to the principle of supremacy (but not direct effect) was in fact made in the Constitutional Treaty adopted in Rome in 2004 to help clarify and legitimise the European Union project. However, this Treaty was rejected by the French and Dutch voters in 2005. A footprint of the newly named 'Reform Treaty' was agreed by the Heads of the Member States in June 2007, a text which draws substantially on the failed Constitutional Treaty. At the time of writing, it appears that the reference to the principle of supremacy has been dropped from the text of the Treaty but is directly referred to in a Declaration. Nevertheless, the principles of direct effect and supremacy are firmly enshrined in the Court of Justice's case law and will continue to apply, whatever the fate of the Reform Treaty.

The Article 234 Reference Procedure

If they feel able, local courts can decide cases such as Bosman's for themselves; if not, as in *Bosman*, they can refer questions to the European Court of Justice under the so-called Article 234 *preliminary reference* or *preliminary ruling* procedure. Under this procedure national courts ask the ECJ questions on the interpretation of European Community law. This process, while apparently complex and certainly time-consuming, is one of the great strengths of the European Community system. At its best, it sees the national courts and the European Court of Justice working in cooperation: the ECJ gives a ruling on the meaning of European Community *law* and the case returns to the national court to apply this ruling to the *facts* of the case. In the UK the rulings of the ECJ form part of the system of precedent and, in recognition of the supremacy of Community law, take precedence over the rulings of all British courts, including the House of Lords.

The European Court of Justice's ruling should always be clear enough for the national court to follow. It helps that there is only ever one judgment—there are no dissents—and each judgment contains a *dispositif* (closing section) at the end summarising the Court's findings. However, the downside of a single judgment is that it is often hard to get all the judges to agree on its wording. Whether the Court of Justice sits as a Full Court (all 27 judges, a rarity), as a Grand Chamber (13 judges), or as a Chamber of three or five judges, the judgment must be agreed by all the judges. The judgment is drafted in French (the working language of the Court) by the *juge rapporteur* (reporting judge). At times, controversial paragraphs are removed from the final version, with the result that the judgment may be difficult to follow in places.

Originally, the decisions of the ECJ were short, following the French model which sees cases as merely expounding the law, not justifying or developing it. However, in recent years the decisions of the ECJ have grown in length and, reflecting the increasing common law influence (following the accession of the UK and Ireland to the EU in 1973), discuss and distinguish other cases more fully. Unlike common law, though, there is no doctrine of precedent in EC law, although in practice the ECJ does generally tend to follow its earlier decisions.

More detail can often be found in the Advocate General's opinion. The Advocate General, a judge at the ECJ, writes an advisory opinion which reads more like a common law judgment (and so is generally much longer than an ECJ judgment). The ECJ is not obliged to follow this opinion but, in many cases, it does in fact do so. In *Bosman* the ECJ did reach the same conclusion as its Advocate General but while the Advocate General placed much emphasis on the challenge to the football association rules as being anti-competitive under Article 81, the Court's sole focus was on the free movement of workers provisions under Article 39.

Having been introduced to some of the nuts and bolts of EC law, it is now time to consider what the Court of Justice actually said in *Bosman*.

THE EUROPEAN COURT OF JUSTICE'S DECISION

The 3+2 Rule

You will remember that Bosman's first claim was that the 3+2 rule (ie, that there could only be five 'foreign' players in a team at any one time) discriminated against him contrary to Article 39 of the EC Treaty on the free movement of workers and Regulation 1612/68; had Bosman been French there would have been no limit on his right to play. The Treaty prohibits discrimination on the grounds of nationality because such discrimination is irrational: employers, including football clubs, must make selection decisions based on the rational criterion of merit, rather than on the irrational and prohibited criterion of nationality. With the opening up of the single market, this means that employers have a much bigger pool of candidates to choose from; using nationality as a criterion to narrow that pool undermines the purposes of the single market.

The Court of Justice recognised this point in *Bosman*. It said that the 3+2 rule related to the essence of the activity of professional players: if Community law did not apply to this situation, then Article 39 would be 'deprived of its practical effect and the fundamental right of free access to employment which the Treaty confers individually on each worker in the Community rendered nugatory'. The 3+2 rule was therefore unlawful.

Three points are worth noting about the ECJ's observations. First, the Court again relied on the 'effectiveness' argument to buttress its reasoning (Article 39 would be 'deprived of its practical effect' if it did not apply to Bosman's case); secondly, the ECJ reiterated the principle of direct effect in the specific context of Article 39 (the 'right of free access to employment which the Treaty confers individually on each worker'); and thirdly, this right of free access to employment was described as 'fundamental'. Traditionally, the epithet 'fundamental rights' is attached to civil and political rights such as the right to life and freedom of expression. It is not usually attached to *economic* rights such as the right to free movement. However, it will be recalled that the European Union was originally established as the European *Economic* Community: the economic freedoms—the free movement of goods, persons, services and capital—lay at the core of the EEC and therefore achieved 'fundamental' status. In the past this has led to a certain imbalance between the economic freedoms and other fundamental rights. However, as the EEC has evolved from Economic Community to European Union, greater recognition has been given to fundamental civil and political rights, and the adoption of the Charter of Fundamental Rights 2000, which brought both civil/political rights and economic/social rights under one roof, has helped to redress the initial imbalance.

So, the ECJ held that he 3+2 rule was directly discriminatory: it overtly discriminated against non-nationals such as Bosman. Direct discrimination is considered the worst type of discrimination—because it is so obviously connected with the prohibited ground of nationality—and so the defendant Member States/sporting associations could defend such discrimination only by reference to one of the express *derogations* (defences) provided by the Treaty. These derogations (public policy, public security and public health) are all narrowly interpreted and it is only in the rarest of cases that the defendant successfully relies on one of them. *Bosman* was not such a case.

The defendant football associations also tried to defend themselves by pointing out that the European Commission had been involved in the drafting of the 3+2 rule: surely, it argued, if the EU's own Commission had said the 3+2 rule was acceptable that amounted to a good defence. But the ECJ said no, dryly observing that the Commission did not have the power 'to authorise practices which are contrary to the Treaty'.

In light of the Court of Justice's ruling in *Bosman*, how then do national sports teams (ie, England, France, Germany) get away with fielding a team of only national players? This question had been addressed in the earlier case of *Donà v Mantero* where, in respect of national teams, the ECJ essentially created a new exception to the rule prohibiting non-discrimination. Relying on the rather contentious justification that *national* games are not commercial in nature, the Court of Justice said that Community law did not prevent the adoption of rules 'excluding foreign players from participation in certain matches for reasons which are not of an economic nature'. Therefore, in the context of matches which are of sporting interest only, such as, for example, matches between national teams from different countries, Community law does not apply.

The upshot of these rulings is that clubs (eg, Manchester United and Chelsea) are subject to Community law in respect of the nationality of players that can be fielded, while national sides (eg, England and France) are not. The decision in *Donà v Mantero* shows that the Court of Justice has rather well-tuned political antennae and decided not to make itself, and EC law, a laughing stock by requiring national teams to field a mixed nationality squad (no matter that some national sides would benefit from the injection of some foreign blood).

One final question. Given that Article 39 stops sports associations from limiting the number of EU nationals that can play for club sides, what is the position of nationality rules in respect of players coming from non-Member States of the European Union, so-called third country nationals (TCNs)? Well, if the EU has an agreement with the third country, and that agreement contains a non-discrimination clause, then again discrimination can be prohibited. This can be seen in *Simutenkov*. The Spanish football association had a rule limiting to three the number of TCN players who were allowed to participate at any time in the Spanish first division. Following *Bosman,* Simutenkov, a Russian footballer who played for a Spanish club, challenged this rule as being contrary to Article 23(1) of the European Communities-Russia Partnership Agreement which prohibited discrimination against Russian nationals legally employed in the territory of a Member State. He won his case.

The Transfer Fee Rule

Establishing a Breach of Community Law

Jean-Marc Bosman challenged not only the 3+2 rule but also the requirement to pay transfer fees. As we discussed earlier (see diagram on page 169), on the expiry of a contract with club A, a professional footballer could not play for club B until club A had released his registration. This was usually conditional on club B paying a transfer fee to club A. Did this rule breach Community law? The problem facing the Court was that this rule, unlike the 3+2 rule, was not discriminatory on the grounds of nationality because it applied equally to transfers between clubs belonging to different national associations within the same Member State (eg, between Manchester United and Celtic) and was similar to the rules governing transfers between clubs belonging to the same national association (eg, between Manchester United and Chelsea). Nevertheless, the Court concluded that the transfer rules breached Article 39 because they 'directly affect[ed] players' access to the employment market in other Member States' and were 'capable of impeding freedom of movement for workers'.

This was an important ruling by the Court of Justice because the Court recognised that Community law was no longer simply about removing *discrimination* (as the Treaty had said) but was also about ensuring that goods and people from other Member States enjoyed *access to the market* of other Member States even where the rule was non-discriminatory. The Court said that Bosman should have had free access to the football market in other Member States unless there were 'objectively justifiable' (ie, good) reasons why he should not.

The Court of Justice's new approach has serious implications for the Member States. Under the *discrimination* model, Member States/ sporting associations had the freedom to set their own rules and these rules would not be challenged unless they were discriminatory either directly (such as the 3+2 rule in *Bosman*) or indirectly (a rule which on its face applies to all workers but which in fact imposes a particular burden on the migrant). By contrast, under the *market access* approach, nearly all national rules risk being challenged as interfering with the Community rights to free movement because, by their nature, most national rules interfere with trade or free movement in some way.

The difference between the discrimination and market access approaches can be seen in the following example. Greek law prohibited qualified opticians from operating more than one optician's shop. This rule was challenged by the European Commission as being contrary to the EC Treaty because the rule interfered with the right of opticians from other Member States to set up a chain of opticians in Greece. If the ECJ had applied the discrimination model the Commission would have lost its case because Greek law treated Greek and foreign opticians the same: nobody could set up a chain of opticians shops. The rule therefore would not have breached the Treaty.

However, the Court of Justice in fact applied the market access approach and found the Greek rule did breach the Treaty because the rule interfered with the right of opticians from other Member States to set up a chain of opticians' shops in Greece. The fact that Greek opticians also could not set up a chain of opticians' shops was irrelevant. The Court's focus was instead on the restrictions experienced by traders and entrepreneurs from other Member States trying to break onto the Greek market. Because such restrictions existed they breached the Treaty and were thus unlawful unless they could be justified.

This choice between the non-discrimination approach to trade and the market access approach has troubled not only the EU but other international organisations such as the World Trade Organisation (WTO). While, on the one hand, the market access approach risks undermining social, environmental and consumer legislation enacted by democratically-elected national governments, on the other, it is more likely to achieve market integration (ie, the creation of a single market).

By contrast, the discrimination approach is less likely to interfere with national regulation but it is less effective in achieving market integration.

In the field of free movement of persons, the Court of Justice has opted very much in favour of the market access approach, now increasingly referred to as the 'obstacle' or 'restriction' approach. In many cases the Court now simply asks the question 'Does the national rule being challenged constitute an obstacle or restriction on free movement?'. If, as in *Bosman,* the answer to this question is yes, then the national rule breaches the Treaty. The burden then shifts to the defendant state to come up with a good reason to justify the existence of the rule.

Justification, Proportionality and Fundamental Human Rights

What, then, are these justifications? They are an open-ended list of 'good' reasons for the rule developed by the ECJ on a case by case basis. They supplement the express derogations (defences)—public policy, public security and public health—laid down by the Treaty. The price for adopting the broad market access test is that the Court has had to recognise an ever wider range of justifications (including consumer protection, environmental protection and worker protection) which Member States can invoke to prevent the wholesale dismantling of national rules.

However, Member States cannot just point to a good reason for the existence of the rule. They must also show that any steps taken to achieve one of the derogations or justifications are proportionate (ie, the measures must be *suitable* for securing the attainment of the objective and must not go beyond what is *necessary* to attain it) and must respect fundamental rights. The case of *Carpenter* provides a good illustration of how these principles work together.

Mrs Carpenter, a Filipino national, overstayed her entry permit to the UK. She then married a British national. The UK tried to deport her for overstaying her visa. In contesting her deportation, Mrs Carpenter came up with an ingenious argument. Since she was Filipino (a so-called 'third country national') she could not invoke EC law herself. However, she said that if she was deported this would restrict her *husband's* ability to carry on business as a service provider in other Member States since she looked after his children while he was away. Her deportation therefore contravened Articles 49 and 50 of the EC Treaty on freedom to provide services. The Court of Justice accepted Mrs Carpenter's argument and said that her deportation would constitute an obstacle to Mr Carpenter's ability to provide services under EC law.

However, the UK argued that Mrs Carpenter's deportation could, nevertheless, be justified on grounds of public policy. While recognising that the UK had a point, the ECJ said that the UK had to balance the public interest in deporting Mrs Carpenter with the fundamental rights of Mr and Mrs Carpenter, in particular the right to family life under Article 8 of the European Convention on Human Rights. While the right to family life is not itself unlimited, the Court said that the decision to deport Mrs Carpenter was disproportionate: even though Mrs Carpenter had infringed UK immigration laws (by overstaying her entry visa) she did not constitute a danger to public order and safety. Therefore, as a result of European Community law, Mrs Carpenter was entitled to stay in the UK.

Establishing Justification and Proportionality in *Bosman*

So how did the principles of justification, proportionality and human rights apply in *Bosman*? Well, the Court of Justice began by recognising that transfer fees might be justified. It said:

> In view of the considerable social importance of sporting activities and in particular football in the Community, the aims of maintaining a balance between clubs by preserving a certain degree of equality and uncertainty as to results and of encouraging the recruitment and training of young players [the transfer fees] must be accepted as legitimate.

In other words, the ECJ has recognised that sport is special and different because it is based on a notion of mutual interdependence. To help explain the significance of the Court's observation, one academic commentator, Stephen Weatherill, contrasts the sport 'market' with the widget market. On the widget market producers aim to gain the largest market share, if necessary by driving their rivals off the market. By contrast, in sport, opponents are there to be beaten but the whole point of the endeavour is destroyed if opponents are, literally, beaten out of sight.

Having recognised that sport was special, the Court of Justice said that there were good reasons to justify the existence of transfer fees: as a way of transferring funds from rich clubs to poor clubs and as a way of providing incentives to clubs to invest in the training of young players.

However, the ECJ then turned to the question of the proportionality of the existing transfer fee rules and found them to be disproportionate (it never got to the question of fundamental rights). It said that the transfer fee rules were not an adequate means of maintaining financial and competitive balance in the world of football because they neither precluded the richest clubs from securing the services of the best players nor did they prevent the availability of financial resources from being a decisive factor in competitive sport. It also said that the prospect of receiving transfer fees was neither a decisive factor in encouraging recruitment and training of young players nor an adequate means of financing such activities. The Court of Justice therefore concluded that the transfer fee rules, like the 3+2 rule, breached EC law and so were unlawful. Jean-Marc Bosman had won his case.

THE IMMEDIATE CONSEQUENCES OF THE *BOSMAN* RULING

The Belgian football authorities paid Jean-Marc Bosman £312,000 and he in turn agreed not to pursue the case any further. This happened in December 1998, more than eight years after the expiry of his contract with RC Liège. But in reality the litigation did not pay for Bosman. He was left heavily in debt as a result of his legal fight with the football authorities and, with his professional career over and his marriage in tatters, he moved back in with his parents. In early 1997 some of the world's top players planned a testimonial for him involving Barcelona and a Europe XI. However, the Spanish FA and FIFA objected to the match, blaming Bosman for the large number of foreign players in the Spanish league (B Oliver, 'Sport Around the World: Bosman out in the cold in Spain', *The Daily Telegraph*, 1 March 1997, 18). The match did eventually go ahead but Bosman's name was not officially connected with the event.

However, the *Bosman* ruling had ramifications for the world of professional football going way beyond the immediate circumstances of

Jean-Marc Bosman at home now his career has come to an end.
© Gary Carlton, 2006.

Jean-Marc's case. With the abolition of the 3+2 rule the nationality composition of many teams has changed dramatically (look at Chelsea). With the abolition of transfer fees for players whose contracts have come to an end clubs have responded by hiring stars on longer contracts, with money previously used for transfer fees being diverted into wage packets. This has made millionaires out of many European players. The football industry has also revised its rules on transfers of players. These new rules include a system of training compensation to encourage and reward the effort of clubs, especially small clubs, in training young players, as well as the creation of a restricted transfer period prior to each season, and a further limited mid-season window, with a maximum of one transfer per player per season.

However, there remains considerable disquiet in the world of football that Community law should apply to it at all. There is a strong feeling of resentment that Community law rules which were intended to apply to 'public' laws of the Member States (eg, Acts of Parliament and statutory instruments) have been extended by the Court of Justice to the 'private' world of football. Those in charge of football argue that because sport is special it should be exempted from the Community free movement rules altogether (R Blitz, 'EU labour movement rules threaten football, says Platini', *Financial Times*, 21 May 2007). Football, they argue, should be left to footballers and not 'unelected bureaucrats' such as European Commissioners (those in charge of the European Commission) and the ECJ who have 'never played sport'.

THE LONGER-TERM CONSEQUENCES OF *BOSMAN*: THE DEVELOPMENT OF UNION CITIZENSHIP

For better or for worse, *Bosman* has changed the face of European football. *Bosman* was also an important staging post in another more fundamental political transformation occurring in the European Union. As we saw in the earlier part of this chapter, the original EEC Treaty gave rights to those who were 'economically' active (such as workers) who could move from one country to another to take up a job. By contrast, those who were not economically active had no rights to move to another Member State. In a European *Economic* Community this distinction made sense: those who were economically active were able to contribute to the economy of the host state, largely through paying taxes. They would therefore be a benefit, not a burden, to the economy of that state. The same would not be true for those who were not economically active (for example, the unemployed). These individuals risked becoming a burden on the social welfare system of the host state.

However, the Court of Justice began to erode the distinction between the economically and the non-economically active by extending the Treaty rights to those who were not economically active, in the traditional sense, such as work-seekers and tourists. This led some to suggest that the ECJ was developing a concept of EU 'citizenship', ie, giving rights of free movement to anyone holding the nationality of a Member State regardless of their economic status. This in turn reflected a changing attitude by the ECJ towards the EU: the EU was no longer just a glorified free trade area but it was also a *political* body assuming state-like qualities. One key aspect of any state is to have a 'people', ie, its own citizens; and citizens have human rights which need to be protected. Cases such as *Carpenter* can be understood as part of this development.

The adoption of the Maastricht Treaty in 1992 (properly known as the Treaty on European Union) helped reshape the understanding of what 'Europe' was about. Not only did this Treaty change the name of the foundation Treaty (from European Economic Community (EEC) to European Community (EC) Treaty, thereby dropping the reference to 'economic'), but it also renamed the whole body of Treaties associated with the EC. The new name was European Union, a name which is to be applied more generally if the Reform Treaty, negotiated in 2007 to replace the failed Constitutional Treaty, enters into force. This shift from European *Economic* Community to European Union was given real substance by the inclusion at Maastricht of new Articles in the EC Treaty on EU citizenship. These provide that all those holding the nationality of one of the Member States of the Union are Union citizens, which, according to Article 18(1) of the EC Treaty, gives them the right to move to and reside in another Member State, subject only to the limits laid down by the Treaty (such as the public policy, security and health derogations).

The *Bosman* case marked an important staging post in this changing perspective from economic community to political union. Bosman was relying on his economic rights as a worker. Yet the Court talked of him not just as a worker but also as a citizen. For example, it said that the provisions of the Treaty relating to freedom of movement for persons were intended 'to facilitate the pursuit by *Community citizens* of occupational activities of all kinds throughout the Community, and preclude measures which might place *Community citizens* at a disadvantage when they wish to pursue an economic activity in the territory of another Member State' (emphasis added).

But what is now the position of those who, unlike Bosman, are not economically active? Are they entitled to enjoy the rights of free movement too? And, if so, are they entitled to enjoy social welfare benefits in the state they move to (the host state) on the same terms as nationals? In the leading case of *Grzelczyk* the Court suggested that the answer was a qualified yes.

Grzelczyk was a French student studying at a Belgian university. Having supported himself financially for the first three years of his studies he applied for a *minimex* (a Belgian social security benefit guaranteeing a minimum income) at the start of his fourth and final year. While Belgian students could receive the benefit, migrant students could not, and so Grzelczyk complained that he was being discriminated against, contrary to European Community law. However, the difficulty with his claim was that, under the relevant Community law rules on students, he was supposed to have sufficient resources to support himself during his studies and so not become reliant on the Belgian social welfare system. However, the Court did a remarkable thing. It said:

> Union citizenship is destined to be the fundamental status of nationals of the Member States, enabling those who find themselves in the same situation to enjoy the same treatment in law irrespective of their nationality, subject to such exceptions as are expressly provided for.

Those 'exceptions' included the need to have sufficient resources. However, the Court then said in effect that the requirement to have sufficient resources had to be read subject to the principle of proportionality, and that it would be disproportionate to deport Grzelczyk during his fourth and final year of study. Furthermore, and more controversially, the Court said, given the 'solidarity' (ie, the sense of common feeling) that now exists between migrant students, such as Grzelczyk, and the Belgian taxpayer, the Belgian authorities should pay him the minimex for so long as he did not become an unreasonable burden on the Belgian public finances. As a result, Grzelczyk, a migrant EU citizen, did enjoy a certain amount of equal treatment in respect of social security benefits in Belgium.

The position of individuals such as Grzelczyk has been strengthened by the adoption of the Citizen's Rights Directive 2004/38. In part this Directive consolidates the secondary measures, like the Workers' Regulation 1612/68, adopted in the 1960s to encourage free movement. However, the Directive goes further than these earlier measures because it expressly gives rights to those who are not economically active. For example, the Directive provides that any national can move to another Member State for up to three months, whether they are economically active or not, and that they will enjoy equal treatment with nationals in the host state once there. However, the Directive contains an important limitation: they will not enjoy equal treatment in respect of social welfare benefits or student benefits. This helps to reduce immediate concerns about 'welfare tourism'.

For periods beyond three months migrants also enjoy the right to move but only if they are engaged in economic activity in the host state as a worker or a self-employed person; or they have sufficient medical and financial resources for themselves and their family members; or they are students. These individuals also enjoy the right to the same treatment as nationals of the host state, including in respect of social assistance but not student support. After five years, Union citizens do not need to show they are workers, self-employed, students or adequately resourced. Thus, after five years, the link with economic activity is truly severed. These migrants are deemed to be sufficiently assimilated into the life of the host state that they are considered, for all practical purposes, to be nationals, with the result that they enjoy equal treatment not only in respect of social assistance but also as regards student maintenance in the form of grants or loans.

Such developments prompt further, more fundamental, questions: where is the EU to go from here? Should it continue down the path of further integration, giving the EU ever more state-like qualities (a defence force, a foreign policy, a social security system?), or should the EU stand still, draw breath and take stock, or should the EU look to retrench and focus again on the four freedoms? The period of reflection following the rejection of the Constitutional Treaty by the Dutch and French voters was supposed to give the prime ministers and presidents of the Member States time to think these thoughts but the negotiation of the Reform Treaty indicates there is little appetite to engage with these difficult issues.

CONCLUSIONS

Bosman is an important case. At a legal level, its importance lies in the shift from a non-discrimination model to a market access approach and in the ECJ's willingness to embrace 'Union citizenship'. At a practical level, *Bosman* is important for Jean-Marc himself, in that the Court of Justice sent out a very strong message that he had been wronged, and for the world of professional football where the rules on nationality and transfer fees have been radically overhauled. For the purpose of this book, the case is important because it shows us how Community law works and it tells us about the method of reasoning of the European Court of Justice.

The EU is a political entity and a legal system that you may—or may not—agree with but it is exciting, dynamic and transformative. The debates about the EU matter, not least because so much is yet to be decided. As lawyers, we have an important role in the continuation of this debate.

Cases

Case C-415/93 *Union Royale Belge des Sociétés de Football Association ASBL v Bosman* [1995] ECR I-4921

Case 26/62 *Van Gend en Loos v Nederlandse Administratie der Belastingen* [1963] ECR 1

Case 6/64 *Costa v ENEL* [1964] ECR 585

Case 13/76 *Donà v Mantero* [1976] ECR 1333

Case C-265/03 *Simutenkov v Ministerio de Educaión y Cultura, Real Federación Española de Fútbol* [2005] ECR I-2579

Case C-140/03 *Commission v Greece (opticians)* [2005] ECR I-3177

Case C-60/00 *Mary Carpenter v Secretary of State for the Home Department* [2002] ECR I-6279

Case C-184/99 *Grzelczyk v Centre public d'aide sociale d'Ottignies-Louvain-La-Neuve* [2001] ECR I-6193

S Weatherill, '"Fair Play Please". Recent Developments in the Application of EC Law to Sport' (2003) 40 CMLRev 51

Websites

The EU's own website is at <http://europa.eu>.
The European Court of Justice's website is at <http://www.curia.europa.eu>.

Further Reading

Introductory Reading

Ward, *A Critical Introduction to European Law* (2nd edn, Lexis Nexis Butterworths, London 2003)

Weatherill, *Law and Integration in the European Union* (Clarendon Press, Oxford 1995)

More Detailed Reading

Barnard, *The Substantive Law of the EU: The Four Freedoms* (2nd edn, Oxford University Press, Oxford 2007)

Chalmers, Hadjiemmanuil, Monti and Tomkins, *European Union Law* (Cambridge University Press, Cambridge 2006)

Craig and De Búrca, *EU Law: Text, Cases and Materials* (4th edn, Oxford University Press, Oxford 2007)

9
Conclusions: Drawing Some Threads Together

Janet O'Sullivan, Catherine Barnard
and Graham Virgo

So, what about law? You should, by now, have a pretty good idea of the sorts of issues studied by students in an academic law course at a good university. This chapter aims to take a step back and reflect on some of the themes and ideas that you will have encountered throughout the rest of the book. Its aim is to provide some further insights into legal problems and legal reasoning, and ultimately to help you decide what *your* answer is going to be to our title question, what about law?

First of all, you have probably spotted that, like it or not, there is no getting away from the fact that you have to acquire the building blocks of the subject. Studying law involves a lot of hard work, reading, understanding and learning difficult rules, and much of this will be the result of *independent* study. Law will not be spoon-fed to you in bite-sized pieces. A good analogy is perhaps with the study of architecture. An architect must spend years learning the basics of his profession—rules about materials, geometry, mathematics, the history of design and so on. But, like architecture, there is *so* much more to mastering the law than merely learning the rules and assembling building blocks. In this chapter, we will give you a taste of some deeper, more creative ideas and questions that await you, once you have mastered the basics of law.

For example, you may have noticed something surprising throughout this book, about the sort of process the judges are engaged in, when applying the law to decide a case. Students often think mastering the law is all about learning all the laws, like memorising lots of encyclopaedias. They assume that, having learnt them all, they will be able to scroll through their mental index and produce the 'right' answer to any legal problem: a bit like putting the facts into the top of a vending machine and expecting the 'right' answer to pop out of the bottom. As you will have realised by now, happily, the process of legal reasoning is much more complex and *much* more interesting than this, particularly in a common law system built on precedent. Simmonds explains the point very clearly in the first edition of his book, *Central Issues in Jurisprudence*:

> But if the law consists of rules which have been positively established and which can be ascertained without difficulty, how does it come about that expert lawyers frequently disagree? Rival QCs or law professors may disagree about what the existing law is. Many appellate decisions adjudicate between rival views of the existing law. But how can this be if the law is so unproblematic? When Professor X and Professor Y disagree about the law of tort, does that show that one of them has not done his homework, and has overlooked some statute or case that the other one has discovered? But we know that in most disputes all the statutes and cases are, as it were, on the table and known to both parties. So why can they not just *see* what the rules are?

Perhaps our notion of a doctrine of precedent lulls us into a false sense of confidence that the law will always be clear-cut and easy to identify: surely new cases are simply to be decided in accordance with past *authority*, in other words, decided following an earlier binding decision on the same facts? But there's the problem: it is extremely rare for the facts of a case to be *exactly* the same as the facts of an earlier precedent. This rarely matters at all, because usually the differences between a new case and the earlier precedent are obviously irrelevant when it comes to applying the earlier legal rule. The following example illustrates this point.

In 1975 the Court of Appeal established in *Froom v Butcher* what should happen when a car driver is injured in a head-on collision caused by the defendant's negligent driving, but whose injuries are exacerbated because the driver was not wearing a seat-belt. The court decided that, where the driver sued the defendant in tort, the driver's damages should be reduced by 20 per cent because of the driver's *contributory negligence* (a partial defence under the Law Reform (Contributory Negligence) Act

1945). This became a precedent for what should happen in such cases in future. Now, in *Froom* the victim's car happened to be a Jaguar, but it is obvious that the rule *Froom* established (about deducting 20 per cent for contributory negligence) does not apply only to unbelted *Jaguar* drivers, but to unbelted drivers of any sort of car. So obvious, in fact, that after *Froom*, cases involving drivers of Fords, Volvos and Toyotas whose injuries were exacerbated because they failed to wear seatbelts were straightforwardly treated as governed by the same precedent. More to the point, the question would never have been argued in court in those cases, because the lawyers acting for both parties would know precisely what the applicable law said about contributory negligence and would readily agree to a 20 per cent reduction in damages.

However, sometimes it is nowhere near this obvious whether an earlier precedent should apply or not. In such a case, the judge has to decide whether the differences between the facts of the earlier precedent and those of the new case are insignificant or important. Sticking with the seatbelt example, a judge might have to decide whether the *Froom* rule should apply if the un-belted driver was pregnant or suffering from a medical condition that made wearing a seatbelt dangerous. What if the driver was obese and so found wearing a seatbelt uncomfortable? And what if the unbelted victim was a passenger not the driver? It is quite plausible that different judges might come to different conclusions about the significance of these distinctions. One judge might regard them as significant enough to distinguish *Froom*, while another judge might decide that *Froom* should apply because the difference did not really matter. Sometimes, both points of view will surface in the same case, with decisions reversed on appeal or with an appellate court divided into majority and minority views. Yet all the judges reached their views in accordance with and using the same legal texts and rules.

You will have noticed many instances throughout this book of judges having to decide whether to apply or distinguish an existing legal rule, based on their view about the importance of factual differences between the precedent and the case in front of them, as well as many examples of judges disagreeing about what the law is in a given situation, what it means and how it should be applied.

The potential for disagreement is not confined to judges—commentators and law students often disagree too. The following two examples will give you a sense of where the disagreements might lie when facts differ, even slightly. The first involves the serious criminal offence of rape. Most people know what 'rape' means and could make a good attempt at working out what the essential elements of the criminal offence are likely to be (the *actus reus* and the *mens rea,* to recap from chapter 2). In essence, the offence of rape involves sexual intercourse with a victim without the victim's consent. You probably imagine that working out whether a particular set of facts falls within this definition is unlikely to be problematic (although *proving* those facts is often extremely difficult). But in 1923 the Court of Criminal Appeal had to consider the case of *R v Williams.* Williams was a singing teacher, who was giving singing lessons to a naïve 16 year old girl. He told her that she had problems with her breathing and that he could improve it by using his body to 'make an air passage'. He then had sex with her. She consented to what he was doing, not realising that it was sexual intercourse. Was Williams guilty of rape?

His barrister argued that as the girl had consented to penetration, Williams could not be guilty of rape (although he might be guilty of a less serious offence). This forced the court to confront exactly what the word 'consent' means in the definition of rape and, unsurprisingly, found that Williams was indeed guilty of that serious crime, despite the fact that his actions were not quite as obviously within the definition as the stereotypical situation of rape by a stranger on an obviously unwilling victim. But would the same apply if a slightly less naïve woman consented to penetration, knowing the 'facts of life' but having been led to believe that intercourse would nevertheless improve her singing voice? This is even further away from the stereotypical rape situation, and subtly different again from the facts of *Williams.* So has such a victim given consent within the definition of rape or not? (There is a similarity here with the victims who were infected with HIV in *Dica,* discussed in chapter 2.) It is entirely plausible to imagine two lawyers disagreeing about whether *Williams* should be applied or distinguished in such a case, yet both might be equally consistent with existing law and logically reasoned. As you will discover, lawyers frequently read majority decisions of the House of Lords and find, disconcertingly, that the dissenting speech is just as convincing as the majority speeches and it is very difficult to decide which side to support.

Interestingly, nowadays the offence of rape is defined in a statute (the Sexual Offences Act 2003) and its provisions deal with the problem in *Williams*. The victim will not be considered to have consented to sex where 'the defendant intentionally deceived the complainant as to the nature or purpose of the relevant act' or where 'the defendant intentionally induced the complainant to consent to the relevant act by impersonating a person known personally to the complainant'. But this statutory wording brings its own grey areas about interpretation. What if a defendant agrees to have sex with a prostitute, intending not to pay her? Has he 'intentionally deceived' her as to the nature of the act? What if the defendant is desperate to have sex with the victim, who tells him that she will agree to have sex with him only if he says that he loves her? He does not love her but tells her that he does in order to have sex with her? Has he intentionally deceived her as to the nature of the act? What if the defendant pretends to be a famous pop star and he has sex with the victim? Has the defendant impersonated somebody 'known personally' to the victim? What does 'personally' mean here? For example, what if she has met the pop star on a number of occasions or merely attended all his UK concerts?

The second example is much more recent and, as the Court of Appeal's 2:1 decision shows, much more difficult to resolve. In *Corr v IBC Vehicles* Mr Corr suffered a very serious injury as a result of his employers' negligence, while working at a plant producing vehicle panels. His ear was almost completely severed in the incident and he narrowly avoided decapitation. Following the accident, Mr Corr began to experience bouts of psychiatric illness known as post-traumatic stress disorder (a common result of a serious accident), which led in turn to depression, something he had never experienced before. Tragically, medical treatment was unable to resolve Mr Corr's depression and he committed suicide six years after the accident at work. His widow sued the negligent employers, claiming damages for the loss of the family breadwinner under the Fatal Accidents Act 1976. To succeed in this statutory claim, she had to prove (among other things) that the employers *caused* and were *responsible* for her husband's death.

In one sense, his death *was* certainly *caused* by the employers' negligence, because were it not for their negligence (in legal jargon, *but for* their negligence), he would not have become depressed and eventually committed suicide. Yet this is only half the story. Just because X's negligence is a 'but for' cause of harm to Y does not necessarily mean that it is appropriate for the law to attribute blame to X. Imagine that X negligently knocks Y off her bike and stops to call an ambulance; while Y is sitting dazed on the pavement, a mugger snatches Y's bag and runs off—X's negligence is undoubtedly a 'but for' cause of the theft of the bag, but it would be seem wrong to hold X *responsible* for the theft. (The same sorts of problem arise in history. It is often said that, with the benefit of hindsight, the terms of the peace settlement after the First World War were too hard on Germany and paved the way for Hitler's rise to power in the 1930s, but that does not mean that the statesmen who devised that peace treaty are held responsible for the death of six million Jews in the Second World War.) So we need other legal rules to decide whether someone whose conduct is undeniably a 'but for' cause of harm should or should not be legally *blamed* for that harm.

Those rules are not easy to express in general terms (after all, it is hard to come up with general principles that will be appropriate in all the different situations where blame is to be attributed), but there are two that are often mentioned. First, lawyers tend to say, with heavy use of metaphor, that the defendant won't be held responsible where the conduct of some third party, or even of the claimant himself, 'intervened' between the defendant's fault and the claimant's ultimate harm. This will normally involve intervening conduct that is wholly 'unreasonable' or 'deliberate', so that it seems to 'eclipse' the defendant's fault and make the defendant's fault 'fade into the background'. This principle would obviously apply in the example of the mugger and the cyclist to exonerate the driver from responsibility for the theft of the bag.

You might imagine that the *suicide* of the claimant would count as a classic example of such deliberate, voluntary conduct, but there have been cases in which a negligent defendant has been held responsible for a person's suicide. For example, where the police know that a person in custody was depressed and suicidal but failed to take the required precautions (such as removing his belt and shoe-laces) so that he was able to commit suicide, the police have been held liable to pay compensation to his widow.

The second principle, useful in attributing blame in slightly different sorts of situation, says that the defendant won't be responsible for ultimate harm if he could not *reasonably have foreseen* the *type* of harm which materialised, although this is usually qualified by saying that as long as the type of harm is foreseeable, its ultimate *extent* doesn't have to be. This qualification is necessary to ensure that the defendant can't escape liability just because he could not have foreseen that the claimant had, for example, brittle bone disease and so suffered much greater harm than the average person (usually called the 'eggshell skull' principle). This distinction between the *type* and *extent* of harm sounds sensible, but it is not always straightforward. Is psychiatric illness the same type of harm as personal injury? Is death by suicide just an extreme form of depressive illness, or is it harm of a different type?

Returning to *Corr*, it was noteworthy that all three members of the Court of Appeal agreed on the relevant legal rules and precedents, yet disagreed on how they applied to the facts of the case. The majority thought the employers should be held responsible for Mr Corr's suicide: for them, psychiatric illness was harm of the same 'type' as the more obviously foreseeable personal injury, committing suicide was merely psychiatric harm of a greater extent, and Mr Corr's deliberate act was neither voluntary nor unreasonable. Ward LJ's dissent is interesting: he agreed that psychiatric harm was harm of the same type as personal injury and that Mr Corr's suicide was not 'unreasonable', but felt that committing suicide six years after the accident could not realistically be said to be a reasonably foreseeable type of harm. For him, the suicide was a tragic accident—it was not right to hold the employers responsible for such a far-removed 'but for' consequence of their negligence.

Once you appreciate that all three Court of Appeal judges in *Corr* agreed on the applicable legal rules and principles, you are forced to think carefully about *why* those judges disagreed about the result in the case. Essentially, the answer is that they had to make *value judgments* about whether those rules should be applied or distinguished, and how they should be interpreted, as lawyers invariably have to do when faced with a new factual situation.

When doing so, some of the considerations taken into account are obviously legal (such as whether extending an existing rule to this new situation would 'flood' the courts with too many new claims or disrupt existing legal rights too drastically), but many other sorts of question are relevant too, such as considerations of morality, economic theory and ethics. For example, you will recall from chapter 2 that all the judges in *R v Brown* made certain assumptions about the moral framework underlying the criminal law—if the judges hadn't made a value judgment (one way or the other) on that non-legal issue, it would not have been possible to decide the case 'according to the law'. In chapter 3 we saw that economic assumptions underpin much of the law about remedies for breach of contract, based on the functioning of a market in a capitalist economy. And in the failed sterilisation cases discussed in chapter 4 the courts came face-to-face with ethical judgments about the value of human life and questions of distributive justice in a society such as ours with a publicly funded health service.

Precisely the same sorts of disagreement arise about the proper interpretation of European Community law and other international legal texts. In this context other issues also come into play—such as the multilingual environment in which the texts were drafted and different cultural norms. Some of these issues can be seen in *P v S,* a decision of the European Court of Justice where the Court's interpretation was swayed less by a literal reading of the text and more by underlying values. P, a male-to-female transsexual, was dismissed on the grounds that she was undergoing a sex change (or 'gender reassignment' as it is properly known). Because, at that time, English law did not prohibit discrimination on grounds of gender reassignment, P argued that European Community law, in particular the Equal Treatment Directive 76/207, nevertheless did cover her situation. The question for the Court of Justice was whether the word 'sex', in the phrase 'there shall be no discrimination whatsoever on the ground of sex' used by the Directive, was broad enough to include 'change of sex'. The Court said yes. Its judgment was influenced by the passionate opinion of the Advocate General who urged the Court to take a 'courageous' decision and interpret the word 'sex' to include change of sex because such an interpretation is 'undeniably based on and consonant with the great value of equality'. The result was that P won her case and her victory benefited many other transsexuals, because the UK government adopted the Sex Discrimination (Gender Reassignment) Regulations amending the British law to prohibit discrimination against transsexuals.

The realisation that judges are often making value judgments prompts the question—are unelected lawyers, judges in particular, the best equipped and most appropriate people to decide these sorts of issue and to mould the law by reference to them? Some people suggest that since judges are predominately from a very elite social and educational background, they are not sufficiently representative of the community. To make matters worse, stories about High Court judges not understanding references to pop groups and websites serve only to undermine further the public's trust in them. On the other hand, most people's experience of the judicial system in operation is extremely positive (at least in so far as the intelligence, sharpness and impartiality of the judges is concerned). Some people have argued that recent legislation, such as the Hunting Act discussed in chapter 7 and some of the recent criminal law reforms, suggest that our elected representatives cannot always be relied on for commonsense and independence and cannot be guaranteed to protect citizens' fundamental rights.

You have probably also noticed throughout the book that some judges are more willing than others to be *creative* when moulding the law. Perhaps the clearest example was the 2003 case of *Rees v Darlington Memorial Hospital Trust* discussed in chapter 4, in which the House of Lords invented a new £15,000 damages award to be given in future to parents of 'unwanted' babies, a remedy that appeared to be plucked out of thin air and with no precedent to support it, as astonished commentators have pointed out. More recently, the House of Lords disagreed openly about whether another new tort rule could be developed by the judges at common law or whether it was too radical and should therefore be left to Parliament. The case involved an unusual tort called *conversion* which covers taking someone else's property (roughly speaking it is the tort equivalent of the crime of theft, but does not require the same level of fault as the criminal offence).

Conversion usually applies to tangible goods, but the House of Lords were pondering whether it should be extended to cover intangible 'things' like contractual rights (see the discussion of 'choses in action' in chapter 6). Under the existing law, conversion does apply if the intangible right is embodied in a physical document like a cheque or a share certificate. So, for this reason, Lord Nicholls thought that the common law could and indeed should extend the law to purely intangible rights. In his view:

> The time has surely come to… recognise that the tort of conversion applies to contractual rights irrespective of whether they are embodied or recorded in writing. I would so hold. This would be a modest but principled extension of the scope of the tort of conversion.

In contrast, Lord Walker took entirely the opposite view:

> Lord Nicholls makes a powerful case for extending the tort of conversion so as to cover the appropriation of choses in action. But in my opinion his proposals would involve too drastic a reshaping of this area of the law of tort … It would have far-reaching consequences which this House is not in a position to explore or assess fully. This is an area in which reform must come from Parliament, after further consideration by the Law Commission.

Perhaps the most famous (some would say notorious) exponent of judicial creativity was Lord Denning, a brilliant lawyer who reached the Court of Appeal just after the Second World War at the remarkably young age of 49 and did not retire until the 1980s. His attitude to inconvenient precedents standing in the way of reaching the 'right' result is seen in the following characteristically sweeping passage from *Hill v C A Parsons Ltd*, a 1971 case about whether a court could, in exceptional circumstances, order an injunction to prevent an employer from wrongfully dismissing an employee:

> The judge said that he felt constrained by the law to refuse an injunction. But that is too narrow a view of the principles of law. He has overlooked the fundamental principle that, whenever a man has a right, the law should give a remedy … This principle enables us to step over the *trip-wires of previous cases and to bring the law into accord with the needs of today* [emphasis added].

In stark contrast, other judges take a much more conservative approach to what they can do when faced with a 'problematic' precedent or statute. This is well illustrated by the decision of the House of Lords in *Hicks v Chief Constable of South Yorkshire*, another tort case which arose (like *Alcock*, discussed in chapter 4) from the Hillsborough football stadium disaster in 1989. Almost 100 Liverpool fans were crushed to death against barriers separating the crowd from the pitch when the police negligently opened gates at the rear of the stand allowing more fans to surge in. Sarah and Victoria Hicks, aged 19 and 15, were amongst those killed and their parents sued the police for damages in the tort of negligence; they did this, not for financial motives, but as Lord Bridge explained, 'to mark the anger of these parents and other bereaved relatives as to what occurred' (although you will remember that an award of damages is not intended to be punitive).

The Fatal Accidents Act 1976 provides for bereavement damages of £7,500 to be awarded if a claimant's spouse or *minor* child was killed by the defendant's negligence, so this sum was awarded in respect of Victoria's death. (Does it surprise you that a bereaved mother whose young child is killed by the defendant's negligence receives only *half* the amount of damages that *Rees* gives to the mother of a child who would not have been born without the defendant's negligence?) But Sarah was over 18 and so this provision did not apply in her case. However, an entirely separate statute also provides that if a legal claim has accrued to a deceased person during his or her lifetime, most such claims will *survive for the benefit of the deceased's estate*—in practice, this means that the deceased's personal representatives are permitted to bring a claim if the deceased could have done so just before their death. The sisters died without leaving a will, but their parents became their personal representatives (known as administrators) and sued the police on behalf of their deceased daughters' estates, to recover damages for the pain and suffering experienced by the girls before they died.

The problem with this claim lay in existing case law, which said that a distinction had to be drawn between pain and suffering experienced *before* death and the pain and suffering *of* death—the deceased accrued a right of action in respect of the former during his or her lifetime, but (by definition) not the latter, so only the former survived for the benefit of the estate to be claimed by the deceased's personal representatives. The judges in *Hicks* felt compelled to decide that this existing case law prevented any damages being awarded in respect of the deaths, despite expressing 'regret' at this conclusion. Had he been judging the case, Lord Denning would almost certainly have found a way to avoid the 'trip-wires' of those existing precedents so as to give damages to the bereaved parents. Very few lawyers and commentators would have objected had that (opposite) result been reached in *Hicks*, but more generally justice is not necessarily better served by judicial creativity—there are sometimes considerable advantages in judicial conservatism, at least where that means that the law is certain and predictable.

In fact, you will have noticed throughout this book that there is invariably tension between two inconsistent characteristics, both of which can claim to make 'good' or 'just' laws, namely certainty and flexibility. It is very important that legal rules are clear, predictable and consistently applied, but too much certainty can bring inflexibility and injustice. On the other hand, although it is vital that the law is flexible enough to produce fair results tailored to the individual merits of a given situation, too much flexibility can bring uncertainty and unpredictability. Getting the balance right is not easy and different areas of law will strike that balance in different ways. For example, the law of contract operates for the most part in the commercial sphere, where businesses need predictable, clear rules so that they can enter into transactions knowing precisely where they stand and what the law's response will be if things go wrong (remember Lord Hobhouse's convincing dissenting speech in the *Blake* case). Too much emphasis on tailoring results to the individual merits of a case would be highly undesirable in commercial contracts (less so, perhaps, in consumer transactions). In criminal law, on the other hand, where the liberty of citizens is at stake, flexibility is very much more important—the same sentence for everyone who commits the same offence would be extremely clear and easy to apply, but it would not do justice to the individual defendant for whom there may have been mitigating—or indeed aggravating—factors. But even in criminal law, too much discretion would be a bad thing—no decent legal system could function if, for example, the law gave judges discretion to 'tailor' the elements of offences or the rules of evidence to match the 'merits' of a case.

This tension was particularly evident in chapter 6, when we considered the role of equitable principles in modern society. Equity began as a flexible, discretionary jurisdiction to do justice by reference to the conscience of the parties, in response to the obvious harshness of the early common law's strict, 'letter of the law' attitude. But in the twenty-first century, equitable principles have very important functions in commercial and property transactions, both of which need certainty to ensure the security of investments and proprietary rights.

The same tension is apparent in the law of negligence, especially in setting the standard of care against which the defendant's conduct is judged. You will remember that English law sets an objective standard, comparing the defendant's conduct with that of the hypothetical reasonable person placed in the same situation. This makes for certainty and ease of application—imagine how hard it would be to administer a subjective standard of care requiring evidence of whether the defendant fell short of his or her own normal standard of care—but can lead to apparent unfairness, as when a person of below-average intelligence or ability is judged against a standard that they could not possibly be expected to attain. This is acceptable as a civil law standard of 'wrongdoing', but would be much more controversial if used as a criminal level of fault.

Indeed, if we step back from the detail of the law we can see the same tensions at a more general, theoretical level. It is vitally important for any decent legal system to have clear, publicly ascertainable rules, so that the public can know in advance what they may or may not do, what rights they have and how their disputes will be resolved. This goal is best served by a small number of very basic, rigid rules, not complicated by exceptions or discretionary qualifications, yet this is inconsistent with doing justice in the individual case, also a vitally important goal of a decent legal system. Think, for example, about whether it would be feasible for a western, capitalist legal system to operate its law of contract on the basis that a promise must be kept unless the welfare of the majority of the citizens would be maximised if it were broken. You will briefly have considered this notion of *utilitarianism* in chapter 2. Lawyers really ought to consider general issues of this sort, unless they are content to accept the existing legal regime without questioning it at all.

We are starting to see that identifying, understanding and applying the law involves all sorts of considerations and values that are not straightforwardly legal issues. This should prompt us to ask even deeper, jurisprudential questions about the law: for example, do non-legal considerations and values form part of the law or not? There are echoes here of the discussion in chapter 7 about the fundamental notion of the rule of law. What would happen if English judges started to decide difficult cases by reference to *unacceptable* values or prejudiced considerations? Would those decisions have the status of 'law' or not?

This issue was explored from the opposite perspective in chapter 7, which raised the question of whether judges must apply an obviously immoral statute (eg, one which allows the state to lock up citizens without any access to courts) just because it was 'properly' enacted by Parliament. Given the supremacy of Parliament, would it be consistent with the rule of law to apply or refuse to apply such a statute? The House of Lords' decision in *Jackson*, especially the speeches of Lord Steyn and Lord Hope, raised the prospect of substantive limits on the supremacy of Parliament in such a case, suggesting that the courts could legitimately refuse to enforce bad statutes.

Related issues arose in chapter 8, with consideration of what membership of the EU means for parliamentary sovereignty in the UK, and are apparent whenever English courts apply the European Convention on Human Rights. You might be interested to hear the final twist in the tale of George Blake, the notorious traitor we met in chapter 3 whose autobiography provided the opportunity for the House of Lords to introduce the controversial remedy of the 'account of profits' into the English law of contract. Blake subsequently took the UK to the European Court of Human Rights (ECtHR) and succeeded in his claim that the UK breached his human right to have a fair hearing because it took an inordinately long time to resolve the litigation about the profits from his autobiography (over nine years from start to finish). Blake was awarded damages of 5,000 euros by the ECtHR—can you imagine the House of Lords reaching that conclusion if the question had been raised in the domestic courts?

The fundamental question of whether non-legal considerations and values form part of the law takes us to some very difficult debates about the meaning of law and, in particular, its relationship with morality. What does 'law' mean? Is it separate from morality or inextricably linked? Chapter 2 provides a good introduction to some of the different views on this important relationship. Until the nineteenth century, most legal philosophers (influenced by Aristotle) believed that there was an underlying body of *natural law* with a moral content and that the role of lawyers was to unearth and expound it. Later commentators sought to separate the question of whether a particular rule or principle counts as a *valid* law from the equally important question of whether that law is a morally *good* law—an approach known as *positivism*. Positivists say that it is possible to identify that something is 'law' by reference to its source and whether that source is recognised as legitimate by the population, without making any claim about its *moral* authority. After all, the Nazi government in Germany scrupulously enacted laws to give dubious authority to its barbarous regime. But positivism still doesn't tell us precisely what is going on when a judge is interpreting a given law, in the light of his or her moral, ethical and other values, so as to decide whether the law should be applied to a new situation or distinguished.

Finally, you will have noticed throughout this book that you can never ignore the *context* in which a particular legal problem has arisen. The common law system of precedent sometimes tempts us to look for higher levels of generality than are actually appropriate; common lawyers are always keen to identify general principles that connect diverse situations. Yet, very often, a rule cannot simply be transplanted into a different factual context—the same answer may not be appropriate, even where apparently the same principles apply. For example, you may well have been surprised in chapter 3 to read that a nineteenth-century case about a fire department from Louisiana failing to provide the contractually agreed level of service was cited to support the creation of an exceptional new remedy for a treacherous breach of a government contract of employment. Lawyers are so used to generalising that they sometimes fail to notice how odd it is to cite and rely on such diverse cases in this way. The same point was made in chapter 8, when discussing the extent to which EU laws made in one context (the promotion of the single market via the free movement of workers) should apply in the very different, rather special, context of sport. You will probably have appreciated too that predicting how precedents will be applied in the future also requires a keen sensitivity to context. For example, was the *Blake* 'account of profits' remedy appropriate only because of the non-commercial, espionage context of the decision itself, or is its rationale potentially wide enough to catch all contracts, even those in a wholly commercial context? Only time will tell.

Context is sometimes the most important aspect of a decision. Think again about *Chhokar v Chhokar*, discussed in chapter 5, with its wholly unusual, indeed shocking, storyline involving collusion between the legal owner, Mr Chhokar, and the third-party purchaser, Mr Parmar. How far do you think the judges in *Chhokar* were influenced by this exceptional factual context when considering the meaning of the crucial statutory phrase 'actual occupation'? If you are not sure, ask yourself how an analogous case should be decided involving an equally wicked husband who, while his wife is temporarily away from the family home, hides most of her obviously feminine possessions, then purports to sell the house to a wholly innocent, if very naïve, purchaser who knows nothing about the wife's interest in the house. This time there is no reconciliation between wife and husband (he has disappeared with the proceeds of sale), just a dispute about whether the innocent purchaser is bound by, or free of, the innocent wife's beneficial interest. It would be much harder for a court to justify a conclusion that the wife remained in *actual occupation* in this situation by virtue of the symbolic presence of her belongings. Indeed, a court might well decide in favour of the naïve purchaser here, perhaps by pointing out that the statutory word 'actual' must mean something, arguably the opposite of 'symbolic'? And, in turn, the reasoning chosen to support this conclusion might well depend, as we saw in chapter 7, on whether the judge wants the precedent being set by the case to be confined to its precise facts or to be potentially relevant in a broader context.

In conclusion, as a law student you will spend many hours reading, learning and understanding details, principles and techniques. But, as we have tried to show in this chapter, you will also spend a lot of time on more creative endeavours—making connections and thinking about the implications of one legal rule (whether from a statute, a case or some other source) in other areas, recognising similarities and drawing distinctions, considering arguments and ideas from all sorts of disciplines outside the law. If you find this an exciting challenge and are ready for lots of reading, thinking and questioning, then we think you will relish studying law at university.

Cases

Blake v UK, Application No 68890/01 [2006] All ER (D) 126 (case law of the European Court of Human Rights can be found at <http://www.echr.coe.int/echr>)

Corr v IBC Vehicles [2006] EWCA Civ 331

Froom v Butcher [1976] QB 286; [1975] 3 All ER 520

Hicks v Chief Constable of South Yorkshire Police [1999] 2 All ER 65

Hill v C A Parsons Ltd [1971] 3 All ER 1345

Case C-13/94 *P v S and Cornwall County Council* [1996] ECR I-2143

R v Williams [1923] 1 KB 340

Further Reading

N Simmonds, *Central issues in jurisprudence: justice, law and rights* (2nd edn, Sweet & Maxwell, London 2002)

J A G Griffith, *The Politics of the Judiciary* (5th edn, Fontana Press, Bodmin 1997)

H L A Hart, *The Concept of Law* edited, with a postscript, by Penelope A Bulloch and Joseph Raz (Clarendon Press, Oxford 1994)

Epilogue

Now that you have been introduced to some of the key principles of the law, why not go back, take a look at the image on the front cover and see how many legal issues you can identify? (Of course, it is an American street scene, but imagine that it is set in England or Wales for this purpose.)

Most obviously, it looks as if a criminal offence is being committed in the foreground, where a businessman is being held up and robbed at gunpoint. The robber, if arrested and subsequently prosecuted, is likely to be sent to jail for a substantial period. Meanwhile, on the left hand side of the picture, a postman is collecting letters from a post box. Perhaps one of the letters is a reply to a contractual offer, in which the writer agrees to enter into a contract to buy a rare painting. If this reply subsequently gets lost in the post and the painting is sold to someone else, the writer of the letter might nonetheless be able to argue that a valid contract has already been made by post to sell the painting to him, so be able to sue the seller for damages.

In the background there has been a road traffic accident. This accident may also raise criminal issues (perhaps one or both of the drivers may have been driving carelessly or dangerously), but the law of tort may also be relevant. Anyone injured might sue the drivers for damages in the tort of negligence. If it was a passenger who was injured, but she wasn't wearing a seatbelt, her damages might be reduced in proportion to her contributory negligence. A relative of the injured passenger might even have a claim for damages, if he or she suffered a recognised psychiatric illness caused by shock on seeing the accident happen or coming upon its immediate aftermath.

Plenty of people are out and about, but as a matter of land law who owns the highway, the pavement and the land beneath? Not the drivers and pedestrians, that's for certain, yet they have rights of way over the land, to use it for passage to and fro. In fact, there appears to be a gathering of people in the middle of the picture. Is this a protest? If so, it raises issues of constitutional law as well. The European Convention on Human Rights, incorporated into domestic law by the Human Rights Act, protects freedom of assembly and freedom of expression. But these rights are not unlimited. If the protest gets out of hand, the police can intervene to prevent breaches of the peace and other public order offences from being committed. And what if the police discover that some of the protesters are nationals of other EU Member States? As EU citizens they have a right to be in the UK. And EC law will provide them with protection against any police decision to put them on a plane and deport them simply because they have been involved in a breach of the peace.

Finally, the picture itself raises important questions of property law. Who owns the picture (and for our purposes the photograph of the picture)? This involves a special type of property law, called intellectual property law, and, in particular, the law of copyright. For your information, the publisher of this book has entered a contract with the copyright holder to reproduce the picture. And you have entered into a contract with the bookseller to buy this book or with the publishers if you ordered the book directly from them. Law is all around you—and that makes it fun and rewarding to study.

Catherine Barnard, Janet O'Sullivan and Graham Virgo

Index